KIERKEGAARD AND THE
CATHOLIC TRADITION

INDIANA SERIES IN THE
PHILOSOPHY OF RELIGION

Merold Westphal, editor

Kierkegaard and the Catholic Tradition

CONFLICT AND DIALOGUE

JACK MULDER, JR.

Indiana University Press

Bloomington & Indianapolis

This book is a publication of

Indiana University Press
601 North Morton Street
Bloomington, IN 47404-3797 USA

www.iupress.indiana.edu

Telephone orders   800-842-6796
Fax orders   812-855-7931
Orders by e-mail   iuporder@indiana.edu

Manufactured in the United States of
America

Library of Congress Cataloging-in-
Publication Data

Mulder, Jack.
  Kierkegaard and the Catholic tradition :
conflict and dialogue / Jack Mulder, Jr.
    p. cm. — (Indiana series in the phi-
losophy of religion)
  Includes bibliographical references (p.   )
and index.
  ISBN 978-0-253-35536-2 (cloth : alk.
paper) — ISBN 978-0-253-22236-7
(pbk. : alk. paper) 1. Kierkegaard,
Søren, 1813–1855. 2. Catholic Church—
Doctrines. I. Title.
  BX4827.K5M84 2010
  230′.044092—dc22

                            2010007347

1 2 3 4 5   15 14 13 12 11 10

FOR FATHER CHARLIE BROWN

Should I misunderstand or be mistaken on some point, whether I deduce it from Scripture or not, I will not be intending to deviate from the true meaning of Scripture or from the doctrine of our Holy Mother the Catholic Church. Should there be some mistake, I submit entirely to the Church, or even to anyone who judges more competently about the matter than I.

ST. JOHN OF THE CROSS

Just as in Catholic books, especially from former times, one finds a note at the back of the book that notifies the reader that everything is to be understood in accordance with the teaching of the holy universal mother Church, so also what I write contains the notice that everything is to be understood in such a way that it is revoked, that the book has not only an end but has a revocation to boot. One can ask for no more than that, either before or afterward.

JOHANNES CLIMACUS

CONTENTS

ACKNOWLEDGMENTS

I must of course thank my wife, Melissa, and my young daughter, Maria, for encouragement and support on this work (though Maria is too young to have known about it). Certainly, I thank my families, Mulders and Manchesters, for support as well. After that, I must thank Nick Engel and Robin Litscher for much help with the early stages of the manuscript. Were it not for their help, I doubt very much that it would have been completed. For that reason, I must also thank Jim Boelkins and the Provost's Office at Hope College and David Cunningham and the CrossRoads Project at Hope, a Program for the Theological Exploration of Vocation, funded in part by the Lilly Endowment, Inc., for faculty development funds that made the collaboration with Nick and Robin possible.

Many scholars have kindly assisted me at various stages of the project. Merold Westphal and Steve Evans gave many helpful comments on earlier editions of the whole manuscript. My friend and colleague Lyra Pitstick has had many helpful conversations with me about Catholic theology and read the introduction very carefully as well. Everyone in Hope College's Philosophy Department has helped with some aspect of this book, and they each deserve a hearty word of thanks. Hope's Philosophy Department is an extremely supportive environment, and I am grateful to be a former student of it as well as a faculty member. Several in the Religion Department have helped as well (with Jeff Tyler being notable among them for help with Luther, and Wayne Brouwer for friendly conversation on the book's themes). Curtis Gruenler of the English Department also provided valuable assistance, especially on the introduction. External scholars who have helped at one stage or another include: Niels Jørgen Cappelørn, John Lippitt, John Davenport, George Connell, Gordon Marino, Søren Landkildehus, Jamie Ferreira, George Pattison, Benjamin Olivares Bøgeskov, Bob Perkins, Jon Stewart, Joseph Ballan, Myron B. Penner, Tom Flint, Martin Matuštík, Louis Mancha, Ada Jaarsma, Michael Paradiso-Michau, Joel Krueger, Bertha Alvarez Manninen, Shannon Nason, Erik Hanson, and a smattering of anonymous reviewers. I would also like to thank Dee Mortensen, Peter Froehlich, Marvin Keenan, the Indiana University Press staff, and Carol A. Kennedy for their work on the present publication.

I also owe a debt of gratitude to the publishers of my earlier work, here reprinted and, in most cases, substantially revised. Springer Science+ Business Media has kindly granted me permission to use material from my article "Must All Be Saved? A Kierkegaardian Response to Theological Universalism," originally published in *International Journal for Philosophy of Religion* 59 (2006): 1–24. Walter de Gruyter Publishing has also kindly granted me permission to use material from my essay "On Being Afraid of Hell: Kierkegaard and Catholicism on Imperfect Contrition," originally published in *Kierkegaard Studies: Yearbook 2007*, ed. Niels Jørgen Cappelørn and Hermann Deuser (Berlin: de Gruyter, 2007), 96–122. Tom Flint has graciously allowed me to reprint most of the material from "Kierkegaard and Natural Reason: A Catholic Encounter," *Faith and Philosophy* 26 (2009): 42–63. Thanks also to Marc Jolley at Mercer University Press for permission to use material from "The Catholic Moment? The Apostle in Kierkegaard's 'The Difference between a Genius and an Apostle,'" in *Without Authority,* ed. Robert L. Perkins, International Kierkegaard Commentary, vol. 18 (Macon, Ga.: Mercer University Press, 2007). A small amount of material was also reprinted by permission of the publishers from "Bernard of Clairvaux: Kierkegaard's Reception of the Last of the Fathers," in *Kierkegaard and the Patristic and Medieval Traditions,* ed. Jon Stewart (Aldershot: Ashgate, 2008), 23–45. The material that appears now in print should be taken to be a more accurate reflection of my viewpoints than was articulated in this earlier work.

Scholarship is a calling, and the voice is God's. For the working of God's grace in me along my own path of conversion I offer this book as "a small installment on the debt—in which I still wish definitely to remain."

ABBREVIATIONS AND
FREQUENTLY CITED WORKS

The following abbreviations for Kierkegaard's works are used in parenthetical references throughout the main text:

Kierkegaard's Writings, ed. Howard V. Hong and Edna H. Hong (Princeton, N.J.: Princeton University Press, 1978–2000). The titles and abbreviations from Kierkegaard's works (shown below) are from this edition.

BA   *The Book on Adler* (Hong and Hong, 1995)

CA   *The Concept of Anxiety* (Reidar Thomte in collaboration with Albert B. Anderson, 1980)

CD   *Christian Discourses* and *The Crisis and a Crisis in the Life of an Actress* (Hong and Hong, 1997)

CI   *The Concept of Irony* together with "Notes on Schelling's Berlin Lectures" (Hong and Hong, 1989)

CUI   *Cumulative Index to Kierkegaard's Writings* (Nathaniel J. Hong, Kathryn Hong, and Regine Prenzel-Guthrie, 2000)

CUP   *Concluding Unscientific Postscript,* 2 vols. (Hong and Hong, 1992). Volume 1 is the only one referred to in this book.

EO   *Either/Or,* 2 vols. (Hong and Hong, 1987). Both volumes are used; I indicate which volume is being referenced in the main text.

EUD   *Eighteen Upbuilding Discourses* (Hong and Hong, 1990)

FSE/JFY   *For Self-Examination* and *Judge for Yourself!* (Hong and Hong, 1990)

FT/R   *Fear and Trembling* and *Repetition* (Hong and Hong, 1983)

M   *The Moment and Late Writings* (Hong and Hong, 1998)

PC   *Practice in Christianity* (Hong and Hong, 1991)

PF   *Philosophical Fragments* and *Johannes Climacus* (Hong and Hong, 1985)

PV   *The Point of View for My Work as an Author* (Hong and Hong, 1998)

SLW   *Stages on Life's Way* (Hong and Hong, 1988)

SUD   *The Sickness unto Death* (Hong and Hong, 1980)

TA   *Two Ages: The Age of Revolution and the Present Age:
A Literary Review* (Hong and Hong, 1978)

TDIO *Three Discourses on Imagined Occasions* (Hong and Hong, 1993)

UDVS *Upbuilding Discourses in Various Spirits* (Hong and Hong, 1993)

WA   *Without Authority* (Hong and Hong, 1997)

WL   *Works of Love* (Hong and Hong, 1995)

Other Kierkegaard editions:

ASKB *The Auctioneer's Sales Records of the Library of Søren Kierkegaard,*
ed. H. P. Rohde (Copenhagen: The Royal Library, 1967)

JN   *Kierkegaard's Journals and Notebooks,* ed. Niels Jørgen Cappelørn
et al. (Published in cooperation with Søren Kierkegaard Research
Centre Copenhagen. Princeton, N.J.: Princeton University Press,
2007–.). *JN* is in progress and will replace *JP* as the standard
English edition of Kierkegaard's *Journals and Notebooks.* When
available, this volume will be referenced for Kierkegaard's journal
entries, as this edition and *SKS* happily use the same, now standard,
notation for the entries (e.g., AA: 12). When this translation is not
available, I will cite the entry by *JP* volume and entry, along with
an accompanying reference to *SKP* (about which see below).

JP   *Søren Kierkegaard's Journals and Papers,* ed. and trans.
Howard V. Hong and Edna H. Hong, assisted by Gregor
Malantschuk (Bloomington: Indiana University Press,
(1) 1967; (2) 1970; (3) and (4) 1975; (5–7) 1978)

SKP   *Søren Kierkegaards Papirer,* 2nd enlarged edition by Niels
Thulstrup, with index vols. 14–16 by Niels Jørgen Cappelørn
(Copenhagen: Gyldendal, 1968–78). References to this edition
will be cited along with all references to *JP* (see above).

SKS   *Søren Kierkegaards Skrifter,* ed. Niels Jørgen Cappelørn,
Joakim Garff, Jette Knudsen, Johnny Kondrup, and Alastair
McKinnon. (Published by Søren Kierkegaard Forskningscenteret.
Copenhagen: Gads Forlag, 1997–.) The reader is referred to
this edition, which is nearing completion, as the standard
critical edition of Kierkegaard's works in Danish.

SV1   *Samlede Værker,* ed. A. B. Drachmann, Johan Ludvig Heiberg, and H. O. Lange, vols. 1–24 (Copenhagen: Gyldendalske Boghandels Forlag, 1901–1906). The reader is referred to this edition for ease of reference, as the standard English edition of *Kierkegaard's Writings* (as abbreviated in the English editions above) includes marginal page numbers keyed to this edition. For a concordance of *SV1* page numbers to approximate page numbers in *SKS,* see the following: www.sk.ku.dk/konkord.asp.

Other works:

Luther's Works will be cited by volume number and page number. All Catholic magisterial documents will be referenced using paragraph numbers, and not page numbers, and the *Summa Theologica* will be cited by part, question, and article.

LW   *Luther's Works,* ed. Jaroslav Pelikan and Helmut Lehmann (St. Louis: Concordia, 1955–86)

DH   Heinrich Denzinger and Peter Hünermann, *Enchiridion Symbolorum, definitionum et declarationum de rebus fidei et morum,* 41st ed. (Freiburg im Bresgau: Herder, 2007)

SCD   *Sources of Catholic Dogma,* trans. Roy J. Deferrari from the 30th edition of Denzinger's *Enchiridion Symbolorum* (1957; repr., Fitzwilliam, N.H.: Loreto Publications, 2007)

CCC   *Catechism of the Catholic Church,* 2nd ed. (Washington, D.C.: United States Catholic Conference, 1994)

ST   St. Thomas Aquinas, *Summa Theologica,* 5 vols., trans. the Fathers of the English Dominican Province (1948; repr., Allen, Tex.: Christian Classics, 1981)

For Vatican documents appearing after 1950 or otherwise not included in available editions or translations of Denzinger, refer to the following URLs for:

· Papal documents
  www.vatican.va/holy_father/index.htm

· Documents from the International Theological Commission (unless another source is given)
  www.vatican.va/roman_curia/congregations/cfaith/cti_index.htm

· Documents from the Congregation for the Doctrine of Faith
  www.vatican.va/roman_curia/congregations/cfaith/index.htm

· Documents from Vatican II
  www.vatican.va/archive/hist_councils/ii_vatican_council/index.htm

· *Joint Declaration on the Doctrine of Justification*
  www.vatican.va/roman_curia/pontifical_councils/chrstuni/documents
  /rc_pc_chrstuni_doc_31101999_cath-luth-joint-declaration_en.html

· *Response of the Catholic Church to the Joint Declaration*
  www.vatican.va/roman_curia/pontifical_councils/chrstuni/documents
  /rc_pc_chrstuni_doc_01081998_off-answer-catholic_en.html

KIERKEGAARD AND THE
CATHOLIC TRADITION

INTRODUCTION

The purpose of this book is to stage a conversation between the work of the Danish philosopher and theologian Søren Kierkegaard and the Catholic tradition on the issues where such a conversation would bear the most fruit. The more ecumenical tone that has prevailed in post–Vatican II Catholic thought often refers to Kierkegaard sympathetically. Yet, while many Catholic writers have read Kierkegaard and even written helpfully on Kierkegaard's overall project, there has been no sustained analysis of where Kierkegaard and the Catholic tradition converge and diverge.[1] This is what I develop in the following chapters.

In addition, although Kierkegaard has exerted considerable influence on philosophy and theology in his own right, readers may find it helpful that this book will also note relationships between the Lutheran Kierkegaard and his "master," Martin Luther himself. For the most part, I follow M. Jamie Ferreira in thinking that it is best to assume that Kierkegaard agrees with Luther except where he explicitly or markedly departs from Luther or Lutheranism.[2] Although Kierkegaard does not receive Luther uncritically, and is often innovative with his reception, the main lines of his thought suggest a profound debt to Luther. In many such cases, Luther's position is widely held in Protestantism more generally. Thus, the investigation offered in this book ends up revealing promising points for dialogue between Protestantism and Catholicism as well as points where the two seem fundamentally to diverge. In either case, we will glimpse something of the essence of both traditions.

This book also has a history in the personal life of its author. I was a Kierkegaardian before I became a Catholic, and I entered into full communion with the Catholic Church in the same academic semester in which I defended my dissertation on Kierkegaard's religious thought. As an author, I have been deeply influenced in formative ways by the twin foci of this book. I hope that this fact has allowed me to understand the views of both participants in this dialogue in uniquely sympathetic ways, but in any case to write the book was for me a personal necessity. Thus, as much as the book is a work in philosophical theology, it also reflects the way in which my own theological imagination has participated in the conversations that follow. At times, my growing commitment to the Catholic Church stretched but did not break my Kierkegaardian intuitions about the relationship between God and the human person. At other times, the shift involved in me could only be described as one of conversion. Yet, since Kierkegaard insisted that what he wanted was honesty (*M*, 46), the honest disagreement I found myself having with Kierkegaard himself has always seemed to me deeply Kierkegaardian in spirit.

Of course, honesty does not by itself a Kierkegaardian make. I am a Catholic, and where my convictions (and sometimes those of the Catholic tradition itself) run into conflict with Kierkegaard, I say so. Indeed, I will, at times, give reasons for why I part ways with Kierkegaard, who in many ways I still regard as my teacher. Still, the content of this book is not intended to be polemical; the point is not to refute Kierkegaard from the point of view of Catholicism. The point is rapprochement and dialogue, not polemic. Sometimes dialogue can go only so far within the limits of honesty, and that is why we must talk about conflict between Kierkegaard and the Catholic tradition, but my reason for writing the book is dialogue.

As will be seen in what follows, there are a variety of ways in which the Catholic tradition can engage with Kierkegaard's thought. Some of these encounters in various chapters will be almost entirely harmonious (as with chapter 5 on the question of hell); some will exhibit more harmony than might otherwise have been thought (as with chapter 1 on natural reason); some will suggest that Kierkegaard's inspiration for a particular idea is best captured by a concept in the Catholic tradition (as with chapter 2 on natural law); and some will argue that Kierkegaard's thought can be a helpful lens for viewing a problem and envisaging a solution in Catholic theology that might not otherwise have been glimpsed with such clarity (as with chapter 6 on imperfect contrition). I make no pretense that I am an utterly neutral party; I am a Catholic Christian. Perhaps another sort of reader might discover elements in Kierkegaard's thought that would lead him or her away from the Catholic tradition and closer to some other corner of the diverse Christian tradition. Such elements assuredly exist in Kierkegaard's work. I simply wish to point out that the limits of this particular study are in many ways the limits of this particular author.

There is a main line of argument that runs through the chapters of this book. Despite the fact that an individual chapter may be read with profit by itself, the book is not simply a collection of essays. I think that the eight areas represented in these chapters represent the main "talking points" on doctrine and dogma for Kierkegaard and the Catholic tradition, but the discussion of them advances in stages. The chapters may be grouped according to two major themes, with each chapter treating a question from the point of view of both Kierkegaard and the mainstream Catholic tradition. These guiding questions are shown below.

PART 1: NATURE AND GRACE

Chapter 1: Is it possible for an individual to become aware of God's existence without the benefit of special revelation (and if so, how)?

Chapter 2: Are an individual's ordinary ethical obligations grounded in something other than special revelation or God's commands?

Chapter 3: How are our ethical obligations and relationships to loved ones transformed by the advent of the Christian revelation?

Chapter 4: How can God work through human individuals ("apostles") to reveal doctrines that may be inaccessible without special revelation?

PART 2: SIN, JUSTIFICATION, AND COMMUNITY

Chapter 5: Is there a case study of a revealed doctrine, concerning which helpful dialogue can be had between Kierkegaard and the Catholic tradition? (This chapter focuses on the question of eternal damnation, a prospect that Kierkegaard and the Catholic tradition regard as a revealed truth.)

Chapter 6: If hell awaits the unrepentant sinner, how must the individual behave in relation to this prospect?

Chapter 7: How is the individual delivered from the prospect of hell, justified before God, and readied for beatitude?

Chapter 8: Is it possible for a third party, or community of faith, to assist in this spiritual transformation of an individual?

These questions constitute the main thread of the argument that runs through the book. I now turn to what this book offers specifically to Catholic readers and to readers of Kierkegaard.

To Catholic Readers

Although Kierkegaard is widely recognized as an important influence in Protestant theology as well as contemporary continental philosophy, not to mention theology and philosophy of religion generally, he is also unique in being someone who both understood himself as a Lutheran and sought to modify the Lutheran picture in a more rigorously Christian way than Luther himself had espoused. Many Catholics have noted that his changes suggest movements toward Catholicism. When we pair Kierkegaard's fascinating experiments in Lutheran theology with the more ecumenical spirit of Catholic thought since Vatican II, we have the makings of a very fruitful dialogue between Protestants and Catholics. Indeed, we stand to learn more about what really divides the Catholic and the Protestant positions, and where possibilities exist for rapprochement.

Catholics should also note that Pope John Paul II, in his important encyclical *Fides et Ratio,* accorded Kierkegaard a rather high honor, as one of only two modern representatives of the subjective aspect of Christian philosophy who were mentioned explicitly. John Paul II wrote: "Christian philosophy therefore has two aspects. The first is subjective, in the sense that faith purifies reason. As a theological virtue, faith liberates reason from presumption, the typical temptation of the philosopher. Saint Paul, the Fathers of the Church and, closer to our own time, philosophers such as Pascal and Kierkegaard reproached such presumption."[3] Kierkegaard might seem a poor choice here, since many have thought him a fideist and Kierkegaard disputes the natural theology that the Catholic Church has affirmed since the First Vatican Council.[4] However, John Paul II also wrote that "closer scrutiny shows that even in the philosophical thinking of those who helped drive faith and reason further apart there are found at times precious and seminal insights which, if pursued and developed with mind and heart rightly tuned, can lead to the discovery of truth's way."[5] Kierkegaard may indeed have held faith and reason further apart than they should ultimately be, but reading him deeply can teach reason the humility that the late pontiff saw as necessary to understand the entire Christian message.[6]

The Catholic tradition is vast and variegated. One simply cannot (at least not without conceit) claim to plumb the full depths of its resources on any one problem, even without bringing the additional complication of an outside thinker such as Kierkegaard into the mix. For this reason, many of the limits of this book are determined by the parameters of Kierkegaard's thought, and not by the history of Catholic doctrine. Thus, for instance, there is no chapter here on the Eucharist, despite its being of such importance to Catholicism that Vatican II called it "the source and summit of the Christian life."[7] There are two reasons for this omission. First, Kierkegaard's reflections on the nature of the Eucharist are in the form of "upbuilding discourses" (as in the "Discourses at the Communion on Friday"[8]); they meander in the direction of dogma occasionally, but do not constitute a sustained dogmatic reflection on the nature of the Eucharist.[9] Second, Michael Plekon has already authored an excellent article, "Kierkegaard and the Eucharist," to which I have little of substance to add. Another omission here that might strike a reader is the absence of discussion on the dogmas concerning the nature of the Godhead or Christology. Kierkegaard clearly thought a great deal about Christology in his published works (and to a lesser extent about the Trinity), but his Christological reflections (many of which are found in *Practice in Christianity*) do not usually serve to isolate his as a theoretically distinct perspective within the larger Christian tradition. He took such Christological dogmas for granted, but insisted on their existential importance, an orientation from which Catholic readers can best profit by simply reading Kierkegaard.

Kierkegaard is not so much a speculative theologian as he is a pastoralist, whose flock is Christendom.[10] He referred to dogmatic issues when he felt they were important for understanding and remedying the predicaments of his age. One such concern he had was with the way in which Hegelian speculation attempted to exempt one from the existential demands of the Christian life. One cannot save one's soul with speculation, and this truth led Kierkegaard to oppose the overemphasis on the intellect of which he saw natural theology as an instance (on this point, see chapter 1). Another example of Kierkegaard's pastoral instincts leading him to make interesting moves in dogma is when he argues that Luther's accentuation of Christ as redeeming gift has been taken to its logical limit and that Danish Lutheranism needed to be reminded that Christ was also a pattern to be imitated (on this point see chapter 7). Many of Kierkegaard's works, on their way to making pastoral points, engage particular dogmatic or doctrinal issues with distinction, and manifest interesting points of convergence or divergence with those very issues in Catholic theology. These cases form the basis for the chapters that follow.

What I stage in this book are joint inquiries between Kierkegaard's work and the Catholic tradition, not textual scavenger hunts to determine the extent to which Kierkegaard *saw himself* as moving closer to Catholicism on a particular point. The work in this book is exegetical, comparative, theological, and philosophical. It is not primarily concerned with features of Kierkegaard's biography. The question in each chapter is not simply whether Kierkegaard's preexisting thought does in fact accommodate a particular Catholic view, but whether and how far it has the *potential* to do so, and, indeed, where it is possible for the Catholic tradition to assimilate Kierkegaard's greatest insights.

To Readers of Kierkegaard

Although I do not ignore the pseudonymous status of many of Kierkegaard's works, I will not be entering into protracted debates about how we should regard each pseudonymous work. My working assumption is that Kierkegaard takes the enormous trouble of writing the pseudonymous works because he himself wants to convey something important to the reader in and by that pseudonymous work. Still, when a passage comes from a pseudonym, it will always be referenced as written by that pseudonym, in accordance with Kierkegaard's stated wishes (*CUP*, 627). I also caution the reader not to get too absorbed in what Kierkegaard meant by the use of a particular pseudonym. When Kierkegaard's writing project was under way, it was usually not a matter of secrecy whether a published work was "really" written by Kierkegaard. In fact, in his journals, Kierkegaard often explains why he uses a particular pseudonym. In one case, Kierkegaard's use of a pseudonym appears to have been for a reason no more complex than that the pseudonym's judgment of his fellows was so harsh that Kierkegaard wanted it known that he (i.e., Søren Kierkegaard) was also implicated in this critique.[11] The basic idea behind much of Kierkegaard's pseudonymity, however, seems to have been that he wanted to "deceive" people into the truth (see *PV,* 53) by showcasing what he saw as stages of individual human existence through creating personae that were actually living within those stages. Thus, despite their philosophical interest, some of the pseudonymous works are both philosophical treatises and, as far as their accompanying narratives are concerned, fiction.

As happens with any important historical figure, a scholarly community has developed around the study of Kierkegaard and his work. I have some acquaintance with (and perhaps even a kind of membership in) this delightful community, and anticipate a certain reticence on the part of some of its members to hear Kierkegaard's name mentioned in the same context as such words as "doctrine" or "dogma."[12] Indeed, these words are often taken to entail some kind of slavish, unreflective, and quite quotidian adherence to a doctrine for no better reason than that it is a doctrine.

If that is what we mean by dogma, then I take it as obvious that Kierkegaard would have no truck with it. To see this, we need only consult his famous 1835 journal entry at Gilleleje:

> What I really need is to be clear about *what I am to do,* not what I must know, except in the way knowledge must precede all action. It is a question of understanding my own destiny, of seeing what the Deity really wants *me* to do; the thing is to find a truth which is truth *for me,* to find *the idea for which I am willing to live and die.* And what use would it be in this respect if I were to discover a so-called objective truth, or if I worked my way through the philosophers' systems and were able to call them all to account on request, point out inconsistencies in every single circle? . . . What use would it be to be able to propound the meaning of Christianity, to explain many separate facts, if it had no deeper meaning for *myself* and *my life*? (*JN,* 1:19 / AA: 12, italics in original)

Commenting on this entry, Josiah Thompson claims that Kierkegaard rejects explanations of the meaning of religion "because they are totally irrelevant to himself and to his situation."[13] Another commentator, Roger Poole, explicitly hopes that the "bad old tradition of seeking univocal meaning" in Kierkegaard's work will end, as this kind of meaning is ultimately irrelevant, so we are told, to Kierkegaard's larger project.[14]

There seems to be some basis for these claims in Kierkegaard's writing. For example, Kierkegaard and his pseudonyms appear to be of one voice in denying that Christianity is a "doctrine,"[15] and instead insisting that it is an "existence-communication" that must be taken up into one's life.[16] Indeed, in one of the most famous passages in Kierkegaard's entire body of work, we read (from the pseudonym Johannes Climacus):

> If someone who lives in the midst of Christianity enters, with knowledge of the true idea of God, the house of God, the house of the true God, and prays, but prays in untruth, and if someone lives in an idolatrous land but prays with all the passion of infinity, although his eyes are resting upon the image of an idol—where, then, is there more truth? The one prays in truth to God although he is worshiping an idol; the other prays in untruth to the true God and is therefore in truth worshiping an idol. (*CUP*, 201)

In this context, the word "dogma" might suggest the arid context in which Kierkegaard was still groping for something more. What I think can be correctly inferred from the episode of the passionate pagan is that Kierkegaard was, in fact, more concerned with inward religious commitment than with whether individuals "got it right" with respect to matters of the intellect. However, proponents and opponents of this view often throw the baby out with the bathwater and claim that Kierkegaard is the witting or unwitting herald of Christian doctrine's ultimate demise.[17]

Thankfully, we also need not take religious passion to preclude dogmatic commitment. Consider Cardinal Newman's shorthand definition of dogma, namely, "supernatural truths irrevocably committed to human language, imperfect because it is human, but definitive and necessary because given from above."[18] If we leave the door open to definitive revelation from God, as I think Kierkegaard ultimately believes we must do, then this definition of "dogma" is as Kierkegaardian as the Kierkegaardian apostle who would proclaim the relevant dogma.[19] To illustrate what would seem to be this very point, one of Kierkegaard's pseudonyms imagines an apostle saying, "I cannot, I dare not compel you to obey, but through the relationship of your conscience to God, I make you eternally responsible for your relationship to this doctrine by my having proclaimed it with divine authority" (*WA,* 97).[20] What "dogma" ultimately boils down to is the question of whether there is or has been a religious authority sufficiently certified to guarantee its truth.

However much Kierkegaard himself disavowed having this authority, he made it quite clear that God intended some individuals to have it.

Readers of Kierkegaard, following his entry at Gilleleje, may regard "dogma" as the very sort of thing for which no one would live or die. To the contrary, Cardinal Newman pithily writes, "Many a man will live and die upon a dogma: no man will be a martyr for a conclusion."[21] The Catholic tradition and Kierkegaard agree that there is such a thing, to speak somewhat loosely, as apostolic authority. This type of authority is what is necessary in proclaiming Christian truths, for both Kierkegaard and the Catholic tradition, and our receipt of such truths into the essence of Christianity can be fittingly called dogma.

‡

While neither the choices for chapters nor the order of their presentation is arbitrary, this book by no means provides a comprehensive survey of all the profitable conversations possible between Kierkegaard and the Catholic tradition. These interrelated inquiries are a start, determined in large part by Kierkegaard's own contributions. My use of the Catholic tradition in this work is driven by a desire to have Kierkegaard interact with a fair representation of what many in the mainstream of the Catholic tradition hold and have held. By taking some theologians to represent this tradition on some topical matters, I do not thereby intend to endorse all of what any theologian has said. I have chosen the theologians and texts I have because I think they lend best to dialogue between Kierkegaard and the Catholic tradition, and I think that this dialogue is eminently worth having, to bring out honest disagreements between Protestants and Catholics when they cannot be avoided, and rapprochement where that is possible.

Kierkegaard scholarship of recent years has achieved marked success in showing that Kierkegaard was not, as the late Richard John Neuhaus has noted, an "intellectually upmarket Holden Caulfield."[22] Rather, Kierkegaard is passionately concerned with issues in dogmatic theology, and readers who wish to follow the lead of his contagious passion must, if they wish to be consistent, answer some difficult dogmatic questions.[23] It is high time to bring the resources of contemporary research on Kierkegaard to bear on the dogmatic questions that animate both the Catholic tradition and Kierkegaard's own work.

PART ONE

Nature and Grace

ONE

Kierkegaard and Natural Reason:
A Catholic Encounter

Many a man will live and die upon a dogma:
no man will be a martyr for a conclusion.

JOHN HENRY CARDINAL NEWMAN

For many people, if they know anything about Kierkegaard at all, they "know" that he is a fideist, or someone who relies entirely on the deliverances of faith for religious knowledge, often at the expense of reason itself. This charge, that Kierkegaard is a fideist, is a very common one.[1] Indeed, many have gone so far as to argue that Kierkegaard is an irrationalist and so concerned with passion at the expense of reason that, they surmise, there is virtually no positive role for reason to play in making the "leap of faith."[2] Kierkegaard scholarship of recent years has been at very great pains to dismiss this charge, and it has achieved some success.

In the Catholic tradition, fideism is a heretical extreme of which so-called rationalism is the other pole.[3] The one affirms that faith in authority is the only means of certainty (at least in regard to knowledge of the divine), and the other affirms that unaided human reason is the only means of certainty. Kierkegaard has, for the most part, been vindicated of the charge of outright, or at any rate irrational, fideism.[4] However, for the Catholic tradition, his repudiation of natural theology generally keeps him too close to the extreme of fideism.[5] Nevertheless,

John Paul II, while unlikely to embrace the full range of Kierkegaard's thought, identified him as a very profitable thinker for Catholics to consider. Accordingly, one prominent pope has, as it were, an official position on Kierkegaard's work: his work, while having widened the gap between faith and reason, nevertheless contains the kind of insight that "can lead to the discovery of truth's way."[6] In this chapter, I examine this claim in the context of Kierkegaard's larger thought, to see just where exactly the disagreement between Kierkegaard and Catholicism on the question of "natural reason" appears to lie, and where the profit in his work may be found on this question.

The most obvious reason for reservations about Kierkegaard's work in the Catholic tradition is the anathema the First Vatican Council pronounced upon those who would deny natural theology, in a dogmatic constitution promulgated in 1870, just short of fifteen years after Kierkegaard's death. The canon simply reads, "If anyone shall have said that the one true God, our Creator and our Lord, cannot be known with certitude by those things which have been made, by the natural light of human reason, let him be anathema."[7] Of course, as with most dogmatic pronouncements of this kind, this one hardly arrived without historical and theological precedent. As Linda Zagzebski notes, even contemporary Catholic epistemology, echoing influences roughly concurrent with or prior to the Reformation, tends to prize both natural theology and a certain kind of voluntarism, or choice, about one's beliefs.[8]

Although Kierkegaard is sometimes thought to be sympathetic to forms of voluntarism, C. Stephen Evans and others have done much fine work in showing that Kierkegaard is unjustly lampooned as an irrationalist and an irresponsible fideist. This has had the consequence of pulling Kierkegaard further away from the heresy of fideism, from the Catholic point of view. It also, however, raises the question that I will attempt an answer in the rest of this chapter: just how far apart are Kierkegaard and the Catholic tradition? I will begin by briefly discussing the attack on natural theology that often captures the attention of Kierkegaard's readers, and go on to discuss how the Catholic tradition has approached the matter of natural theology, taking care to see where and why Kierkegaard's position ultimately differs.

Kierkegaard's Attack on Natural Theology

As we shall see, Kierkegaard is no irrationalist. However, Kierkegaard's Lutheran heritage had a profound, if ambiguous, relationship to his thought, and Luther is not known for an appreciative approach to natural theology and natural reason, the latter of which he claims is "superstitious and ready to imagine."[9] Perhaps one of the clearest verdicts we get from Luther on the value of reason is when he notes, in the *Table Talk,* that "prior to faith and a knowledge of God, reason is darkness, but in believers it's an excellent instrument. . . . As our body will rise [from the dead] glorified, so our reason is different in believers than it was before, for it doesn't fight against faith, but promotes it."[10] The idea here seems to be that prior to an individual's acquisition of Christian faith, reason "fight[s] against faith," but when it is cleansed by Christian faith, reason becomes useful for the promotion of faith. This perspective makes sense in the light of Luther's generally dismissive attitude toward what scholasticism called "nature."[11] Luther seems to consider unredeemed "nature" as positively pernicious, rather than good or even neutral. Elements of this attitude can be glimpsed, and even in some cases intensified, in Kierkegaard's work,[12] and these facts may have helped to fuel his antipathy to "natural" theology.

While this chapter is concerned with Kierkegaard's attitude toward reason generally, its focus is more particularly on the matter of natural theology. The first task before us, then, is to provide an examination of some of Kierkegaard's salient views (or at any rate, those of his pseudonyms) on natural theology. The first place to turn is the pseudonymous writings, and especially those of Johannes Climacus. There, we find the traditional critique of natural theology in *Philosophical Fragments.*

In that work, Climacus gives a dilemma for the natural theologian. He writes:

> If, namely, the god does not exist, then of course it is impossible to demonstrate it. But if he does exist, then it is foolishness to want to demonstrate it, since I, in the very moment the demonstration commences, would presuppose it not as doubtful—which a presupposition cannot be, inasmuch as it is a presupposition—but as decided, because otherwise I would not begin, easily perceiving that the whole thing would be impossible if he did not exist. (*PF,* 39)

Since Climacus is clearly right that it is impossible to (successfully) demonstrate the existence of a nonexistent entity, the only horn that concerns us from the above dilemma is the horn that tells us that if "the god" does exist, then it is "foolishness" to want to demonstrate it. Let us call this the "Foolishness Objection" (FO). What could Climacus mean here?

I think we can be aided somewhat in our attempt to understand the FO by considering what follows it. Climacus writes: "If, however, I interpret the expression 'to demonstrate the existence of the god' to mean that I want to demonstrate *that the unknown, which exists, is the god,* then I do not express myself very felicitously, for then I demonstrate nothing, least of all an existence, but I develop the definition of a concept" (*PF,* 39–40, italics mine). In this passage, Climacus argues that if we mean something else by "demonstrating" God's existence, namely of moving from "the unknown" to "the god," then this sort of "demonstration" will prove nothing. In that case, we are only proving that a given entity, whose existence is no longer being doubted, is in fact the theistic God. This will hardly convince doubtful parties of God's existence. Let us call this the "Infelicity Objection" (IO). The FO and the IO, then, seem to be the two relevant objections to natural theology.

At this point, it will be helpful to consider William L. Rowe's distinction between the two parts of a theistic argument for God's existence, of which the first part is the effort "to prove the existence of a special sort of being."[13] The second part takes the efficacy of the first part for granted, moving from the existence of God to "the effort . . . to prove that the special sort of being whose existence has been established in the first part has, and must have, the features—perfect goodness, omnipotence, omniscience, and so on—which go together to make up the theistic idea of God."[14] That is, one would perhaps not think to bow down and worship, for instance, the first cause of the universe (even if proof for its existence were made manifest), but if the first cause were sufficiently (and successfully) delineated so as to resemble the theistic God, theistic devotion could enter into the picture.

Turning our attention back to Climacus, if we distinguish the two parts of theistic argument, it is not clear why the IO is especially serious, especially if the first part, that of demonstrating the existence of a special sort of being, were successful. That is, since it is the job of the second part not to establish the truth of an existential claim, but to expound upon one that has already been established, the IO cannot mount an interesting and independent charge against theistic argument in general. Thus, the FO is the real issue in considering Climacus's criticism.

The FO contains Climacus's insistence that if we were to take God's existence to be doubtful, we would never "begin" with the argument. This is because natural theology, or at any rate that version of it of special interest to both Climacus and Catholicism, undertakes to demonstrate God's existence from God's works (or alternatively, God's "effects"). The reason that Climacus thinks we would never begin is that we would be using God's works (i.e., creation) to prove the existence of a Creator, but the argument would never get off the ground were it not to premise that the works in question are precisely *God's* works, which would not themselves exist without God. The situation, Climacus notes, is much as if we were going to try to prove the existence of Napoleon by premising that losing the battle of Waterloo was an (actual) action performed by none other than a historical personage named *Napoleon* (*PF,* 40). Climacus, however, recognizes that God's case is different than that of Napoleon's case, since "between the god and his works there is an absolute relation. . . . God's works, therefore, only the god can do" (*PF,* 41–42).

Nonetheless, the FO is more interesting than it looks at first. Climacus writes: "The works from which I want to demonstrate his existence do not immediately and directly exist, not at all. Or are the wisdom in nature and the goodness or wisdom in Governance right in front of our noses? Do we not encounter the most terrible spiritual trials here, and is it ever possible to be finished with all these trials?" (*PF,* 42).[15] The idea here seems to be that in attempting to prove the existence of God using God's works, we will need to have it assured that they are indeed God's works, and thus that all of the creation is under the providential care of the theistic God. This is tantamount to supposing that the problem of evil is definitively solved before even attempting to marshal the evidence for God's existence. The lot of this arguer is not to be envied. The argument, however, is not only difficult; it is confused, according to Climacus. One is, in effect, taking the second, if you will, "thicker" conclusion of the theistic argument and using it as a premise to prove the first, and "thinner," conclusion of the theistic argument.

This critique may suffice for some versions of the teleological argument for the existence of God, or the argument from design, but Climacus nowhere restricts his attack on natural theology to the teleological argument.[16] Rather, Climacus clearly means to cut short all efforts at demonstrating God's existence. Climacus's arguments are directed at the enterprise of natural theology in general, and the effort to demonstrate God's existence on the basis of God's works in particular.[17] A good candidate for further consideration is the cosmological argument. Indeed, there are relevant differences between the cosmological and teleological arguments.

While I am not interested here in rendering a verdict on whether Climacus is correct with regard to all forms of the teleological argument, it is worth noticing that this style of argument may appear more likely to play into his hand than the cosmological argument. The reason for this is that the teleological argument begins immediately with considerations about God's having designed objects in the natural world for an end. Thus, Aquinas's fifth way "is taken from the *governance* of the world."[18] Climacus is likely to argue that it is precisely the governance that is supposed to be noticed in the creation. But how does one recognize that things behave "designedly" unless one already supposes what the divine purpose might wish to accomplish? That is, perhaps we surmise that some events in the world transpire much as if they were purposed by a benevolent creator. This benevolence is then precisely what is in question when we arrive at the vexed problem of evil, which is especially troublesome when the traditional theistic understanding imputes benevolence on a maximal scale to the Creator. Climacus's worry here might be expressed by saying that he develops the suggestion that theistic arguments *themselves* conflate the two parts of theistic arguments, and that actually the first part cannot get off the ground without presupposing the soundness of the second part, which is simply to beg the question. With regard to the teleological argument, the suggestion deserves the sort of scrutiny I cannot give it here. But with regard to the cosmological argument, Climacus's suggestion may not be as plausible. My purpose in this chapter is not to mount or defend any single theistic argument. However, it is worth briefly noting one example of an argument that does not appear to commit the errors Climacus notes.

In the *Summa contra Gentiles,* Aquinas uses a cosmological style of argument to prove the existence of an unmoved mover. Using this procedure, Aquinas then argues that the required sort of unmoved mover must also be, among other things, eternal, purely active, immaterial, simple, and, finally, good.[19] Climacus appears to allege that theistic arguments presuppose the goodness of the Creator so as to move from God's works to the conclusion that God exists. In the case of the cosmological argument, however, this objection may be more difficult to sustain. Without making the vaunted claim (a serious defense of which would require a wholly separate inquiry) that the cosmological argument itself is somehow on more secure footing than the teleological argument, we can notice that Aquinas's treatment of the latter purports to reason from the *governance* (one of Kierkegaard's favorite ways of referring to God) of the world to the conclusion that there is a God. Climacus's complaint is that one cannot speak of governance without a governor, and here we will need an intentional agent.[20] With regard to the cosmological argument, however, it is not so clear whether we will need an intentional agent when it is the phenomenon of motion that we are trying to explain. To establish the existence of a prime mover (or uncaused cause, or self-existent being, etc.) is, of course, the first part of the cosmological argument. The fact that the second part will then argue that the entity whose existence has been established must also be the theistic God need not affect the argument for the primary existential claim, namely, that an independent or self-existent being exists. Since Aquinas drew much of his inspiration for this argument from Aristotle, the resources for mounting this argument are as likely to be found in pagan antiquity as in a religiously loaded theistic metaphysic.[21] For this reason, Climacus's critique of natural theology, as found in *Philosophical Fragments,* is, at best, incomplete.

When our topic is widened, however, to a concern over natural (though non-inferential) knowledge of God, independent of special revelation, Climacus receives the idea much more positively. While Climacus notes that "without risk, no faith, not even the Socratic faith," he nonetheless insists that Socratic faith is not faith in the strict sense (*CUP,* 210). He also insists that "Socrates did not have faith that the god existed" (*PF,* 87). Here it is important to contrast the belief in the eternal God's existence and the fact that the eternal God deigned to enter into time in the incarnation. On this point, Kierkegaard writes, explicitly of *Fragments,* "I do not believe that God exists [*er til,* eternally is], but know it; whereas I *believe* that God has existed [*har været til*] (the historical)" (*JP,* 3:3085 / *SKP,* VI B 45). Socratic faith is an "analogue" to Christian faith because Socrates believes in the face of objective uncertainty, whereas Christian faith believes in the face of the "absurdity" of the incarnation (*CUP,* 205). How then is there risk, or objective uncertainty, for Socrates, if God's existence is supposed to be the object of knowledge?

The idea here seems to be that the risk has to do with the source of the knowledge, for Climacus. There is objective uncertainty, precisely because scouring nature for evidence for God, *in the abstract,* generates a conflict between the evidence for wise governance and the evil present in the world (*CUP,* 203–204). This is the evidence available to a distanced and objective observer. But the individual who rubs the wonderful lamp of freedom with "ethical passion" finds that God comes into existence for her (*CUP,* 138).[22] That is, the true and natural knowledge of God's existence is obscured by one's failure to relate to one's own life with passion. Without this impediment, or rather by actively relating to one's own life with passion, there is a natural (though again, non-inferential) knowledge of God, according to Climacus. He writes, "[God] is in the creation, everywhere in the creation, but he is not there directly, and only when the single individual turns inward into himself (consequently only in the inwardness of self-activity) does he become aware and capable of seeing God" (*CUP,* 243). That is, because God is not an object, but a subject, the individual has only a subjective way to knowledge of God, as opposed to an objective way.[23] Sin can thus provide an impediment to knowledge of God, but ethical passion can reopen the way to knowledge of God, independently of special revelation.

From the first critique in *Fragments,* we can see that Climacus appears to regard the effort to prove God's existence using demonstrative and objective reason as at best irrelevant, and at worst pernicious. In particular, it can often distract one from the real existential claim that faith makes upon a Christian. The more one hangs one's hat on a proof, the more one's faith is simply a matter of intellect, which, as it turns out, Kierkegaard does not think is very secure as far as its ability to prove God's existence is concerned. On the other hand, there is knowledge of

God available to human beings that we might fittingly call "natural" in that it can be acquired without special revelation.

In one of his journal entries, Kierkegaard writes:

> To stand on one's foot and prove the existence of God is altogether differ-ent from falling on one's knees and thanking him. The former is a deli-cate silk ladder which one throws up like a romantic knight of cognition and somehow uses in a curious manner to get aloft, simultaneously se-curing the ladder while standing upon it (unlike firemen who enter each floor to secure the shinning rope)—the latter is a solid stairway, and even if one advances more slowly, he is on the way and all the more securely. (*JP*, 2:2279 / *SKP*, III A 145)

The idea here seems to be that the natural theologian is assigning himself a really impossible task, namely, to (rationally) secure the very edifice upon which he is constructing his faith. Faith has primarily to do with the will,[24] for Kierkegaard, and thus to construct one's faith on the basis of an intellectual argument is ultimately inappropriate. Faith and de-monstrative reasoning are the operations of, if you will, different organs of the person. The former is the one thing needful, and the latter does not help us acquire it, for Kierkegaard.

While I think that Climacus's arguments against the attempt by natural theology to demonstrate God's existence ultimately miss their mark, this does not mean that Kierkegaard and Climacus have nothing important to offer us in a related connection.[25] Rather, Climacus's attack on natural theology is a narrow (if erroneous) instance of a wider (and ultimately correct, in my view) suspicion of reason's capabilities in rela-tion to faith. Having things reasoned out in a distanced and objective way can assure one of only so much, and cannot cancel the "pain and crisis of decision" (*CUP*, 129), as Climacus puts it. As Merold Westphal comments, "Far from providing support to faith, objectivism leads the individual to the place where faith is not even possible."[26] This is an area where Kierkegaard and the Catholic tradition will likely disagree, since, as we shall see below, the Catholic tradition thinks that reason actually makes faith possible.

This way of approaching the matter, however, is not the whole truth. It is surely important for Catholics to approach Kierkegaard "with mind and heart rightly tuned," but it is also important for Catholic thinkers and natural theologians to beware of distorting reason and removing it from its theological moorings. On this point, Pope Benedict XVI writes that we have "cut ourselves off" from a kind of "primordial knowledge" and that "an increasing scientific know-how is preventing us from being aware of the fact of creation."[27] Faith is at least partly a human act of will, for the Catholic tradition,[28] and this act of will can still be denied and even obscured in various ways, many of which have to do, as we shall have occasion to note later, with the presence of evil in the world. This is the reason for Climacus's "most terrible spiritual trials." This may suggest that the Climacan and Catholic notions of "objectivity" are relevantly different. For Climacus, the notion may be exaggerated by the conceits of the Hegelian system, and reliance on it may very well inhibit the possibility of faith.[29] We can now turn to the Catholic tradition to consider a version of its view of the promises of natural theology.

On Natural Theology and Epistemology in the Catholic Tradition

The *Dogmatic Constitution on the Catholic Faith,* from which the canon anathematizing natural theology's naysayers is taken, makes it clear that the Church regards its original source for this doctrine on natural theology to be none other than St. Paul in Romans 1:20. That passage reads, "Ever since the creation of the world, his invisible attributes of eternal power and divinity have been able to be understood and perceived in what he has made. As a result they have no excuse." Thus, the point of natural theology seems to be that it provides a kind of "public" confirmation of the fact that humans should worship a God. In the aforementioned dogmatic constitution we read, "The same Holy Mother Church holds and teaches that God, the beginning and end of all things, can be known with certitude by the natural light of human reason from created things."[30] Commenting on this passage, the *Catechism of the Catholic Church* writes, "Without this capacity, man would not be able to welcome God's revelation. Man has this capacity because he is created 'in the image of God.'"[31] Thus, another of the primary reasons that the Church defends natural theology is that it actually makes it possible for human beings to receive God's revelation.

The Catholic Church thus claims that certainty can be achieved using natural reason about such matters as whether or not there is a God. Yet, the type of certainty that is being pleaded for is sometimes a bit unclear. The *Catechism* notes, "Created in God's image and called to know and love him, the person who seeks God discovers certain ways of coming to know him. These are also called proofs for the existence of God, not in the sense of proofs in the natural sciences, but rather in the sense of 'converging and convincing arguments,' which allow us to attain certainty about the truth."[32] A proof in the natural sciences, at least as they are often construed, would seem to be out of the question, since the natural sciences have as their subject precisely the physical world, and theology has as its subject the things of God that transcend the physical. The *Catechism* goes on to say that "the world, and man, attest that they contain within themselves neither their first principle nor their final end, but rather that they participate in Being itself, which alone is without origin or end."[33] This is precisely the kind of reasoning that generates a cosmological argument for the existence of God.

For instance, consider Rowe's famous formulation of the cosmological argument:

1. Every being (that exists or ever did exist) is either a dependent being or a self-existent being.
2. Not every being is a dependent being.

Therefore,

3. There exists a self-existent being.[34]

Rowe goes on to argue that the celebrated Principle of Sufficient Reason (PSR) is "the fundamental principle" on which the premises of the cosmological argument rest, but that, in his view, we are simply unable to know the truth or falsity of PSR.[35] PSR, as Rowe lays it out, requires that, "*there must be an explanation (a) of the existence of any being and (b) of any positive fact whatever.*"[36] Rowe and the Catholic Church may part ways on the question of our knowledge of PSR, but Pope Pius XII appeared to insist, along with Rowe, on its importance, in particular, for natural theology.[37] In his encyclical *Humani Generis,* he wrote, "Indeed, this philosophy, recognized and accepted within the Church, protects the true and sincere value of human understanding, and constant metaphysical principles—namely, of *sufficient reason,* causality, and finality—and, finally, the acquisition of certain and immutable truth."[38] Thus, while the relevance of such metaphysical principles is not primarily what is under dispute, the fact of our knowledge of such metaphysical principles does appear to be a matter of dispute.

Curiously, however, the Church never appears to "legislate epistemology," at least with regard to such metaphysical principles. We are thus left asking how we might come to know them. This is indeed a question that Rowe asks, but there might be some reason, in our current epistemological climate, to wonder whether he has adequately surveyed the epistemological options available to the theist. Rowe considers whether we might be able to know PSR intuitively, but dismisses the suggestion for the reason that able philosophers fail to apprehend its truth. At that point, he writes:

> Here, perhaps, all that one can do is carefully reflect on what PSR says and form one's own judgment on whether it is a fundamental truth about the way reality must be. And if after carefully reflecting on PSR it does strike one in that way, that person may well be rationally justified in taking it to be true and, having seen how it supports the premises of the Cosmological Argument, accepting the conclusion of that argument as true.[39]

One might be quick to remind us that if Catholicism is in the picture, then we need to be discussing *certainty,* and not simply *rational justification.* Certainty is what Vatican I claimed for reason's ability to know God.[40] But it is worth inquiring into just what we mean by the term "reason."

Aquinas, for instance, has it that natural reason "begins from sense," and thus, "can go as far as it can be led by sensible things."[41] That is, natural reason operates on the data given to us by the senses in such a way as to draw conclusions from it, given the sensible things, and the abstract principles that allow deduction from them. Aquinas does not, for instance, grant a serious hearing to a kind of Cartesian global skepticism, of the sort that would have me wondering whether 2+3=5 on the basis of the far-fetched possibility that an evil genius might be manipulating my brain. On this point, Thomas Hibbs writes, "Aquinas would urge . . . that reasonable doubts are always local, never global; they are formulated against a set of background assumptions that could never all at once be successfully put in question. If doubt were to become truly global, it would be fatal."[42] Thus, natural reason does not begin, nor need it begin, where Descartes does in his *Meditations,* in the search for indubitable truths in the face of global skepticism. Rather, Aquinas tells us that natural reason "contains two things: images derived from the sensible objects; and the natural intelligible light, enabling us to abstract from them intelligible conceptions."[43] What this means is that Aquinas's conception of knowledge already assumes that certain capabilities (among them the hotly contested power of abstraction) are in place, and, to a certain extent, functioning properly.

To employ this sort of account, one might include a number of principles that are necessary *before* conducting the kinds of demonstrations that Aquinas saw as paradigms of *scientia,* or demonstrative knowledge, as propositions apprehended by the natural light in a non-inferential way. John I. Jenkins writes, "Presented with certain *phantasmata,* one spontaneously forms an idea in the intellect's first operation, and in the second operation the intellect is moved to make a non-inferential judgment. Such judgments are justified as basic."[44] To say that these judgments are basic is to say that they have the right sort of positive epistemic status; the right sort of warrant that, if the belief is also true, could certify it as known, even if the belief has such warrant without being inferred from other beliefs, and even if the subject is not aware that each of the conditions for its having this kind of warrant are met.[45] Jenkins makes it explicit that principles of the sciences, in the mold of Aristotle's *Posterior Analytics,* are the objects of this basic knowledge. It seems to me, however, that Jenkins's account suggests that Pius XII's "constant metaphysical principles," among them that of sufficient reason, might well also be included in the kinds of judgments that, on Jenkins's account, the Angelic Doctor might deem basic.[46] We thus might be able to construct an authentically Catholic hybrid of natural theology and basic beliefs.[47]

Accounts of basic beliefs are often objected to because they simply absorb claims with prominent objectors into a privileged and sacrosanct set, thereby relieving the believer of any obligation to provide reasons for her belief in these claims. In answer to this charge, the defender of this brand of Catholic epistemology can reply that what is claimed to be basic is not a privileged proposition available only to partisans of Catholic Christian truth, but rather a set of metaphysical principles that are constantly assumed by many, from respected philosophic voices in pagan antiquity to crime scene investigators.[48] One might object to this that the reason that our knowledge of the principle is justified, or warranted as basic, is that God intends for our faculties to deliver these true beliefs to us. This seems to reduce to the claim that we *know* the universe is ordered because it *is* ordered (and theistically ordered at that), and this seems circular. In response, I would claim that the circularity is not vicious. For the circularity to be vicious, it ought to use as a premise the very thing it intends to prove. It is not doing that; it is simply taking advantage of the penchant people have for believing that events and facts have explanations and exploiting this to show that this overarching general principle entails the existence of a self-existent Being. Is this a moderating of the Church's position? Perhaps it is, but only because we live in an epistemological environment where global skepticism has entered into the fray. Post-Cartesian radical doubters were never Aquinas's audience. Aquinas never took global skepticism seriously, and did not think he needed a direct response to it. I think there is little reason to believe that the dogmatic documents of the Church take global skepticism any more seriously than Aquinas did.

Thus, the view we are examining here would hold that God's existence can indeed by known with certainty, and by no other capacity than natural reason, but that it is precisely natural reason that would infer God's existence on the basis of foundational principles that are not themselves inferred. In this context, it means something to call reason "natural." It means that it is ordinary and natural for humans to correctly believe that certain principles are in fact true, which they constantly take for granted in their everyday lives and only venture to call into question when the conversation shifts to abstruse philosophical discussion. Thus, one might undertake Rowe's suggested introspection, and find that PSR just does seem compelling. We must, however, leave open the possibility that one could *know* (and not just be rationally justified in believing) PSR just because one is, in effect, *designed* to know PSR. Perhaps one is also aware that from PSR (and the contingency of created things) one can infer the existence of a self-existent being, and perhaps also knows of arguments that might convince her that this self-existent being is the theistic God. If so, these beliefs might then qualify as certain knowledge if the foundational beliefs are known, and the inferential relations are clear. All of this appears to be consistent with what the Church wants to claim, namely, that nonsectarian (but nonetheless natural and human) reason can make a powerful contribution to belief in God, but that reason might first need to exorcise itself of any skeptical worries about, among other things, evil demons and brains in vats.

Basic Belief in God in Kierkegaard and Catholic Theology

Thus far we have discussed how knowledge of PSR could be basic. In this section, we will consider a different, but related, question, namely, whether and how a belief in God's existence might also be basic. To claim that belief in God is basic is a tenet typically associated with Reformed Epistemology, and has often been taken to distinguish the latter from Catholic views.[49] Recently, however, Stephen R. Grimm has argued that Cardinal Newman's epistemological views are substantially in harmony with those of Reformed Epistemology.[50] Newman, for instance, takes the case of a child (he supposes the age of five or six), who forms his belief in God through the development of his awareness of a moral governor without inferring it from other beliefs.[51] There is an interesting comparison to be made here with Kierkegaard, especially with his pseudonym Judge William's account of his childhood. In *Either/Or*, part 2, Judge William describes the way his first homework assignment (at age five) inculcated within him a sense of duty, and that this eternal duty was a proof of the immortality of his soul (*EO*, vol. 2, 270). Now, it is certainly true that Newman's views on conscience are thought to be a clue to our awareness of God's existence, whereas Judge William draws this out more explicitly to the immortality of the soul. However, the similarities on this point suggest that Kierkegaard can countenance an awareness of God and the eternal even in the natural human being.

When we shift our focus more squarely to the question of a basic knowledge of God, we must notice that Kierkegaard, in his own journals, writes, in 1848, "I cannot get away from the thought I have had from the beginning: does not every man in his quiet mind think about God" (*JP*, 6:6158 / *SKP*, IX A 55). It is also significant that in a draft for *Philosophical Fragments*, Kierkegaard has Climacus say, "Just as no one has ever proved it [i.e., God's existence], so there has never been an atheist, even though there certainly have been many who have been unwilling to let what they knew (that the God [*Guden*] exists) get control of their minds" (*JP*, 3:3606 / *SKP*, V B 40:11).[52] Thus, although Kierkegaard does not appear to endorse the soundness of a proof for God's existence in the ordinary sense, he cannot quite pull himself (or even the pseudonym most opposed to arguments for God's existence) away from the idea that humans might have some kind of fundamental knowledge of God, whether they recognize it explicitly or not.

This line of thought has many distinguished proponents. For our purposes here, let us consider briefly the contributions of two, namely, the Reformed philosopher Alvin Plantinga and the Catholic theologian Karl Rahner. One of Plantinga's major contributions has been his development of what he has called the "Aquinas/Calvin Model" of basic belief in God for human beings.[53] According to this model, we human beings naturally have implanted within us (by God) a tendency to form true beliefs about God. Plantinga, following Calvin, calls this the *sensus divinitatis.* He writes, "The *sensus divinitatis* is a disposition or set of dispositions to form theistic beliefs in various circumstances, in response to the sorts of conditions or stimuli that trigger the working of this sense of divinity."[54] However, a difference between Plantinga and the Catholic natural theological tradition here is that Plantinga does not think that this natural knowledge is arrived at by an inferential process. In fact, he even argues against a natural theological interpretation of Romans 1:20, suggesting that it aligns more neatly with his *sensus divinitatis* than with natural theology.[55] What, then, is the difference between natural theology and the *sensus divinitatis* on this score? The answer has to do with how the theistic beliefs are formed. Plantinga writes, "Upon the perception of the night sky or the mountain vista or the tiny flower, these beliefs just arise in us. They are *occasioned* by the circumstances; they are not conclusions from them. The heavens declare the glory of God and the skies proclaim the work of his hands: but not by way of serving as premises for an argument."[56]

While Plantinga is here distancing himself from natural theology in the ordinary sense, it is worth noting that many Catholic theologians find a similar, though not necessarily identical, way of talking about the knowledge of God to be attractive. Plantinga's Aquinas/Calvin model is intended to be a rather broad presentation of non-inferential ways of naturally knowing God. It is broad enough to encompass the idea that God's presence is understood by the subject to be exterior or interior. One aspect of Aquinas's work that may be fruitful in a slightly narrower way, however, argues that "the light of natural reason itself is a participation of the divine light."[57] This suggestion in Aquinas, further developed by Karl Rahner, proposes that if external circumstances "trigger" a *natural* awareness of God, we should nonetheless understand God's presence as interior, rather than exterior, and in some sense phenomenologically prior to our own act of understanding these ordinary perceptual stimuli. Both are non-inferential modes of knowing God, but Rahner's method suggests a particular specification of a broader Aquinas/Calvin model.

Rahner made an especially memorable mark on theology in his doctrine of the "anonymous Christian," which is often cited in discussions of religious inclusivism.[58] However, he also believed in what he called an "unthematic and anonymous" knowledge of God.[59] This "transcendental" knowledge was said by Rahner to be co-present with every act of knowledge, because it was different from and necessary for an individual apprehension of any single object of knowledge.[60] This is why Rahner writes, "All clear understanding is grounded in the darkness of God."[61] Rahner even claims that this transcendental knowledge "has to be called a posteriori insofar as every transcendental experience is mediated by a categorical encounter with concrete reality in our world, both the world of things and the world of persons."[62] While never directly repudiating the traditional "proofs" for God's existence, Rahner insists that a posteriori proofs should not be "misunderstood in the sense that God could simply be indoctrinated from without as an object of our knowledge."[63]

Thus, while Rahner does not wish to impugn the a posteriori character of the natural knowledge of God, he appears to want to insist that natural knowledge is never identical with what we might call *purely secular knowledge* (which is ultimately a chimera). That is, even our "natural" experience is already saturated with the presence of God, and while Rahner himself constantly points out that we can deny, or "suppress," this,[64] we nevertheless always have this primordial awareness as a part of our very being, especially as prior to, and necessary for, any act of understanding.

Despite his clear disavowal of natural theology (in contrast to Rahner's measured and somewhat tepid reception), Kierkegaard would likely approve of much of what Rahner has said in connection with a transcendental knowledge of God. As early as 1838, he wrote:

> Developing a priori basic concepts is like prayer in the Chr. sphere, for one would think that here man placed himself in relation to the Deity in the freest, most subjective way; and yet we are told that it is the Holy Spirit that effects prayer, so that the only prayer left to us would be to be able to pray, although upon closer inspection even this has been effected in us—similarly there is no deductive development of concepts, or whatever one wants to call that which has some constitutive power—man can only call it to mind, and willing this, if this willing is not an empty, unproductive gaping, is what corresponds to this single prayer and, just like it, is effected in us. (*JN*, 1:261 / DD: 176)

In the margin for this entry, Kierkegaard also notes, "One can therefore also say that all knowing is like the drawing of breath, a *respiratio*." (*JN*, 1:261 / DD: 176.a). The point of these entries, though not easy to discern, seems to be that, in the Christian sphere, one would think that one could simply pray to God, much in the same way that one would lay his entreaties before a king. However, it is not like this, since the Spirit effects prayer, and indeed makes us capable of it. In a similar way, our concepts and our understanding are not the job of our autonomous deductive reason, but rather, all our knowing is connected with the Holy Spirit, who makes each knowing act possible.

What the foregoing has shown is that while atheists can come to knowledge of a great many things, ultimately the atheist's project is unworkable, for both Kierkegaard and Catholicism. This is because even our ability to grasp truths that are not strictly religious or supernatural is already overrun with God's active presence. Perhaps this means that Climacus is partly right in his attack on natural theology in that we do already know, in some sense, the existence of God prior to proving it. However, the sense in which we know God's existence prior to its proof is the sense in which we are all aware of God's existence in our innermost being, and yet there are significant impediments, having to do with the reign of sin in our lives, that can hamper our ability to make this knowledge explicit. Natural reason can make us aware of God's existence using faculties generally available to all rational beings. As a result, according to Paul, we have "no excuse." Our sinful tendency to attempt to live without God is checked by our ability to discern clear signs of God's existence, whether that be through Newman's route of conscience (where a significant parallel exists in Kierkegaard's writings), Plantinga's basic beliefs, Rahner's transcendental knowledge, or more traditional demonstrative evidence. No doubt this is why the *Catechism* tells us that this natural knowledge enables us to receive God's revelation.[65]

My view here comes to this: natural theology is helpful and available, but this does not mean that we have demonstrative knowledge of the principles that undergird the premises of the traditional arguments for God's existence. Some of these principles, such as PSR, can be had by way of a more basic, non-inferential knowledge that has everything to do with the proper functioning of our cognitive faculties in the right sort of environment. As it happens, strong similarities between Kierkegaard and Plantinga along the lines of properly basic belief in God have already been shown.[66] If Kierkegaard is a proper functionalist of sorts, we might ask ourselves whether Kierkegaard would find some basic metaphysical principles, such as PSR, to be properly basic. If so, what would prevent him from endorsing the cosmological argument?

In addition, there are even parallels (or at any rate, analogues) in the Catholic tradition along the lines of a properly basic belief in God to be glimpsed in Newman and in Rahner. Properly basic knowledge of metaphysical principles (such as PSR) and properly basic knowledge of God are certainly distinct, but they are related. While the Catholic tradition is somewhat more reticent to believe that the claims of faith per se are properly basic,[67] and I share this reticence, there is still much that Kierkegaard and Catholicism have in common with respect to the epistemological underpinnings of theistic belief. In the following section, I will briefly consider the consequences of sin and just how much it is said to dull our epistemic faculties.

The Consequences of Sin in Kierkegaard and Catholicism

In this brief section I want to discuss how Kierkegaard and the Catholic tradition can both give accounts of the deleterious consequences of sin for natural knowledge of God without the need to deny natural knowledge altogether or implausibly claim that all atheism is culpable. To do this we need to briefly consider the pseudonym Anti-Climacus's claims about sin in *The Sickness unto Death*.

Anti-Climacus contrasts Socrates' view of sin with the "Christian" view of sin. The difference is taken to be that Socrates believes that sin is most deeply rooted in ignorance, and thus, "The Socratic principle works out in the following way. When someone does not do what is right, then neither has he understood what is right" (*SUD*, 92). By contrast, what Anti-Climacus is pleased to call the Christian view of sin insists that "sin is not a matter of a person's not having understood what is right but of his being unwilling to understand it, of his not willing what is right" (*SUD*, 95). For Anti-Climacus, the reason for this refusal to will to understand the truth, this lying to oneself, is that the individual is in despair. Thus, one way to account for the origin of atheism in Kierkegaard's work is that the reason for the phenomenon of atheism is that people are sinful and that they defiantly refuse to recognize the truth of God's existence and thus their creaturely dependence upon God.

While I see no need for a Christian or theist to deny that this possibility exists, it is highly implausible if interpreted as the *only* explanation for the phenomenon of atheism (even from a theistic point of view) for the very good reason that many atheists are honestly persuaded of the truth of their position and seem not to be numbered among the world's gravest sinners. On the other hand, the reason for the Catholic insistence on the competence of reason, and thus the availability of natural theology in the first place, was rooted in Paul's claim that, because all can come to know God, all are left with "no excuse." How can we resolve this issue?

There are two things that I think are important to note here. First, while the route of natural theology is considered to be generally available, Aquinas, for instance, makes it clear that there exists a "common and confused knowledge of God" which is found, he thinks, in practically everyone.[68] This "common and confused" knowledge is said to arise from observing nature's order, but it does not entail knowledge of the "orderer's" attributes, or indeed of whether there is only *one* "orderer."[69] This type of natural knowledge does not depend upon an especially acute demonstrative intellect (and so is available to the greater mass of uneducated people), but it also has fewer payoffs for that reason. Notice here that, while *monotheism* is within the scope of natural theology, it may be partially hidden without an intellect suited for demonstrative proofs.

This, claim, however, would seem to only accentuate the problem. After all, is not Vittorio Messori right, in his question to John Paul II, when he claims that it is precisely atheism that has often been confined to the "*elite* and intellectuals?"[70] If so, this would seem to be a counterexample to the claim that everyday people possess a "common and confused" knowledge of God, but that intellectuals possess a finer and more sophisticated knowledge of God.[71] For this reason, we must turn to investigate the consequences of sin. We have already noticed Anti-Climacus saying that sinful humans can (culpably) deny their own knowledge of God and other Christian truths. But, under the assumption that natural knowledge of God is available, can atheists deny God's existence without being culpable for this denial?

One way to respond to this is to use a Kierkegaardian tack helpfully articulated by Evans. Evans uses 1 Samuel 3 to demonstrate how it is possible to have an encounter with God without knowing that it is God whom one encounters.[72] In that episode, Samuel is being called by God's voice, but Samuel does not learn that it might indeed be God's voice until Eli the priest instructs him. Evans goes on to argue that an atheist might well have an encounter with God through the experience of moral conduct. Just as Newman argued that conscience provided a way for awareness of God, Evans sees Kierkegaard as arguing for something similar, and in a way that might permit atheists to have this awareness. Evans writes, "If they are truly responsive to the voice of conscience and truly seek the Good, then they may in fact be in a situation analogous to Kierkegaard's pagan:[73] someone who has more truth in his or her life than another person who may assent to true propositions about God but who does not truly respond to God's call as that call manifests itself through conscience."[74]

One might compare this claim with Vatican II's own statement on the possibility of salvation for those outside the readily visible confines of the Catholic Church. In *Lumen Gentium,* we read:

> Those also can attain to salvation who through no fault of their own do not know the Gospel of Christ or His Church, yet sincerely seek God and moved by grace strive by their deeds to do His will as it is known to them through the dictates of conscience. Nor does Divine Providence deny the helps necessary for salvation to those who, without blame on their part, have not yet arrived at an explicit knowledge of God and with His grace strive to live a good life.[75]

I think there would be one significant difference between the view of Catholicism and the view Evans is articulating as Kierkegaardian here. I think Evans is right to think that, for Kierkegaard, even a non-theist could encounter God *in* the moral life of Kierkegaard's ethical sphere without recognizing God therein. Where I think there is a difference between Kierkegaard and Catholicism on this point is that Kierkegaard would hold that *fulfilling* the moral requirement would be to obey the divine command to love the neighbor, which Kierkegaard takes to be a revelation (*WL,* 44).[76] Even if the atheist can fulfill this obligation without knowing God as its origin, the knowledge of the requirement would not be natural knowledge. For Catholicism, natural knowledge, as we will see in the next chapter, can make us aware of particular ethical requirements that can be fulfilled without the special grace of Christian charity. Fulfillment simply of the natural law does not save a person for Catholicism, though, and so perhaps there is an implicit faith also being referenced.[77] These facts might explain how someone could be entering into a relationship with God as an atheist, but the question that remains is how does our individual obtain the false belief that there is no God without culpability?

On this point, we might consider the phenomenon of social sin. In his apostolic exhortation *Reconciliatio et Paenitentia,* John Paul II described one important aspect of this phenomenon. He writes:

> To speak of social sin means in the first place to recognize that, by virtue of human solidarity which is as mysterious and intangible as it is real and concrete, each individual's sin in some way affects others. Consequently one can speak of a communion of sin, whereby a soul that lowers itself through sin drags down with itself the church and, in some way, the whole world. . . . With greater or lesser violence, with greater or lesser harm, every sin has repercussions on the entire ecclesial body and the whole human family.[78]

In this way, sin always drags down the world by its very nature. In fact, as we saw earlier, Benedict XVI argues that, presumably through sin, we have cut ourselves off from a primordial understanding of creation. Benedict appeared to be insisting that the kind of scientific methodology that comes with an a priori prejudice against God is a sinful mentality into which it is too easy to get caught up.[79] Thus, we can certainly find, in the Catholic tradition, an insistence that personal sin has social effects, and there is no reason to restrict these effects to the individuals who perpetrated the sin, where original sin is the obvious paradigm case.[80] These social effects can also have epistemic repercussions.

The epistemic repercussions that social sin can have can obscure the natural knowledge that might ordinarily come much easier.[81] John Paul II discusses an example of this in connection with Gandhi and specifically Christian knowledge. He notes that, for many, the negative connotations that are associated with life in Western society "present a considerable obstacle to the acceptance of the Gospel." Of Gandhi, he asks, "Could a man who fought for the liberation of his great nation from colonial independence accept Christianity in the same form as it had been imposed on his country by those same colonial powers?"[82] While John Paul's example is of specifically Christian knowledge, what we have seen in the foregoing provides support for extending this analysis to the case of natural knowledge of God.

In addition, Vatican II also insisted that atheism all too often arises from a well-meaning protest against the evil in the world and, in some cases, the inadequate Christian credentials of the faithful.[83] The distinction between implicit and explicit faith (common in Catholic circles) is not one that Kierkegaard clearly made, but the category makes some sense of his insistence that the passionate pagan has more truth than the nominal Christian. It also helps us to understand what religious harm individuals can do to others without necessarily robbing them of their eternal reward.

‡

Kierkegaard's pseudonymous attacks on natural theology's attempts to prove God's existence go only so far. So long as there is an acceptable epistemological option available to ground our awareness of the principles that undergird the premises of demonstrative arguments, then some demonstrative arguments may in fact prove God's existence with certainty by natural reason (so long as natural reason is properly understood). In fact, it has been argued elsewhere that Kierkegaard himself accepts some aspects of the epistemological picture that would make this possible.

Kierkegaard has a positive role to play in helping to "purify" reason, as John Paul II had it, since he urges us to remind ourselves of the theological moorings that enable reason to discern what Benedict XVI called "the fact of creation." Further, Kierkegaard and the Catholic tradition appear to share a sense that the knowledge of God's existence should be available to all, independently of whether these individuals have the capacity for digesting complex demonstrative arguments. Parallels to aspects of Kierkegaard's work can be found in Newman's understanding of conscience and in Rahner's notion of transcendental knowledge of God. All of this would seem to be a natural knowledge independent of a particular revelation by God.

Kierkegaard and the Catholic tradition can also be mutually reinforcing on the issue of non-culpable atheism. There are resources in both for implicit theism in the face of explicit atheism. In addition, the phenomenon of social sin in the Catholic tradition may indicate an advance upon Kierkegaard's thought on this issue, but Kierkegaard's depth in probing human despair can also be helpful in imagining cases of what we might, following Evans, call "motivated atheism."[84] In some cases, the motivation is understandable, but it is not ultimately an "excuse."

TWO

Is Abraham a Hero?
The Natural Law and a
Problem in *Fear and Trembling*

We realized that we would have to suffer, and that from
now on we would no longer have any hope in this life.

THE MARTYRDOM OF PERPETUA

One of the things that Kierkegaard does better than anyone else is to take
a problem that so many others have considered from a purely theoretical
point of view and to consider it for its real-life implications. In Kierkegaard's famous work *Fear and Trembling,* the pseudonym Johannes de
Silentio takes this approach to the near-sacrifice of Isaac by Abraham.
The work may perhaps never be surpassed for its insistence on arguing out in detail what the psychological and existential character of
Abraham's experience was in being commanded to do something so
horrific. In the text, we are not asked theoretical questions about God's
commands so much as we are given an engagingly frank discussion
about what sort of anguish Abraham must have been going through in
the course of the episode related by Genesis 22.

Fear and Trembling has sometimes been taken to give Kierkegaard's
ethical theory. Thankfully, it does not. Kierkegaard's Christian ethic
of love is to be found in *Works of Love,* the subject of the third chapter in this book. Still, I believe that Evans is right in his contention
that the foundation of Kierkegaard's ethic of love is to be sought in
a sophisticated version of what is known as divine command theory.

Significantly, the essence of divine command theory is fairly well, and favorably, articulated by none other than Luther himself when he writes, "The first thing to know is that there are no good works except those works God has commanded, just as there is no sin except that which God has forbidden."[1] That is, for divine command theory, ethical actions that are obligatory acquire their binding status from divine commands, preferences, or volitions. Likewise, ethical actions that are prohibited acquire this status from divine prohibitions of one sort or another. In addition, this theory of ethics often, though not always, carries with it a claim about how ethical obligations cannot be known apart from divine revelation.

By contrast, natural law ethics claims that many of our most basic ethical obligations are epistemologically available to everyone, and need not be the subject of a special divine command to be obligatory. This does not preclude some actions from acquiring from a special divine edict a binding status they would not otherwise have. Yet, natural law claims that our ordinary obligations acquire such binding force not directly from God's special commands, but simply from the fact that human nature flourishes and languishes in particular sorts of environments. An understanding of natural law is indispensable for an understanding of the common approach to morality in the Catholic tradition.[2] Aquinas is, in many ways, the fountainhead of this tradition, and so it will be helpful to consult his views. In this chapter, I argue that Aquinas's system, perhaps surprisingly, upholds the very things that Silentio seems to prize in Abraham's action, and does so better than the text of *Fear and Trembling* does.

My aims in this chapter do not permit me to confine myself to a more modest argument. As much as I admire Kierkegaard's work in general, and this relentlessly disputed text in particular, I believe that *Fear and Trembling* is ultimately inconsistent and that its aims are better understood by Thomistic natural law. Since the argument is somewhat ambitious, to sustain it will take some length and detail. Part of the reason I think that Silentio's text is in need of revision, however, is that I believe that St. Perpetua's martyrdom, the crucial element of which is the leading quotation of this chapter, cannot be embraced on this picture of faith.[3] I believe that Thomistic natural law has the virtue of being able to accommodate her case and that it can also retain the existential absurdity of Abraham's faith, at which Silentio so rapturously marvels. The upshot is that Silentio can have all the existential absurdity he wants and more in natural law.

Silentio goes to a great deal of trouble to explain what Abraham did *not* do when asked by God to offer up his son as a burnt offering on Mount Moriah. Related to this account are three figures in the rest of *Fear and Trembling,* namely, the tragic hero, the knight of infinite resignation, and the knight of faith. The knight of faith is clearly supposed to take pride of place as the exemplar of the life of faith.[4] I argue, however, that Silentio's categories, for all their interest, are not consistent with the claims he makes for them. Yet, for all the helpfulness of what I see as Aquinas's theoretical contribution to understanding this episode, called the *Akedah,* or "binding" of Isaac by the Rabbinic tradition, an investigation into Abraham's experience might never have been glimpsed with such clarity and passion without Silentio's illuminating work.

A Preliminary Issue

I cannot here analyze every view that differs from my own in the vast literature on *Fear and Trembling,* but I want to remark on one trend in that literature before beginning my main argument. Some readers of *Fear and Trembling* take it that a large share of the point of the work is to anagogically point forward to the soteriology of the Christian faith that neither Silentio nor his Abraham professes.[5] This view would have it that the *Akedah* is a symbol of what is to come in the sacrifice of Jesus on the cross. This view has a long and honorable history, particularly in the patristic tradition.[6] I have no argument to raise against the view in question, stated as simply as it is above.[7] I agree, however, with Michelle Kosch when she writes that the "manifest content" of *Fear and Trembling* "suggests an interpretation on which the book's aim is to show exactly how terrifying the situation of someone who believes he has overriding individual obligations to God can be. The price of faith is renunciation of one's most deeply held desires, violation of moral duty, alienation from family and society, inability to explain oneself to others."[8] Yet, Kosch goes on to argue that Kierkegaard actually intends for the text to point to a "hidden message" that, at least in my view,

substantially contravenes a good portion of its "manifest content."[9]
Kosch is certainly right that we would indeed do ourselves a disser-
vice by thinking that Kierkegaard could have had nothing beyond the
"manifest content" up his sleeve in this pseudonymous text. There is
an enigma about *Fear and Trembling* to be sure, but I believe that the
"manifest content" should not be so easily dismissed.[10] Kierkegaard was
at least as fascinated by the *Akedah* as was Silentio, noting "The person
who has explained this mystery has explained my life" (*JN*, 2:156 / JJ:
87; *FT*, 242). Indeed, Kierkegaard himself uses the case of the *Akedah* as
at least a partial example of what is personally required of a Christian
who dies to the world (*FSE*, 79), without any reference to its additional
anagogical meaning.

Accordingly, there is not one and only one point that *Fear and Trembling* makes. However, one indispensable part of what makes it a classic
work is that it looks in earnest at a perplexing and philosophically diz-
zying passage of import for the Judeo-Christian tradition. On the one
hand, Abraham's near-sacrifice of Isaac raises questions about the nature
of ethical theories in relation to putative divine commands that appear
to transgress them. On the other hand, the book raises problems that
are just as serious about what kind of status this earthly life should have
for those with religious commitments. This latter way of looking at the
text treats it as a kind of anticipatory reply to hermeneuts of suspicion
such as Nietzsche. Nietzsche's chief enemy was the nihilism that he saw
in Christianity, a kind that lives for the world beyond, sacrificing this
life, and thus being hostile to life itself, since, for Nietzsche, this life is
the only one to be had.

Now, the idea that Silentio's text might give an incomplete picture
of the life of faith and even of Abraham is nothing new. It is, in fact,
explicitly developed by other pseudonyms and Kierkegaard himself.[11]
Yet, I will focus on the text of *Fear and Trembling*, not because I want to
ignore Kierkegaard's other works, but because I want to ask whether a
careful inquiry into this text actually gives indirect support for natural
law's vision of the relation between religion and ethics. What I argue,
then, is that, whether or not Kierkegaard himself intended the text to
indirectly point this out, the categories used to understand existential
faith in *Fear and Trembling* are in need of revision.

Faith and Hope in *Fear and Trembling*

Silentio's claim is that what makes Abraham so great is decidedly *not* that he simply consented to God's command to sacrifice his son, though that obedience is a necessary condition for the greatness of Abraham. Rather, what makes Abraham great in the work, and what earns him the title "knight of faith," is that he continues to hope against hope that he will *not* lose Isaac, despite having been commanded to offer him as a burnt offering. Accordingly, Edward F. Mooney is certainly right when he says, "Unlike the knight of infinite resignation, the faithful knight embraces the hopeful trusting expectation that Isaac will be restored."[12] Silentio writes:

> Yet Abraham had faith, and had faith for this life. In fact, if his faith had only been for a life to come, he certainly would have more readily discarded everything in order to rush out of a world to which he did not belong. . . . But Abraham had faith specifically for this life—faith that he would grow old in this country, be honored among the people, blessed by posterity, and unforgettable in Isaac, the most precious thing in his life, whom he embraced with a love that is inadequately described by saying he faithfully fulfilled the father's duty to love the son, which is indeed stated in the command: the son, whom you love. (*FT*, 20)

Silentio's point here seems to be that Abraham does not lose hope that God's earlier promises to bring forth progeny through Isaac will be fulfilled even when it is Abraham himself who is called upon, seemingly, to put an end to Isaac's life and all Abraham's hopes. Accordingly, Abraham does not simply put his trust in the fact that God will, in some vague sense, "work things out." Instead, Abraham trusts, very specifically, that God will see to it that Isaac is not permanently lost to this life, which means that Abraham trusts that he will not be called upon to murder Isaac.[13]

It is nonetheless important to note that Abraham believes, on Silentio's telling of the story, that he will not murder Isaac, *even if* he is called to actually go through with offering him as a burnt offering. Silentio writes, "Let us go further. We let Isaac actually be sacrificed. Abraham had faith. He did not have faith that he would be blessed in a future life but that he would be blessed here in the world. God could give him a new Isaac, could restore to life the one sacrificed. He had faith by virtue of the absurd, for all human calculation ceased long ago" (*FT*, 36). Thus, by all of our human knowledge, Abraham is setting out to kill Isaac, and Abraham may have it in view that he will be doing everything *humanly* necessary and even everything within his power to end Isaac's life. He does not believe, however, that this will be the last word, since he believes that God will raise progeny for him through Isaac (according to the first promise, on which see Gn 17:19) and thus that Isaac will live. The only thing that stands in the way of Abraham's ending Isaac's life is the possibility (to which Abraham passionately clings) that God either will not in fact demand Isaac or will raise Isaac up after Abraham fulfills the human conditions for taking his life. Without this possibility, Abraham has simply given up on God's first promise. This is why Abraham has faith for this life.

It is worth noticing that if Kierkegaard intends Abrahamic faith to be a "formal" lesson for all forms of faith, then Silentio's brand of faith will be in an interesting position to respond to the criticisms leveled against religious faith by the likes of Nietzsche. Nietzsche is famous for advancing the claim that Christianity says "no" to this life, and as part of this "no," teaches its adherents to be overly concerned about the afterlife, and thus "hostile to life."[14] In contrast, Silentio's work seems to give a substantive anticipatory reply to Nietzsche by arguing that Abrahamic faith, which is understood as exemplary by both Kierkegaard and the New Testament, hopes for *this* life. In fact, Silentio goes even further, arguing that a "faith" that does not hope for this life is not faith at all (*FT*, 20).[15] Despite the initial promise and interest of Silentio's anticipatory reply, I will argue that this element of hope for this life will ultimately prove deadly to his account of the formal kind of existential faith that must be modeled by any other faith,[16] especially Christian faith.

In addition to the knight of faith, Silentio's account also discusses the knight of infinite resignation. The stage of infinite resignation, I believe, is reached by taking Abraham's obedience to God's command, and subtracting the hope that he retains for this life, which is grounded in God's promise that descendants will be reckoned for him through Isaac.[17] Silentio writes:

> Indeed, if Abraham, the moment he swung his leg over the ass's back, had said to himself: Now Isaac is lost, I could just as well sacrifice him

here at home as ride the long way to Moriah—then I do not need Abraham, whereas now I bow seven times to his name and seventy times to his deed. This he did not do, as I can prove by his really fervent joy on receiving Isaac, and by his needing no preparation and no time to rally to finitude and its joy. If it had been otherwise with Abraham, he perhaps would have loved God but would not have had faith. . . . This is the peak on which Abraham stands. The last stage to pass from his view is the stage of infinite resignation. He actually goes further and comes to faith. (*FT,* 37)

As we see above, the knight of infinite resignation appears to give up the hope that Isaac will be returned in this life. This is not necessarily a shameful path, according to Silentio, who at one point appears to assert that he can "save [his] soul" by this sort of movement (*FT,* 49), but it is not faith, which holds on to the temporal.

It is important to note that knights of infinite resignation exemplify some virtues of the spiritual life. For one thing, they appear prepared to obey God unconditionally. For another thing, their lives are not "dissipated in multiplicity" (*FT,* 43) as, for example, are Kierkegaard's aesthetes, in the first part of *Either/Or.*[18] Rather, the knights of infinite resignation lead lives that must be unified by a single pursuit or desire (*FT,* 42–43), and they must love it. In an effort to describe the movement of infinite resignation, Silentio tells a story of how a young lad falls in love with a princess who is not, so to speak, his socioeconomic equal. Since the lad cannot obtain the princess's love in this life, Silentio writes, "his love for that princess would become for him the expression of an eternal love, would assume a religious character, would be transfigured into a love of the eternal being, which true enough denied the fulfillment but nevertheless did reconcile him once more in the eternal consciousness of its validity in an eternal form that no actuality can take away from him" (*FT,* 41–44).

The lad, as an exemplar of the knight of infinite resignation, preserves his love of the princess, but transforms it and looks to its crowning and ultimate fulfillment in the eschaton. By this method he also, as John Lippitt notes, makes himself immune from hurt, since no actuality can take away this kind of eschatological fulfillment from him.[19] Being immune from all real hurt in this earthly life, the knight of infinite resignation is a stranger and an alien in this world (*FT,* 41, 50). If the lad were a knight of faith, on the other hand, he would hope for the object of his affections, the princess, in this life. Silentio has this sort of lad say, "Nevertheless I have faith that I will get her—that is, by virtue of the absurd, by virtue of the fact that for God all things are possible" (*FT,* 46). The knight of infinite resignation is recognizable for being an alien in this world, over against the knight of faith, for whom one might easily mistake someone who is completely given over to the finite and nothing else (*FT,* 51). As Lippitt notes, "the crucial difference between infinite resignation and faith is that the knight of faith's care for the finite, and ability to dwell in it, remains undiminished."[20]

Let us observe, then, what the knights of faith and knights of infinite resignation have in common. Both knights of faith and of infinite resignation fulfill the following two conditions:

> (1) I have concentrated on some desire[21] with the whole substance of my life (*FT,* 42–43).
>
> (2) I obediently respond to God's command (or at any rate, I capitulate with respect to my circumstances, as in the case of the young lad), even if, from the outward and human point of view, this requires giving up my human grasp on the object of my desire (*FT,* 35).

The knight of infinite resignation and the knight of faith differ; however, in that the former goes on to add:

> (3) I recognize that the object of my desire is impossible for me to acquire in this earthly life by my human capabilities, and so believe that, while its significance will be recaptured in eternity,[22] it is lost to me in time (*FT,* 35, 43).

The knight of infinite resignation, accordingly, reifies the resignation in (2) so that (2) is not a step onto something else, and thus (3) closes off the ("absurd") possibility that the duties and relationships suspended by (2) will be recaptured in this earthly life. As Edward F. Mooney notes, the knight of infinite resignation has "written . . . off, temporally speaking" the desire or pursuit into which the substance of his life was thrust.[23]

In contrast, the knight of faith makes the movement of resignation captured by (1) and (2), but does not reify this resignation. Rather, he believes that Isaac will be returned to him (or that the princess will be his in time) after having seen to it that all human possibilities for this happening have been exhausted. That is, the knight of faith takes (1) and (2) and adds to them the following:

(4) I recognize that the object of my desire is impossible for me to acquire in this life by my human capabilities, but nevertheless believe
that I will acquire it in this life, by God's miraculous intervention,
contrary to all expectations and human possibilities (or "by virtue
of the absurd") (*FT,* 46).

To this one might object that Silentio does not intend faith, perhaps even
Abraham's faith, to be for this earthly life. I think the best way to do
this is to consider the way Davenport recently took in correspondence
with me, arguing that it is "implicit" in the text that the hereafter forms
another temporal sequence, and so even the lad gets the princess in (a
different sequence of) time. The problem with that reading is that it is not
what Silentio means by "this life" at *FT,* 20, where he says that real faith
must be for this life, explicitly distinguishing this from "a life to come,"
and noting very earthly results in which Abraham had faith. It would
not be surprising that Silentio's unrestrained admiration for Abraham
would result in a similarly unrestrained view of existential faith. I believe
that this is what we find.

Thus, the knights of faith and the knights of infinite resignation appear to occupy slightly different territory vis-à-vis Nietzsche's criticism
of Christianity. The knight of infinite resignation appears to have no
response to Nietzsche's criticism that Christianity is, in a sense, hostile
to life, since the kind of religious movement he undertakes makes him
an alien in this world (*FT,* 41), only to find his true home in the next.
Of course, when there *is* a next world, that might not be quite as bad as
Nietzsche thinks. The knight of faith, on the other hand, seems to hold
out some interesting philosophical promise, because he appears to give
one example of how existential faith (and thus Christian faith as an
instance of the former) is not world-negating. Silentio's category of the
tragic hero, I will show, brings some depth and some serious complexity
to the relationship between the knight of faith and the knight of infinite
resignation. Ultimately, I will argue that the three categories must be
mixed in any adequate ideal of faith.

The Tragic Hero and the Knight of Faith

Things get considerably more complicated when we usher in the category
of the tragic hero. The tragic hero is a category that is articulated in

Problema I, whose leading question is, "Is there a Teleological Suspension of the Ethical?"[24] Here, the concern is not so much with affirming this earthly life, but with the status of the ethical, understood primarily as Hegelian Universal, or "social morality."[25] In particular, Silentio is interested in the individual (Abraham) over against the universal (social morality). The tragic hero, by contrast, allows a duty that admits of an ethical (in Silentio's sense) justification to "trump" some other of his ethical duties. Examples of this sort of hero are Agamemnon, Brutus, and Jephthah, all of whom, at least on Silentio's interpretation,[26] were bound to kill at least one of their children in virtue of a higher allegiance to the aims of the state. While our contemporary intuitions would judge such individuals unethical from the start, Silentio never bats an eye at the idea that their actions can be justified within "the ethical." The question is whether Abraham's action is of the same sort, where lying to prevent an innocent person from suffering certain harm is also, qualitatively, taken to be of this same sort. Thus, the question of whether Abraham is a tragic hero is ultimately a question of whether Abraham exchanges one "ethical" duty for another.

Silentio, in the main, evidently believes that the answer to that question is a *negative* one: Abraham is *not* a tragic hero. Instead, Silentio says, Abraham suspends "the ethical" in favor of a higher τέλος altogether. Silentio writes:

> The difference between the tragic hero and Abraham is very obvious. The tragic hero is still within the ethical. He allows an expression of the ethical to have its τέλος in a higher expression of the ethical. . . . Abraham's situation is different. By his act he transgressed the ethical altogether and had a higher τέλος outside it, in relation to which he suspended it. For I certainly would like to know how Abraham's act can be related to the universal, whether any point of contact between what Abraham did and the universal can be found other than that Abraham transgressed it. (*FT*, 59)

Silentio thus notes that Abraham does not perform his act to save a nation or to appease angry gods, as would be true of the other tragic heroes. He writes, "It is not to save a nation, not to uphold the idea of the state that Abraham does it; it is not to appease the angry gods. If it were a matter of the deity's being angry, then he was, after all, angry only with Abraham, and Abraham's act is totally unrelated to the universal, is a purely private endeavor. Therefore, while the tragic hero is great because of his moral virtue, Abraham is great because of a purely personal virtue" (*FT,* 59). Thus, Abraham is not within the "ethical" as we are to understand it in Problema I, because "the ethical" in that sense is intrinsically tied to moral duties that are not private, but corporate, as duties to the state would be.

Yet, Problema II opens with a new question, namely, "Is there an Absolute Duty to God?" Now, if an ethical theory is simply a theoretical algorithm for deciding which actions are taken to be morally right and wrong, then the assertion that Abraham has an absolute duty to God and obeys it appears to give us another answer to the question of whether Abraham is within the ethical.[27] The answer to this question appears to be an *affirmative* one. Silentio writes, in Problema II, "In this connection, to say that it is a duty to love God means something different from the above, for if this duty is absolute, then the ethical is reduced to the relative" (*FT,* 70). Silentio appears to use the phrase "the ethical" with some uniformity in the text, but his sense of the word openly contrasts with what we often mean by "ethical." This is why J. Kellenberger distinguishes two senses of "ethical," where "ethical$_1$" refers to the kind of publicly available social morality that Abraham appears to teleologically suspend, and "ethical$_2$" is the ethical that Abraham obeys and does not teleologically suspend. Kellenberger writes, "The ethical$_2$ is universal in the sense that its obligations bind all who have them, but within the ethical$_2$ some individuals are bound by certain individual duties that may be far from evident to many."[28]

But what exactly is it supposed to *mean* that Abraham teleologically suspends the ethical, in the sense of the ethical$_1$? Kellenberger claims that ethical$_1$ consists of obligations that "are both binding on all and clear to all."[29] But what sort of ethical theory could that be? The two most historically plausible candidates are Kantian and Hegelian ethics. Kant famously had a very strong reaction to the *Akedah,* in which he wrote, "Abraham should have replied to this supposedly divine voice: 'That I ought not to kill my good son is quite certain. But that you, this apparition, are God—of that I am not certain, and never can be, not even if this voice rings down to me from (visible) heaven.'"[30] There are some troubles with taking Kant as Silentio's target here, though. As Lippitt writes, "Agamemnon . . . is quite prepared to kill in the interests of his duties qua king: an action of which a strict Kantian would not be able to approve."[31] That is, the tragic hero is supposed to be "still within the ethical," but it is precisely the tragic hero that perpetrates acts that would never be permissible on Kant's ethical theory.

Take, for example, Jephthah, who, before winning a battle for Israel, vows to sacrifice to God as a burnt offering whatever comes out of his door in the event of victory (thinking perhaps that it might be a farm animal). He grieves as his daughter comes running out to greet him, but nonetheless (on Silentio's reading, at any rate) eventually sacrifices her, knowing that the nation of Israel would be visited by God's wrath in response to an impious refusal by Jephthah to keep his oath (see Jgs 11:29–40). This sort of action could not be justified within a rigidly Kantian ethical scheme, since in that framework one is hardly permitted to murder one's kin because one made an insane pledge to a seemingly vindictive deity.[32] Instead, most commentators now recognize that there are important Hegelian elements in the ethical that Abraham suspends, even if, as Ronald M. Green notes, "we cannot answer the question about the presence of a Kantian ethic in *Fear and Trembling* with certainty because the ethical position presented there, without attribution, seems to combine themes from the entire rationalist tradition begun by Kant."[33]

Supposing, then, that "the ethical" in Problema I has strong Hegelian elements, how exactly should we understand the "ethical-universal" in this context? In general, ethical life in the state is the highest life for a human being in Hegel's thought. Thus, in the ordinary case, Hegel appears to think that following our duties is largely a matter of following one's duties to one's state, and these duties "trump" other duties by their very nature.[34] Thus, on the one hand, Silentio's more-or-less Hegelian conception of the ethical appears to believe that the actions of his tragic heroes were justified within the ethical ideals already in place within their states at particular times.[35] On the other hand, however, particular states have their moment in history, for Hegel, and most of those that capture the limelight at a particular moment are doomed to fail at another. It is the hero, says Hegel, who founds states.[36]

Hegel writes:

> Such are all great historical men—whose own particular aims involve those large issues which are the will of the World-Spirit. They may be called Heroes, inasmuch as they have derived their purposes and their

vocation, not from the calm, regular course of things, sanctioned by the existing order; but from a concealed fount. . . . They are men, therefore, who appear to draw the impulse of their life from themselves. . . . But at the same time, they were thinking men, who had an insight into the requirements of the time—*what was ripe for development.*[37]

Now, my goal is not simply to claim that Abraham is a Hegelian hero in this context (it will still be clear that Abraham is not one), but I want to draw a lesson from what Silentio is saying, and Hegel's concept of a hero, while not being an exact fit for Silentio's concept of a tragic hero, will help us to see the point.

Notice that ethical life is proper within a state, for Hegel, and so he notes, "The rational end of man is life in the state, and if there is no state there, reason at once demands that one be founded."[38] This means, broadly speaking, that some actions, namely, those of heroes, can find their justification without the obvious trappings of ethical life in an already existing state, and in some cases, against them altogether (to found a new state). While Hegel has no patience for those who "seek guidance from the Lord" at the expense of reason,[39] he recognizes the importance of the hero's task, even though the hero sometimes *appears* to be following nothing more than his own individual understanding, *which may not even represent his contribution to reason and the state to his consciousness.* Hegel writes, "It was not, then, his private gain merely, but an unconscious impulse [*Instinkt*] that occasioned the accomplishment of that for which the time was ripe."[40] Thus, within Hegel's ethical theory, there is room for those whose actions can be judged only by their future outcomes, since to all appearances they are motivated only by individual concerns.

Silentio's Abraham differs from Hegel's hero in one important way, however. For Hegel, a hero's action, however arbitrary it may seem, ultimately finds its justification in the ethical imperative to found the state that reason demands be founded. That is, the movement of Hegel's thought (its dialectic) has its τέλος in a progressive, world-historical order—things are always getting better, from the point of view of reason, and this trajectory "rests immanent in [reason] itself" (*FT*, 54). By contrast, Silentio insists that "the paradox of faith, then, is this: that the single individual is higher than the universal, that the single individual . . . determines his relation to the universal by his relation to the absolute, not his relation to the absolute by his relation to the universal" (*FT*, 70). For Hegel, things are not getting better with Abraham; if anything the *Akedah* is a dialectical retrogression.[41] Thus, for Silentio, Hegel is right—if we judge Abraham by the standards of a rational world-history. However, Silentio insists that existential faith requires that those who would take faith upon themselves not judge Abraham in this way, but that individuals of faith instead believe that there is a God who is transcendent with respect to the world-historical, in response to whose commands one can acquire "purely personal virtue" in the way that Abraham did (*FT*, 59).

Tragic heroes must have their action take place within some kind of ethical system, governed by the progress of reason and/or the state in which the individual finds him or herself. By contrast, knights of faith are said to be able to acquire their virtue in a "purely personal" way, just as Abraham is said to do. But this reading of what appears to be Silentio's view faces some challenges in the text. Despite the fact that Silentio believes Abraham's *deed itself* to fall outside the pale of the ethical (*FT*, 59), he first imagines what he would do in Abraham's situation. Let us call this imagined version of Silentio, Silentio's "impostor." Before ever having defined the category of "tragic hero," Silentio writes:

> If I, (*in the capacity of tragic hero,* for higher I cannot come) had been ordered to take such an extraordinary royal journey such as the one to Mount Moriah, I know very well what I would have done. . . . The moment I mounted the horse, I would have said to myself: Now all is lost. God demands Isaac, I sacrifice him and along with him all my joy—yet God is love and continues to be that for me, for in the world of time God and I cannot talk with each other, we have no language in common. (*FT*, 35, italics original)

Silentio also says that, in this imagined episode, his "immense resignation" would have been a substitute for faith (*FT*, 35). Here, Silentio's impostor is called, by God, to sacrifice Isaac, and in obeying, resigns his finite claim on Isaac. The strange part about this is that Silentio has identified the impostor who sacrifices Isaac and loses hope not simply as an exemplar of resignation, but in addition, as a *tragic hero*, who is, by the definition in Problema I, "still within the ethical."

But which ethical is this impostor in? He isn't in Kant's ethical, because it would seem that he means to go through with the sacrifice of

Isaac, which is impermissible in that ethical framework. Nor is this impostor within Hegel's state, since Silentio explicitly distinguishes Abraham's *deed* (and *not* simply the *way* Abraham performs it) from the other
cases of the tragic hero.[42] Abraham won't even count as a Hegelian hero,
since Abraham isn't founding a state by means of Isaac's sacrifice; to
the contrary, and to all appearances, he's destroying one. But if Silentio
sees this fantastic journey as an example of the tragic hero, there must
be a nonstandard ethical to which Abraham belongs. C. Stephen Evans
puzzles over this difficulty as well, explicitly referencing this passage,
and noting that the "ethical" might need to mean something other than
the operative Hegelian concept.[43] I believe Evans is right about this, but
I also believe that Silentio can no longer have recourse to an account
of the "ethical" where this impostor counts as both a knight of infinite
resignation, willing to sacrifice Isaac, and a tragic hero, when one is
ordinarily disqualified from being a tragic hero when one's action does
nothing for the state (*FT,* 59).[44]

The Martyrdom of Perpetua

Suppose, however, that we shift the stage at this point. Instead of considering one of Abraham's impostors, let us consider an exemplar who,
if we trust the relevant historical sources, gave up hope in this life. Our
example is St. Perpetua the martyr, and the relevant passage leads off
this chapter.[45] As Herbert Musurillo points out, the account of her martyrdom became something of an "archetype" for later such accounts.[46]
Perpetua, a young woman of twenty-two, was imprisoned for her faith,
and had to relinquish her charge over her young son. Shortly thereafter she had a vision that indicated to her that her martyrdom was fast
approaching. After relating this vision to her brother, she notes, "we
realized that we would have to suffer, and that from now on we would
no longer have any hope in this life."[47] In ways that parallel some of the
issues at stake in Silentio's understanding of Abraham, Perpetua had to
suffer with the idea that she was abandoning her family. This is clearest
in relation to her father's pleading:

> "Daughter," he said, "have pity on my grey head—have pity on me your
> father, if I deserve to be called your father, if I have favoured you above
> all your brothers, if I have raised you to reach this prime in your life.

Do not abandon me to be the reproach of men. Think of your brothers, think of your mother and your aunt, think of your child, who will not be able to live once you are gone. Give up your pride! You will destroy all of us! None of us will ever be able to speak freely again if anything happens to you."[48]

Clearly Perpetua had to deal with considerable obstacles related to her family and their life in the community. This suggests that her obedience to God stands over against the Hegelian "universal." We shall see that this is significant in grounding our claim that Perpetua can be seen as a lady of faith.[49] Perhaps we can also suppose that Perpetua is thus a lady of infinite resignation, since she gives up her hope in this life, exchanging it for the hope of another. How does her example relate to Silentio's other concept of the tragic hero? After all, one might object, the martyrs sacrificed their *own* lives, whereas Silentio's fantasy involves Abraham preparing to sacrifice *Isaac's* life.

On this point, we should consider the essay, "Does a Human Being Have the Right to Let Himself Be Put to Death for the Truth?" by another of Kierkegaard's pseudonyms, H.H. (*WA*, 50–89). There, H.H., in an essay that, quite notably, exhibits several interesting literary parallels to *Fear and Trembling*,[50] claims that without appeal to Christian revelation (and thus a transcendent God's intervention) one does not have the right, *ethically* speaking, to "let himself be put to death for the truth" (*WA*, 84). This is likely to seem a strange claim until we remember that we are, at least implicitly, dealing with a Hegelian view of the "ethical." In such a framework one's action must find its justification within the movement of reason and its progress in human society. As we noted, Abraham's action is unacceptable in this framework. However, H.H.'s point is that a martyr's willingly dying for the "truth" is also ethically unacceptable unless there really is a transcendent revelation, which is on principle excluded by the Hegelian "ethical."[51] This would seem to count against her being viewed as a tragic hero, because it suggests that Perpetua is outside the "ethical" in the terms put forth by *Fear and Trembling*, because she looks to a transcendent God and a life to come, and not an ethics of immanence.

And yet, it strikes me as highly unlikely that Perpetua conceives of herself as doing nothing positive for a non-Hegelian, transcendent movement of history, or "dialectic" in her martyrdom. Instead, I think it is likely that she believes that she is contributing to the march of the Christian Church through history. This is why the early Church was always keenly aware of the fact that the blood of the martyrs is the seed of the Church.[52] It is also why Silentio is wrong to argue that, qualitatively, there is no difference between the Church and the state (*FT*, 74). The state demands an ethical justification that can find its place in a universe without a transcendent God. A Christian Church, by contrast, can hardly pass itself off as independent of a transcendent God, at least with regard to what it demands of its adherents.

When Silentio equates an ecclesiastical hero to a tragic hero, he denies that either the latter or the former could be a knight of faith (*FT*, 74). But there is a sense in which Perpetua is a lady of faith, a lady of infinite resignation, and now, Silentio's enigmatic passage that we saw earlier has given us a way to see her as a tragic (or ecclesiastical) hero, because she is contributing to the transcendent dialectic of the Christian Church. This dialectic is not immanent, and that is why Silentio is wrong to think that an ecclesiastical hero is the same as a tragic hero such as Agamemnon (*FT*, 35).

The difference between Perpetua's martyrdom and the tragic heroism of the Abraham impostor that Silentio imaginatively portrays is that his tragic heroism is a fault because it could have attained to the heights of faith. By contrast, Perpetua's heroism is a virtue, and it is faithful. Why the contrast? The tragic heroism of the Abraham impostor, in this circumstance, is paired with the kind of resignation that nullifies faith (because giving up hope in this case entails distrusting God's promise of progeny through Isaac). On the other hand, Perpetua's heroism is doing something positive for the dialectic of the Christian Church, whose tree she is causing to flower, and her personal resignation does not nullify her faith, because God's promise of victory in martyrdom to her is *meant* to be fulfilled in eternity, rather than on earth. Further, Perpetua, in obedience to a transcendent truth, sacrifices her life for precisely that truth, which in a Hegelian dialectic would be impermissible. If, as Silentio argues, "faith is precisely the paradox that the single individual as the single individual is higher than the universal" (*FT*, 55), then Perpetua should count as a lady of faith as well. Accounting for the faithfulness of an archetypal martyr such as Perpetua thus entails blending Silentio's categories of faith, infinite resignation, and tragic heroism.

This reading, however, presents us with a choice. Silentio argues that the knight/lady of faith and the knight/lady of resignation are distinct and that the former is superior to the latter. Either Perpetua's resignation hopes for the restoration of something in time and finitude, contrary to her words, and Silentio's account of faith is preserved, or Perpetua's resignation does *not* hope for the restoration of anything in earthly time, but her faith is recognized in preference to Silentio's account (especially proposition (4)). I believe the latter path to be the correct one.

One might try to get out of this dilemma by claiming that Perpetua hopes for the restoration of her life in the eschatological hereafter, which is itself a new, but nonetheless human, life, granted by a transcendent God, to which we can draw a temporal line (of some kind) from her earthly sojourn. My response to this objection is that it is precisely why Silentio's account of faith is inadequate, because he appears not to recognize that whether knights of infinite resignation are hoping in the correct way depends substantially upon whether or not their time has come to hope for the next life. He clearly demarcates the life to be had in eternity so strongly from the life to be had in this temporal order that there seems to be something deficient about the person who hopes only for the next life. But this need not be so, and the example of Perpetua should help us in understanding this point.

Silentio believes that one mark of faith is its continual hope for the fulfillment of its desire in *this* life. Yet, his account of Abraham uniquely privileges one individual desire, namely Isaac, and progeny through him. The experience of other Christian heroes of faith is not like this. Their experience hopes for the ultimate crowning and fulfillment of the projects of their lives, which can be accomplished only outside their earthly lives. Now it is indeed paradoxical to hope for the crowning and fulfillment of these lives at the very moment when they are, to speak in an earthly way, being brought to naught. In this sense, there is still hope in the face of the "absurd." One is no less required to rest one's hope on a possibility that can be accomplished only by a transcendent God, but this possibility does not, and need not, always include the hope that such crowning and fulfillment will take place prior to the "the new heavens and the new earth" (Is 66:22).

Thus, the correction I am arguing for is to claim that faith is constituted primarily by dying to our purely human hopes, and hoping for the fulfillment of the desire into which one has correctly concentrated the "whole substance of [one's] life" (*FT*, 43), *to be fulfilled in the manner that one's life, and thus God's providence, dictates.* Abraham's act is indeed faithful, but it is faithful not *because* he hoped for this life (which, is *not* a sine qua non for existential faith, on my view, contra Silentio), but because God's particular promise to bring progeny through Isaac *required* him to hope for this life, and Abraham obediently and joyfully did so. Thus, faith is a wider category than hoping for the fulfillment of one's desires in the midst of this earthly sojourn. It is possible that a relationship with God may require hoping for the fulfillment of one's desires in this earthly life. It is also possible that it may require abandoning hope in this earthly life, but neither of these is logically necessary for faith, since the martyrs, equally heroes of faith, on my view, either perceived that the providentially appointed time had come to abandon hope in this life for the hope of another, or perhaps simply saw no need to hold out a special hope for this earthly life in light of the likelihood of their impending death.[53]

An attentive reader of Kierkegaard would point out that this is only Silentio's problem. I am happy to agree; not only does Kierkegaard have a deeper ethical vision (on which, see *Works of Love* and the next chapter of this book), but Kierkegaard's later work emphasizes the role of the martyr as a "witness to the truth." There, Kierkegaard himself claims that a real "truth-witness" to Christianity (which hardly seems a lower category than a knight of faith) will be "unfamiliar with everything called enjoyment" (*M*, 5). In the same newspaper article, Kierkegaard notes that a martyr's death constitutes admission into the first order of the Christian faithful (*M*, 6). If Perpetua's martyrdom is indeed archetypical, then it seems clear that Kierkegaard takes a different view on the matter than Silentio. Still, the fact that Kierkegaard's most famous text (a fame that he himself predicted) has problems that can be addressed by turning to the Catholic tradition is a point worthy of careful discussion.

Why Natural Law?

I have come to believe that another perspective in ethics represents more faithfully what Silentio ultimately wants to prize in Abraham: that of the natural law ethics of Aquinas. I want to be clear that I am not here attempting an independent defense of natural law ethics as a freestanding ethical theory. I am simply arguing that natural law provides a particularly appropriate context for approaching the case of Abraham and for preserving the very things that Silentio wants to preserve about his act, while suitably modifying his picture to accommodate the wider picture of faith I have defended above. The two basic things natural law preserves are Silentio's beliefs about the structure of morality and his belief that Abraham's act is especially praiseworthy because in it, Abraham passionately retains the belief in the absurd, namely, that he will get Isaac back.

Natural law is a theory about ethics that simply maintains that there is a law to which everyone in principle has some amount of access and that prescribes certain basic moral norms, according to the most basic principle of human practical reason, namely, that one should seek after the good.[54] This is then expanded to what humans have in common with all substances, animals generally, and other humans. These aims are, respectively, to preserve their own existence (as all substances seek, in their own way, to do); to procreate and to instruct resulting offspring (as all animals seek to do); and to know the truth about God and to live peaceably in society with other humans (as all humans seek to do). Stephen J. Pope writes, "Natural law is 'law' in that it orders the person to act in some ways and to refrain from acting in other ways; it is 'natural' in that these requirements are derived from innate human inclinations and are integral to human flourishing."[55] On the principles of natural law, everyone grasps these basic requirements in some measure, though sin can pervert one's awareness of them in varying degrees.[56]

It is important to note that natural law is, by its very nature, subordinate to, because it is an expression of, the eternal law, for Aquinas, and indeed, for the way the Catholic Church has traditionally conceived of the natural law. This is why Pope Leo XIII wrote, "The natural law is written and engraved in the soul of each and every man, because it is human reason ordaining him to do good and forbidding him to sin. . . . But this command of human reason would not have the force of law if it were not the voice and interpreter of a higher reason to which our spirit and our freedom must be submitted."[57] Thus, when Aquinas asks "Whether the Natural Law Can Be Changed," the second objection to his position claims, "the slaying of the innocent . . . [is] against the natural law. But we find [this thing] changed by God: as when God commanded Abraham to slay his innocent son. Therefore the natural law can be changed."[58] While Aquinas maintains that the natural law can be added to, it cannot, in general, be the sort of thing from which one can subtract. Therefore, with respect to the slaughter of the innocent, Aquinas will want to claim that the natural law cannot be changed. In the response to the objection, then, Aquinas writes, "All men alike, both guilty and innocent, die the death of nature: which death of nature is inflicted by the power of God on account of original sin, according to 1 Kings 2:6: The Lord killeth and maketh alive. Consequently, by the command of God, death can be inflicted on any man, guilty or innocent, without any injustice whatever."[59] Aquinas's point here is not as difficult to discern as it is to swallow. God regulates the length of a person's earthly life, and so, should God determine that this life will be shorter than one might ordinarily expect, God may do so. Notice also that this is not a violation of the natural law at all, for Aquinas. This is because it is written into the very nature of the natural law that the eternal law, from which the natural law is derived,[60] can overrule some, though not all, things that would otherwise be violations of the natural law. This, again, is precisely because the natural law is simply the way in which human beings understand the eternal law of God's wisdom.

It is, however, important to note that, in insisting that Abraham's deed (were the knife to come down and slay Isaac) would not be a violation of the natural law, Aquinas is also insisting *that it would not, for that reason, count as murder.*[61] Rather, since Aquinas takes one punishment for sin (including original sin) to be death, God is just in meting out this punishment, and the only question is when it will be exacted. Further, the eternal law retains unchanging application in all affairs of creation, including the natural law. Aquinas writes, "Accordingly, the eternal law is nothing else than the type of Divine Wisdom, as directing all actions and movements."[62] Earlier, Aquinas is even more emphatic when he notes that "the natural law is nothing else than the rational creature's participation of the eternal law."[63] Thus, for Aquinas, the eternal law governs all things, and the natural law is one instance of that law that is derived from reason and that applies to rational beings, because of their own characteristic nature.

On this point, Denis Goulet writes, "Though St. Thomas agrees with Kierkegaard that personal vocation places a man apart from ordinary law, he did not feel compelled to assert along with the great Danish thinker that God's most intimate personal commands *contradict* those of the 'ethical sphere' or, what is for St. Thomas its equivalent, 'natural law.'"[64] This point needs to be revised with reference to Silentio's thought. The reason is that the natural law simply does not accurately correspond to Silentio's "ethical." Silentio's "ethical," as we have seen, presupposes an immanent dialectic. That is to say, it presupposes that the ethical "has nothing outside itself that is its τέλος" (*FT,* 54). Aquinas, however, unlike Silentio, was not battling with opponents who actually considered the movement of God to be purely immanent to world history.[65] It is true to say that Aquinas's natural law is not suspended, but the reason *why* natural law is not suspended and Hegelian ethics are is that the former never made the vaunted claims to self-sufficiency that were made by the latter. Recall that Kellenberger divides the ethical into ethical$_1$ and ethical$_2$, with the former being suspended, but the latter being the expression of, in Abraham's case, a higher, private, *duty* to God. Silentio, while describing what Abraham is undergoing, writes, "It is an ordeal, a temptation. A temptation—but what does that mean? As a rule, what tempts a person is something that will hold him back from doing his duty, but here the temptation is the ethical itself, which would hold him back from doing God's will. But what is duty? Duty is simply the expression for God's will" (*FT,* 60). Thus, even Silentio grants that there is a construal of duty that is not suspended. The fact that Hegel's ethical, in Silentio's view despairingly, attempts to avoid the providence of a transcendent God is part of why Kierkegaard himself will develop a different ethical theory.

One might object that Kierkegaard's well-known suspicion of natural theology implies a similar suspicion of natural law as an ethical theory, or, at any rate, our "natural" epistemological abilities to grasp such things. This may be right, but whatever Kierkegaard and his pseudonymous cohorts think about the ability of reason to discern truths in ethics, Aquinas already possesses a theory of the eternal law, to which everything is subject and which does not suspend the natural law on those occasions when the eternal overrides the ordinary dictates of the natural law, but rather *is itself expressed in the natural law.* Further, this natural law is nothing other than the divine wisdom retrieved by humans (who naturally live in community) according to the capacity of reason to discern it. The only difference between Kierkegaard's larger theory and Aquinas's on this point is that Aquinas believes that reason can discover the ordinary expression of the eternal law, that is, the natural law, and Kierkegaard's ethic of neighbor love cannot be understood outside Christian revelation.[66] This epistemological difference, however, does not affect the metaethical point that Aquinas, Kierkegaard, and Silentio believe that the ethical that is not relativized is ultimately the expression of the divine wisdom and/or will, and that the expression of ethics that is relativized is the one whose only requirements are generated by a world without appeal to God.[67]

Nonetheless, faith is beyond reason, for both Kierkegaard and Aquinas, and the sacrifice Abraham prepares flies in the face of *ordinary,* natural reason. This does not mean that it is *ultimately* unreasonable, or contradictory. As Goulet points out, even for Aquinas, while God's claims are never contrary to virtue, they are sometimes contrary to the "wonted mode of virtue."[68] Yet, Goulet goes on to claim that "St. Thomas regards it as sheer blasphemy to hold that God commands something impossible, contradictory, or absurd."[69] However, for Silentio (and for Kierkegaard), the absurd is not the same thing as God commanding Abraham to, say, square a circle, nor does it even refer to God's command.[70] Rather, the absurd is when Abraham holds on to his belief that he will get Isaac back, even when he is called to make that humanly impossible by sacrificing Isaac. The "absurd" here is the existential absurdity that God is continuing to promise the very thing that it seems he means to withdraw. If this is the absurd, however, then Aquinas's Abraham, perhaps surprisingly, would make Silentio proud. He had absurdity twice over, for, on the one hand, he needed to first hold together (5) and (6), as did Silentio's Abraham.

(5) I will receive progeny through Isaac.
(6) I am now being commanded by God to sacrifice Isaac.

But, on the other hand, Aquinas's Abraham also had to hold both of these propositions together with another proposition that seems to conflict with them, namely,

(7) I know it to be an unchangeable moral truth that it is always wrong to murder.[71]

Abraham's maintenance of these beliefs does not nullify his situation and its existential absurdity. On the contrary, it heightens it.

Natural law preserves Silentio's sense that the ordinary way the "ethical" is construed can be overridden by God's command without nullifying ethics altogether. Further, natural law does not discard the "absurdity" of Abraham's situation but rather heightens it. Thus, a proper understanding of the ethical in Silentio's text and in Aquinas's work reinforces the point that the natural law is a more appropriate way to render Silentio's overall point about the case of Abraham, without determining the "general conditions of faith on the basis of the particular problems of Abraham."[72] To determine the general conditions of existential faith in this way, as I have argued, is ultimately to claim that no such martyr as Perpetua could have been faithful in realizing that she could no longer hope in this life.

Some Possible Objections

I want to close this chapter by briefly examining two important possible objections to my reading of *Fear and Trembling* and my Thomistic take on the text's ideals. These objections are rooted in John Davenport's recent effort to show that the main point of *Fear and Trembling* is "to present the essence of 'faith' as *eschatological* trust."[73] The first objection would be that I am arguing for a "Strong Divine Command" (SDC) ethics or some such similarly problematic reading of the *Akedah,* on which see below, and fall prey to problems such a reading faces. The second objection might be that we can rescue Silentio's text, and its understanding of existential faith, in another way, namely, by making appeal to the concept of a "eucatastrophe." I will treat these objections in turn.

One must be careful to understand what Davenport means by "eschatological trust." He cannot, of course, mean that Silentio's Abraham has the kind of trust that hopes for the fulfillment of his desire in the eschaton itself, for that would make Abraham a knight of infinite resignation. Davenport knows this. He writes, indicating a broader understanding of the word "eschatological," that "when a story ends with an

ethical victory made possible only by grace, that story has an eschatological quality: it repeats the pattern that distinguishes all eschatological
narratives."[74] Drawing on J. R. R. Tolkien's notion of "eucatastrophe,"
Davenport goes on to argue that, as each story with an eschatological
ending closes with a "good catastrophe" of "sudden and miraculous
grace,"[75] the major eucatastrophe in Abraham's story is the angel's staying Abraham's hand and God's providing for a ram in Isaac's stead.
It will be important to note in what follows that Davenport is largely
concerned about defending the right reading of *Fear and Trembling* and
that I am arguing that the right reading of *Fear and Trembling* ultimately
imperils the text's "rash" understanding of faith (*CUP*, 500). However,
if Davenport's reading of the text is correct, then it will jeopardize my
analysis of the text.

The first objection, then, might be that I am falling prey to the
problems with an SDC reading. SDC interpretations, Davenport notes,
tend to emphasize Abraham's unconditional obedience, rather than the
manner in which he renders his unconditional obedience. Davenport is
right to complain about this sort of reading, since it is clear in the text
that Abraham's faith requires his hope that he will retain Isaac even after obeying God's command to prepare the sacrifice.[76] Davenport then
remarks that SDC interpreters endorse the claim that "God's *power* or
status as creator is the sole ontological source of right or moral obligation. According to this kind of absolute theological voluntarism, God's
commanding X is necessary and sufficient for X to be obligatory, and
God can command anything (even murder)."[77]

I want to differentiate my natural law reading of the *Akedah* from
the SDC reading Davenport is discussing. My reading does not define
the right or the good as whatever God commands, though I do hold that
whatever God commands will necessarily be good. Instead, I hold, as
natural law theorists do, that what the natural law will find to be right
will have everything to do with human nature, and the right context in
which it will flourish. That context, however, has itself everything to do
with the order with which it was set up by its wise Creator, and, ultimately, the relationship that obtains between Creator and creature. As
we noted before, God can override the "wonted mode" of virtue, which is
to say that God can "shift" the context for human flourishing to what remains "natural" (though perhaps unusual), but God cannot violate that

context entirely without destroying the very order God has instituted. Anthony J. Lisska helpfully writes, of Aquinas's theory, that

> Aquinas rejects any form of divine prescriptivism or theological definism. What makes an act right or wrong is that it is either in accord or not in accord with the fundamental developmental properties central to the concept of human nature. . . . That God may have created the structure of human nature differently is not the issue. Of course that could have taken place. But once human nature had been established, certain moral rules follow from the divine archetype of human nature.[78]

Thus, my corrective account of the *Akedah* is not to be counted as one of Davenport's SDC readings, even though it does insist that an important *component* of Abraham's faith is in obeying divine commands in preference to ordinary obligations.

Davenport also believes that a related dilemma presents itself for *any* "higher ethics" interpretation of Silentio's text. While I admit that I depart from Silentio's text, I do claim that my natural law interpretation of the *Akedah* upholds most of the significant ideals in Silentio's text, so a brief reply may be in order. Davenport claims that since Kierkegaard's dialectic characteristically preserves the dialectical elements of the previous stages (such as the aesthetic and the "ethical"), readings like mine must explain what elements of the ethical (or "ethical attitudes" as he puts it) are retained in faith, and, on his view, such readings are not equipped to give this explanation.[79]

Now Davenport is right that the ideals retained cannot be the ethical ideals of *Sittlichkeit* (or "social morality"), but what prevents them from being the kinds of ethical ideals that inspired *Sittlichkeit* in the first place, namely, the desire to foster genuine human flourishing? What is added to *Sittlichkeit* in religious faith is the belief in a transcendent God, a relation with whom has, as it turns out, a great deal to do with human flourishing. This was a point that *Sittlichkeit,* an immanent dialectic, missed. These ideals are preserved and fulfilled when they are suitably modified to take into account a human being's relationship with God. It remains the fact, however, that the ordinary particular ethical requirements of Silentio's "ethical," or *Sittlichkeit,* or virtue's "wonted mode," can be overridden by certain of God's decrees in my natural law interpretation, but this does not nullify human flourishing, and so retains the deeper truth of what *Sittlichkeit* sought.

A second objection might be rooted in the fact that Davenport wants to argue that the correct way to interpret Silentio's "teleological suspension of the ethical" is by reference to what he calls "Eschatological Suspension." If he is right about this, then this may save the text from my own worries. This is because I hold that the "ethical" that is suspended is something like the "wonted mode" of virtue, and Davenport holds that even agapic ethics are eschatologically suspended. Davenport writes:

> [Abraham] "suspends" his duty to Isaac only in this sense: he accepts that he can *fulfill* this duty only if the promised eschatological possibility is actualized by God. His intention toward Isaac remains loving, but he acts in a way that can be consistent with this love only if God's promise is fulfilled by a eucatastrophe. Call this Eschatological Suspension: a duty is E-suspended if and only if our will to fulfill it must rely on an eschatological possibility in which we can only have faith.[80]

I partially agree with Davenport that Abraham's intention can be just only if God eucatastrophically fulfills its ethical character, but I must insist that, among God's eucatastrophes, the new heavens and the new earth should be included. This entails that those who hope for the fulfillment of their desires in that eucatastrophe, such as Perpetua, may also be reckoned as faithful. This amounts to an insistence that Davenport's "eschatological" reading should really be eschatological in the usual sense, and not confine itself to being a somewhat novel "earthly eschatological," despite the fact that I believe that it must be that to save the text of *Fear and Trembling*.

For, consider that the actual sacrifice of Isaac is not the only kind of violence going on in the *Akedah*. For example, in the first scenario of the Silentio's "Exordium," we find Isaac traumatized by his father's actions, even before the knife comes down (*FT*, 10–11). Surely the risk of bringing about such trauma to Isaac is there in the actual *Akedah*, even if this scenario of the "Exordium" should be imaginative. In the absence of outweighing reasons to bring trauma to one's son (or to risk doing so), one would think that this would be ethically wrong, especially from within the perspective of an immanent ethics. The same seems to be true for Abraham's silence with respect to Sarah. After all, *Fear and Trembling* claims that it would be unethical of Abraham to "conceal his undertaking" from Isaac, Sarah, and Eliezer (*FT*, 82), and it would remain this way unless his ethical duties to disclose such matters were eucatastrophically fulfilled by a miracle from God. Can Abraham's duty to his wife, his son, and his servant be eucatastrophically fulfilled in this life?

Perhaps Sarah is visited by an obliging angel; perhaps Eliezer is; all of these are things we know nothing about, whether from Silentio's account or from the biblical text. Although this is an argument from silence, an empirical one is more powerful. The teleological suspension is an instance of "obeying God rather than men" (Acts 5:29).[81] Saintly people who do this, as Perpetua did, to the consternation of her father, do not regularly report such miraculous earthly interventions to be forthcoming. Davenport has suggested to me that the hereafter could play some such role in fulfilling the aspects of Abraham's action that are not directly intended. I respectfully disagree. I do not think that Davenport is allowed this admission, since it again asks for permission to hope for "a life to come" (FT, 20). It is the retention of the hope for this life that distinguishes the knight of faith from the knight of infinite resignation, whether that would be in Abraham's scenario, the lad's, or Silentio's imagined bourgeois philistine's (FT, 38–41). Without the hope for this life, Abraham is essentially an accidental subspecies of the knight of infinite resignation.[82] I believe that change makes very good sense of the *ideals* of the text (and here we come very close to my natural law modification), but it cannot be a successful interpretation of *the text itself.*

As we have noted, H.H. asked the unique question of "whether a human being has the right to let himself be put to death for the truth" (WA, 57). Ultimately, his answer was that Christ (who is the truth) has the right to do so, and that a Christian has this right in relation to non-Christian persecutors, but that a Christian dare not assert that he or she possesses such a hold on absolute truth as to make other Christians guilty of his or her death for the truth (WA, 86–88). Thus, the reason that H.H. thinks a martyr such as Perpetua can justly suffer and die for the truth, even by making others guilty of the crime of her murder, is that she is (one of) the recipient(s) of such a definitive revelation that her maintenance of belief in its truth is more important than her obligation to seek the earthly good of her fellows. It is important to note that, perhaps curiously, in the absence of this kind of revelatory stance, H.H. disallows the martyr the right to be put to death for the truth. That is, Perpetua's death is a teleological suspension of the ordinary, wonted mode of virtue that will be eucatastrophically fulfilled only in the eschaton, when God "will wipe every tear from their eyes, and there shall be no more death or mourning, wailing or pain, [for] the old order has passed away" (Rv 21:4). I believe that any adequate conception of faith should allow for this sort of possibility, and the fact that natural law can do so is precisely its strength. This does not mean that we have nothing to gain from reading *Fear and Trembling*. On the contrary, no other text seems to be so capable of directing our attention to the existential manner in which the *Akedah* should be approached. While our theories can tinker with this unique contribution, for subsequent history, its approach can only be mimicked.

‡

Silentio's discussion in *Fear and Trembling* provides us with a framework for interpreting the movement of faith that cannot square with the experience of martyrs such as Perpetua. I think this is a strong reason to believe that *Fear and Trembling* provides us with an account of existential faith that is actually too "thick." We need an account that can explain a wider array of faithful behaviors. The dialectic of the Christian Church is a kind of transcendent dialectic (which is in some sense "ethical," though not in Silentio's sense) to which Abraham, along with the martyrs, can contribute. In this way, they are heroes, though not in the Hegelian sense.

However, the life of faith can issue in diverse personal vocations, of which martyrdom and even Abraham's (near) sacrifice might be two. This means that whether one resigns or does not resign this life is largely a matter of one's life circumstances and calling by God, within the boundaries of which one lives the life of what Kierkegaard would call faith. No doubt this means that, from a certain viewpoint, Nietzsche is half right: religious faith sometimes is hostile to this earthly life, namely, when God commands that one hold fast to one's faith at the expense of one's societal and familial obligations, and perhaps even earthly life itself (as in the case of Perpetua). Yet if faith is hostile to our earthly sojourn, it is never hostile to the fullness of life that is promised by God, however "absurd" this may seem to others.

I am well aware that Kierkegaard himself developed a much more adequate treatment of the phenomenology of faith than did Silentio. In many ways, this will be the subject of the next chapter. However, considering Silentio's pseudonymous treatment of "the ethical" in this way, I think, allows one to see that Aquinas's treatment of natural law in the Catholic tradition provides a more adequate framework for discussing the life of faith than Silentio's. Aquinas's account also preserves, and in some ways enhances, rather than negates, the anxiety of Abraham's sacrifice, which he obediently prepares in the face of the twin absurdity that progeny will be reckoned to him through Isaac and that it is always wrong to kill.

THREE

The Order of Love: The Love of Preference in Kierkegaard and the Catholic Tradition

There is only one whom a person can with the truth
of eternity love more than himself—that is God.

KIERKEGAARD

In considering where the ultimate difference between Kierkegaard and the Thomistic tradition in Catholicism lies on the question of the love of our fellow human beings, we begin with the Christian command to "love your neighbor as yourself." When Jesus confirms it (Lk 10:25–37) to a "scholar of the law," the scholar asks him a question, which Kierkegaard interprets as an attempt to pull the command apart from its concrete moral exigency (*WL,* 96–97). The question is simply, "who is my neighbor?" The famous parable of the Good Samaritan that follows is clearly meant to deny this attempt at obfuscation, because the kindly Samaritan, we are to assume, does not know the robber's victim whom he helps, and yet he is the one who is a "neighbor" to the abandoned man. Thus, loving one's neighbor, it seems, takes no account of nationality (which, in an important sense, separated the two men), familial relationships (as there were none between the two in this case), ordinary (as opposed to immediate) geographical proximity, or preexisting bonds of friendship. Further, neighbor-love even seems to "trump" institutional religious obligations.[1] This conforms to a widely shared moral intuition that the immediate needs of others override other ordinary obligations we might have. Thus, a dying stranger in need of help takes precedence over the desire to make it to one's child's baseball game in time for the first pitch, even if one promised to do the latter. Both Kierkegaard and the Catholic tradition (in its Thomistic guise) can agree to this basic intuition.[2]

There is, however, another widely shared moral intuition that, when also accentuated, has not always been thought consistent with the other intuition. This second moral intuition holds that, *on the ordinary run of things,* my family and friends take some amount of precedence over individuals who bear no such relationship to me. Consider a brief, and rather commonplace, example. Suppose that Jones's income is modest, but that it can, with little or no remainder, take care of the needs of her family. Suppose next that winter has made an early start, and that Jones has scraped together enough money to purchase an inexpensive but suitable winter coat for her daughter, who has no such coat. Upon making this purchase, she walks back to her home and encounters a young girl, a stranger, who, she comes to find out, has need of such a coat. Jones, perceiving the need, gives the girl the coat, thus depriving her daughter of the coat that she also needs.

In this case, a widely shared moral intuition would regard Jones as blameworthy. Not only is it permissible for Jones to reserve the coat for her daughter, but rather, Jones is morally obliged to reserve the coat for her daughter. This suggests that ordinary moral convictions testify to the fact that individuals in our family have a greater claim on the resources with which we might manifest our love than those whom we do not know at all. Often the Catholic tradition has taken an even further step and claimed that we are actually to love our family *more* than those who are strangers to us. This represents what the Catholic tradition, and especially Aquinas, has called the order of love. Although the Catholic tradition has not been univocal on this point, when magisterial documents register a view on such matters, they often echo the language of Aquinas on the order of love.[3] Kierkegaard, however, appears to dispute at least some of Aquinas's conclusions.

By contrast, Kierkegaard clings to the first intuition, that we have an immediate obligation to our neighbor, who is a human being in need, without regard to such factors as might influence our preference. Kierkegaard articulated a radical view of love on the basis of biblical insights such as the parable of the Good Samaritan. To illustrate this, Kierkegaard writes of Christ's own love that "his love made no distinction, not the tenderest distinction between his mother and other people, for he pointed to his disciples and said, 'These are my mother'" (*WL*, 100). As we shall see, this has often given rise to false views about Kierkegaard's work, to wit, that he is an enemy of erotic love, friendships, and even families. While these extreme views are false, it is true that Kierkegaard ultimately believed in only one kind of love, Christian love (*WL*, 143).[4] The result is that Christian love is extended to all, with no distinction or gradation, but that its particular manifestations (which we will discuss below) are different. Luther, too, urged Christians to "not distinguish between friends and enemies," and to consider "nothing except the need and advantage of his neighbor."[5] However, the deeper convergence between Kierkegaard and Luther has to do with the deeper divergence between Kierkegaard and the Thomistic tradition on this point. That deeper divergence is on the question of how deeply defective nature is, and whether we are capable of "natural love."

One should not overlook the fact that any account of Christian love is at burden to endorse some version of both of the two basic moral intuitions noted above. There is certainly merit in both approaches, as both approaches tend to preserve some of our clearest ideas about love. Christ himself seems to have considered Peter, James, and John to be among his closest friends, and yet, he also indicates that the command to love has a universal scope of one sort or another. What will vary in a Christian account of love is the extent to which that account leans more toward one or the other of our two intuitions noted above.

The Catholic tradition, following Aquinas,[6] often has insisted, though a bit less loudly in recent years,[7] that there is a genuine ordering to love. That is, some persons are fittingly accorded a greater degree of love than others, which often has to do with familial ties. This is to cling to the second intuition noted above, that, ordinarily, my daughter, for instance, should be loved more than another person whom I have not met. In the following I will be interacting with what I take to be the mainstream of distinctively Catholic thought on this question, which is the Thomistic tradition. In the course of elucidating Kierkegaard's views and Aquinas's views on love, I will occasionally note parallels and convergences with other Catholic thinkers. Except where noted, I do not understand these other thinkers, such as St. Francis de Sales, to be incompatible with the relevant Thomistic view, but the influence they have had on Catholic thinking about love is also important to note. Kierkegaard exhibits some parallels to the Catholic tradition, and even to Aquinas, when it comes to the matter of love. However, there are also some divides between Kierkegaard and Aquinas. While these may not always pertain to Catholic dogma in the strict sense, in many cases their roots are so deeply embedded in the Thomistic tradition that their influence on the Catholic tradition writ large has been enormous. On the face of it, these divides have to do with the ordering of love, according to which I am to love certain neighbors more than others, a view with which Kierkegaard will take issue. At a deeper level, however, I believe that the real difference between Kierkegaard and the Thomistic corner of the Catholic tradition in particular is the concept of nature, which grounds the Thomistic understanding of preferential love. In this chapter I will argue for this claim.

Kierkegaard's Vision of Love

Love begins in God, for Kierkegaard, because God is love. Kierkegaard does not mean only that God exemplifies love excellently well, as if it were simply one of God's traits, but rather that God is love itself, so much so that he writes, "The love-relationship requires threeness; the lover, the beloved, the love—but the love is God" (*WL*, 121). It is worth noting that this is one area where Kierkegaard's opinion would seem to be closer to Peter Lombard's than to Thomas Aquinas's.[8] Aquinas maintained, against Peter Lombard, that the love by which we love God and neighbor is not itself the Holy Spirit, but that it is an "interior habit superadded to a natural potency."[9] One of the main reasons Aquinas offered for rejecting Lombard's view is that he could not see how love could be voluntary (and thus meritorious) if it were simply from an "extrinsic principle."[10] Kierkegaard would be at burden to disagree with such an objection because he so strongly emphasized the voluntary character of love.[11]

In fact, Kierkegaard is insistent that love must be understood not just as voluntary but as a duty. Kierkegaard notes that this is an "apparent contradiction," but claims that duty can do what nothing else can; it can preserve the unconditional nature of the obligation to love (*WL*, 29). Although Kierkegaard clearly understands this to mean that the will plays an indispensable role in loving the other, it is important to note that Kierkegaard does not make explicit precisely what role emotions play here.[12] On this point, M. Jamie Ferreira writes, "Kierkegaard does not announce at the outset whether love is to be understood as disinterested benevolence or as attentive, intimate caring, perhaps because no single description could account for all of the occasions in which we are obliged to love."[13] Nevertheless, although Kierkegaard insists that we cannot know in the abstract whether a given action is, or is not, loving (WL, 14), he clearly thinks we can discern a good deal about what takes place in the love-relationship.

For one thing, one must love one's neighbor *as* oneself, and Kierkegaard deduces from this that one must not love one's neighbor *more* than oneself.[14] Of course, we are less often, if ever, tempted to a kind of extreme altruism whereby we might actually love all others more than ourselves than we are to a brand of erotic love or close friendship in which we claim to love the particular beloved more than we love ourselves. Kierkegaard believes that friendship and erotic love are alike in being forms of preferential love that privilege one relationship over others, so my account will alternate between them in what follows (WL, 52–53).

What does Kierkegaard mean by erotic love? He writes, "Erotic love is based on a drive that, transfigured into an inclination, has its highest . . . expression in this—there is only one beloved in the whole world" (WL, 49). By contrast, "Just as unconditionally, and powerfully as erotic love intensifies in the direction that there is but one and only one beloved, just as unconditionally and powerfully does Christian love intensify in the opposite direction" (WL, 49). Thus, erotic love directs its love toward a single beloved, whereas Christian love directs its love to the neighbor, who is, in a sense, "all people" (WL, 21).

Still, one might wonder why erotic love would be so objectionable, since, in ordinary parlance, it marks out a relationship that one only has with one person, and that one simply cannot have with "all people," for whom one might, nonetheless, have due regard. Certainly, when I speak words that express love to my wife, it would make embarrassingly little sense to me or to others to pass along similar sentiments to all and sundry. Kierkegaard's native Danish language allows us to appreciate this point, as it permits several different expressions for the love that we might have in each case. Love of neighbor (*Kjerlighed*) is different from preferential love (*Forkjerlighed*), and under the heading of the latter Kierkegaard places friendship (*Venskab*) and erotic love (*Elskov*).[15] But the linguistic point does not remove the difficulty entirely. This is in large part because we tend to cherish an ideal of love that it is self-sacrificing. I do not think of my love for my wife as *incommensurate* with my love for a stranger, or even for myself; I should be quite tempted to think of it as *greater* than these. Do I not love my wife more than I love my own life, and thus my self? If I do, is my love for her not greater, in some sense, than my love for the neighbor, whom I am to love *as* myself? There is, it seems, a good bit going for erotic love.

Yet, Kierkegaard has at least two problems with erotic love, so construed. The first is theological, and the second is psychological. The first problem is that erotic love of the sort specified above is ultimately nothing short of idolatry,[16] since "there is only one whom a person can with the truth of eternity love more than himself—that is God. Therefore [the commandment] does not say, 'You shall love God as yourself'" (*WL*, 19). In this, Kierkegaard is in agreement with St. Francis de Sales, whose treatise *The Love of God* notes that we should love God more than ourselves for the time-honored, if paradoxical, reason that "God is closer to us than ourselves."[17] It will also become important to note that Aquinas, who insists on an order of charity that will separate him from Kierkegaard, is in agreement with Kierkegaard that we must love God more than we love ourselves.[18]

On the other hand, suppose that I love the beloved *as much as* I love myself precisely in erotic love; it is simply the case that I do not love others *as much as* I love either myself or the beloved. What would be objectionable about this? To this, Kierkegaard replies that erotic love is actually a form of self-love (*WL*, 53–54). Now, we must tread with caution here, since, as Ferreira notes, there is a proper self-love that is implied by the command to love one's neighbor *as oneself*.[19] Indeed, Kierkegaard emphasizes this so strongly that he writes, "To love yourself in the right way and to love the neighbor correspond perfectly to one another; fundamentally they are one and the same thing" (*WL*, 22). On the other hand, though, there is a quite selfish brand of self-love that Kierkegaard deplores (*WL*, 151). Why does erotic love reflect the selfish and not the proper kind of self-love? Briefly put, I think Kierkegaard's answer seems to be that erotic love and friendship leave the beloved or friend as a mere object to be appreciated, enjoyed, and preferred over others by the lover.

To see this, let us take a brief detour into Aristotle's conception of friendship (note that erotic love would itself be understood as a kind of friendship, for Aristotle). Aristotle argued that there were three kinds of friendships that corresponded to the three kinds of lovable things: the good, the pleasant, and the useful.[20] Even vicious people can have friendships of pleasure and utility, because "those who love each other for utility do not love each other for themselves but in virtue of some good which they get from each other. So too with those who love for the sake of pleasure; it is not for their character that men love ready-witted people, but because they find them pleasant."[21] By contrast, "perfect friendship is the friendship of men who are good, and alike in excellence," and such friends "wish well to [each other] for their own sake."[22] Aristotle insists that this kind of friendship is the only kind of friendship where the friend is loved not because of some secondary good that can be obtained through the relationship to the friend, but because of who the friend is him- or herself.

It is important to note, however, that Aristotle is not arguing that we become so taken with the person behind the qualities we esteem that we eventually are in a position to love the person *regardless* of his or her qualities. He writes, "But if one accepts another man as good, and he becomes bad and is seen to do so, must one still love him? Surely it is impossible, since not everything can be loved, but only what is good. What is evil neither can nor should be loved; for one should not be a lover of evil, nor become like what is bad; and we have said that like is dear to like."[23] Aristotle goes on to argue that, while we should try to rescue a friend's character, the friendship cannot continue when the friend fails to exhibit qualities that can be rationally esteemed. In this way, Aristotle's account of love looks to what can be esteemed for its own sake (as in perfect friendships), what can be enjoyed as a result of the friendship (as in friendships of pleasure), and what can be genuinely useful to then achieve some other desirable end (as in friendships of utility). Whatever we think of his reading of Aristotle on this point, Kierkegaard appears to think that Aristotle cannot draw this distinction between a perfect friendship, where the self loves the other for her own sake, and friendships of pleasure and utility, where the other is loved simply as a source of pleasure or utility. Kierkegaard seems to think that all of these friend-ships are relationships where the other is loved selfishly as a source of pleasure of one sort or another. Seemingly to this effect, the pseudonym Anti-Climacus claims that it is misleading to make "the distinction that paganism and the natural man make between love and self-love, as if all this love were not essentially self-love" (*SUD*, 45).

This seems to be the point on the matter of love where Kierkegaard's Lutheranism shines through most clearly, and it may help to elucidate Kierkegaard's negative reaction to Aristotle. We have already seen that Luther deplores Aristotle, whom he calls that "damned, conceited, ras-cally heathen."[24] Aristotle would have it that we have the natural capac-ity to love our fellow human beings and that we are perfectly capable of doing so in the right way, so long as we have the proper resources and upbringing. Clearly a Christian account cannot be satisfied without discussing some kind of divine role (even if not a properly supernatural one) here, but for Aquinas, who receives Aristotle much more favorably, the question would be whether human beings' natural state is one where they are equipped to perform morally good (even if not supernaturally meritorious) actions.[25] For Luther, the answer, in his *Disputation against Scholastic Theology*, seems clear: "everyone's natural will is iniquitous and bad."[26] So, for Aquinas to think, as we shall see that he does, that natural love, on the model of Aristotle, is a good thing, and that grace must elevate, and not destroy, it, is a clear error from Luther's point of view. Luther makes this fairly clear when he writes that "the entire *Ethics* of Aristotle is the worst enemy of grace" and "the whole Aristotle is to theology as darkness is to light."[27] This clear divide between Luther and Aristotle will be important later. For now, it serves to illustrate the kind of objection Kierkegaard may be voicing in thinking that even Aristotle's "perfect" friendship remains within the sphere of sin.

Aristotle carefully distinguishes a bad kind of self-love from a good kind of self-love, noting that "the good man should be a lover of self."[28] Perfect friendships, for Aristotle, are examples of the right kind of self-love. Further, it is in a person's attitude toward him- or herself that "all the characteristics of friendship have extended to others."[29] It is for this reason that Aristotle famously claims that a friend is "another self."[30] Kierkegaard is clearly picking up on this when he notes that the beloved of erotic love is "the *other I*" (*WL*, 57, emphasis original). In opposition to this, Kierkegaard writes that the neighbor is "the first you" (*WL*, 57). Aristotelian love forms an interesting contrast with Kierkegaardian love on this point, since, for Aristotle, love moves out from the self to others (waxing the closer the other is to the self, and waning as the other is further away), whereas for Kierkegaard, loves moves out from God to everyone else equally (including the self). For Aristotle one should love oneself most of all. Indeed, it is only by doing so that one can love others in the right way.[31] For Kierkegaard, "Only by loving God above all else can one love the neighbor in the human being" (*WL*, 58).[32] This is because for Kierkegaard, we love with, and in accordance with, God's own love for all.[33] Our love for ourselves and others arises out of our love for God. In this context it is important to note that Kierkegaard claims the neighbor, whom I am to love with redeemed Christian love, is "just as near" as I am, or ought to be, to myself (*WL*, 21).

One of the reasons for Kierkegaard's claim that we love others through and in our love for God is that the human being has an "inherent kinship" with God and that "God has created him and Christ has redeemed him" (*WL*, 62 and 69). Of this twofold reasoning for why the other is lovable, the first sentiment makes frequent appearances in the writings of the saints. For instance, St. Francis de Sales writes, "Love of our neighbour, through charity, is the love of God in man, or man in God; it is holding God alone dear for his own sake, the creature only out of love for him."[34] Kierkegaard calls this kinship with God an individual's "watermark." We read:

> Take many sheets of paper, write something different on each one; then no one will be like another. But then again take each single sheet; do not let yourself be confused by the diverse inscriptions, hold it up to the light, and you will see a common watermark on all of them. In the same way the neighbor is the common watermark, but you see it only by means of eternity's light when it shines through the dissimilarity. (*WL*, 89)

Here, Kierkegaard argues that we must love one another through and because of our inherent kinship with God, and that this kinship persists despite any dissimilarities in terms of factors such as socioeconomic standing, familial relationship, nationality, prior animosity, and so on. The point, I take it, is that dissimilarities of these sorts cannot be used to excuse one from the demand to love. To the complaint that people think it "impossible" to love the enemy, Kierkegaard writes, "Well, then, shut your eyes—then the enemy looks just like the neighbor" (*WL*, 68). Indeed, because neighbor-love is not concerned about the dissimilarities of human existence,[35] we need waste no time in looking for a suitable person to love, since, "when you open the door that you shut in order to pray to God and go out the very first person you meet is the neighbor, whom you *shall* love" (*WL*, 51, emphasis original).

Despite the appearance of things, Kierkegaard goes on, especially in "Love is a Matter of Conscience," to argue that this form of love does not rule out relationships that we might ordinarily construe as erotic love or as friendship. Thus, erotic love makes a comeback, but only insofar as it "coincide[s] materially" with neighbor-love, for Kierkegaard.[36] It is worth emphasizing this point, and, to this effect, Patrick Stokes writes, "Kierkegaard does allow that we can have a beloved or a friend, but such a relation must be secondary and subordinate to the duty-directed neighbor love."[37] Stokes goes on to cite what is perhaps Kierkegaard's clearest statement on this matter when he writes, "Your wife must first and foremost be to you the neighbor; that she is your wife is then a more precise specification of your particular relationship to each other" (*WL*, 141). Once Kierkegaard has insisted that all such "secondary" relationships must be rooted in neighbor-love, he can even admit that "erotic love is undeniably life's most beautiful happiness and friendship the greatest temporal good!" (*WL*, 267).

Nevertheless, a tradition of interpretation has developed around *Works of Love* that argues that its account of neighbor-love is too abstract or too inward to commit us to anything ethically concrete in the external world. This line of interpretation has representatives no less distinguished than Martin Buber and Theodor Adorno.[38] Adorno is particularly harsh, writing, "Kierkegaard is unaware of the demonic consequence that his insistence on inwardness actually leaves the world to the devil."[39] Although I agree with much of the already vast and growing literature rebutting these charges, I think it should be admitted that Kierkegaard's expression in the text, while often moving, is not always very felicitous.[40] It is not without reason that Kierkegaard's tone has made some readers bristle. But Kierkegaard's critics seldom propose much in place of his account that improves upon its real strengths, whether or not they are as easy to glimpse at a first reading as we would like. To illustrate this, in the next section, I will briefly consider one recent discussion of agapic love, or Christian neighbor-love, which includes certain criticisms of Kierkegaard's work.

A Criticism of Kierkegaard's Vision
and a Kierkegaardian Response

In Sally B. Purvis's article, "Mothers, Neighbors and Strangers: Another Look at a Agape," she writes, "My richest and most powerful experience of agape, of unqualified, unconditional love for another, has come with my experience of being a mother."[41] Purvis claims that this is a reversal of many more traditional accounts of agape, such as Kierkegaard's, which have been more suspicious of such relationships in the name of "disinterested" or non-preferential, love.[42] I take it that the substance of this claim is in line with the school of Kierkegaard criticism noted above, that Kierkegaard's version of love, for the sake of unconditional love, effectively empties the individual of her contingent features. I will briefly discuss some aspects of Purvis's article for two reasons. First, her negative portrayal of Kierkegaard shows a traditional (and erroneous) conception of Kierkegaard, but second, and more importantly, her positive proposal that mother-love be taken as an example of agapic love can, indirectly, show the real resources of Kierkegaard's view when it is called upon to respond.

Purvis's article isolates three basic characteristics of mother-love. The first, she notes, is that mother love is "inclusive."[43] By this she seems to mean that the inclusivity of mother-love embraces all of one's own children equally with the same "fundamental commitment to their well-being,"[44] as opposed to preferring one over another. The second characteristic, which she discusses at more length, is that mother-love is "intensely involved and other-regarding."[45] Purvis writes, "At times there is no clear line between the needs of the lover and the needs of the beloved. The needs of the child as expressed in cries of different volume and tone are experiences by the mother as in some sense internal to her own being. . . . [T]he *mother's need* may be to feed the child, comfort her, rock him, etc."[46] The third characteristic of mother-love that Purvis identifies is that it is "unconditional." She writes, "Even if all her efforts fail, and when her child fails, she continues to love no matter how far her child departs from her interests and her plans for her or his life. . . . Furthermore, the love is not 'located in the agent' as Kierkegaard's account would have it: it remains intensely other oriented."[47] Purvis's account of mother-love focuses on these three characteristics to elucidate what she believes should be a part of agapic love, the former being a useful model for the latter. She writes, "I am suggesting that agape fully experienced would be similar to mother-love extended to the whole of humanity . . . the second part of the love command could be fruitfully restated as 'Love your neighbor as a mother loves her children.'"[48]

The trouble with this account is not primarily its substance, but that it is intended to be an alternative to Kierkegaard's view. Purvis's first characteristic of mother-love, inclusivity, if understood in the way she seems to mean it, is hardly a stumbling block at all for Kierkegaard. On her view, mother-love is inclusive because it includes all the children of the family in the mother's love, even when the mother finds it hard to *like* all of her children. In response, I think a Kierkegaardian should point out two things. First, Kierkegaard's love is inclusive because he clearly thinks that we should love all with an equality that does not change with contingent features of the other that we may or may not like.[49] The second thing that a Kierkegaardian should point out here is that there really is a kinship between all human beings, precisely because all human beings are created in the image of God.[50] We bear this image because God is, in some sense, a parent to us.

Purvis's second characteristic of mother-love includes within itself two characteristics. First, it is "intensely involved," and second, it is "other-regarding." This may seem like a genuine stumbling block to Kierkegaard's view. Close attention to Kierkegaard's text, however, shows that there is an intense involvement to be found in Kierkegaard's understanding of love. Kierkegaard gives us many passages where he remarks that love both needs to love and needs to be loved. This, he argues, is an internal need in love itself. Kierkegaard writes, "Love is a need, the deepest need, in the person in whom there is love for the neighbor; he does not need people just to have someone to love, but he needs to love people" (*WL*, 67). That is, love needs to express itself in action. Kierkegaard notes that "we are saying the utmost when we say of a poet, 'He has a need to write'" (*WL*, 10). It is perfectly easy to imagine him saying, in this context (although he in fact did not), "we are saying the utmost of a mother when we say, 'She has a need to love her child.'"[51] Furthermore, the expression of love that we have within us is elicited by the individual to whom it is an expression of love in such a way that he or she has a "claim" upon it. Kierkegaard writes, "Your friend, your beloved, *your child,* or whoever is an object of your love has a claim upon an expression of it also in words if it actually moves you inwardly. The emotion is not your possession but belongs to the other; the expression is your debt to him, since in the emotion you indeed belong to him who moves you and you become aware that you belong to him" (*WL,* 12, emphasis mine). The idea here seems to be that love essentially has within it a drive to express itself in action, but how it actually does so is given shape by the particular relationships in the context of which we are responsive to the needs of the concrete other. Indeed, this other is not simply an abstract "human being" to whom we are attentive, but someone to whom we "belong." Ferreira helpfully comments on Kierkegaard's use of the Danish word *Trang* for "need." She writes that it is "a kind of passionate craving, a dynamic impulse coming from within and reaching out."[52] Indeed, love, as a need, comes from within, but reaches out to the neighbor because we now *belong* to that person in the need she has, which has now become our own. Ferreira goes on to say, "The neighbor love that is commanded in the case of a spouse or child or friend will in fact be an interested caring, but it will be warm, intimate, or passionate because that is the nature of the relation, not because warmth or intimacy or passion is commanded. . . . The nature of the relationship will shape the response."[53]

From what we have seen in the foregoing, it will be difficult to see how the charge that Kierkegaardian love fails the test of being unconditional can be sustained with any justice.[54] This point is made in a striking way when Kierkegaard references Christ's love for Peter when Peter denied him. Kierkegaard writes, "[Christ] did not say, 'Peter must first change and become another person before I can love him again.' No, he said the exact opposite, 'Peter is Peter, and I love him. My love, if anything, will help him to become another person'" (*WL,* 172). Kierkegaard's point here is simply that Christian love does not vary with the changes in its object. It is difficult to know what more Purvis is looking for here.

Purvis's related charge that Kierkegaardian love is too "detached" presumably because it is "located in the agent" fails to see that neighbor-love for Kierkegaard is not defined by either the object or the agent,[55] but by the love (*WL*, 66), which is God. That is, our love is to be a participation in God's own, unconditional, intensely involved, and inclusive, love, which seems to be the substance of what Purvis would claim for her own account. In the next section, we will consider Aquinas's views on love for a contrast and move toward a partial reconciliation between Kierkegaard's view and a long-standing view in the Catholic tradition, namely, the Thomistic view.

Kierkegaard and Aquinas on Natural Love

Aquinas devotes an entire question of the *Summa Theologica* to the order of love, or charity.[56] Some of the elements of this "order" can be glimpsed in Kierkegaard's text as well. Just as we saw Kierkegaard claiming that we can love the neighbor only by loving God above all else, so Aquinas believes that all love is rooted in the love of God. Stephen J. Pope writes of Aquinas's position, "in charity the various material objects of love in different relationships are all loved under the formality of the love of God."[57] For both thinkers, love for God really does undergird, in some sense, any other expression of Christian love, or Christian charity, and we are called to extend this love, in some sense, to everyone. Yet, the difficulty here is that, for Kierkegaard, the love-relationship I have with my wife is merely a "more precise specification" within my love for her as a neighbor, which must be unconditional and without degree, and be extended alike to a stranger whom I should pass on the street (*WL*, 141). For Kierkegaard, there is only one kind of love, and that love has no quantity, though the manifestations and behaviors of love in particular relationships can be quite different. For Aquinas, however, my relationship to my wife is not a more precise specification of charity; it *is* charity. The ordering of relationships really belongs to love itself, rather than being simply a set of manifestations of the one neighbor-love that is equally extended to the passerby on the street.

Thus, what is interesting from a Kierkegaardian point of view about Aquinas's views on this score is that love has an ordering at all. "Ordering" in this context means principally that some individuals are loved with a different sort of love or with a greater degree of love than others. So, when Aquinas asks, "Whether We Ought to Love One Neighbor

More Than Another?" he notes that there have been two opinions on this question (the second is the one he endorses). The first opinion appears, in some ways, close to Kierkegaard's own view. Here is that opinion: "Some have said that we ought, out of charity, to love all our neighbors equally, as regards our affection, but not as regards the outward effect. They held that the order of love is to be understood as applying to outward factors, which we ought to confer on those who are unconnected, and not to the inward affection, which ought to be given equally to all including our enemies."[58] On this view, which Aquinas will reject, we give equal affection to all out of charity, but the outward manifestation of the charity is different; in fact, that appears to be the *only* difference. Now, this cannot be Kierkegaard's view exactly, because Ferreira, as we saw, was right to point out that the warmth, intimacy, and caring of the Kierkegaardian neighbor fluctuates on the basis of the relationship, and thus the affection that Christian love gives to the other neighbor would seem to do so as well. On the other hand, there is something, in Kierkegaard's view, that is equal, and that is the kinship with God that grounds our love for the neighbor.

Aquinas's response to this view is complicated but instructive. In many ways, Aristotle's ethical system constituted, for Aquinas, the natural way that rational human beings would behave, and indeed love, even without the supernatural virtues of faith, hope, and charity. Pairing this with the well-worn scholastic dictum that "grace does not destroy nature, but perfects it,"[59] Aquinas wishes to affirm that the natural affection we have for those who are closest to us by way of blood-relationships or other such ties is reasonable and is not nullified by Christian charity. He writes, "For the affection of charity, which is the inclination of grace, is not less orderly than the natural appetite, which is the inclination of nature, for both inclinations flow from Divine Wisdom."[60] Accordingly, relationships to family or spouses are part of the order of love that is natural and is affirmed by Christian charity. Although Kierkegaard, in keeping with his more generally Protestant outlook, does not seem to have quite as robust a view of nature and its ethical significance,[61] wouldn't Kierkegaardian Christian love preserve our sense of the importance of our family relationships? The answer to that question is yes, but the reasons that Kierkegaard will give for that response will differ from those given by Aquinas.

As we saw earlier, Kierkegaard believes that "erotic love and friend-ship *as such* are only enhanced and augmented self-love" (*WL,* 267, emphasis original). But for Kierkegaard, it is this very self that is prob-lematic, since it is fundamentally sinful and selfish. Christian faith, therefore, results in a "new creation," or "rebirth," where the person's life is radically new.[62] Kierkegaard's self is, as George Pattison puts it, "not an individual substance of a rational essence, but a being in dynamic and temporally charged ecstatic dependence on God."[63] For Aquinas, the human being is understood not as the relation *from out of* a "psychical-physical synthesis" (to use Anti-Climacus's words) relating to itself and then to God (*SUD,* 13, 25), but as the body-soul composite *itself.*[64] The significance of this point is hard to overestimate. Because the human be-ing, for Aquinas, is a decidedly natural animal and grace *perfects* nature, the Aristotelian self-love that was in place prior to the infusion of the supernatural virtue of charity remains fundamentally intact, though it is elevated and put upon a new foundation. "Natural love," to use Pope's definition, is "the natural orientation and innate affinity of a finite being for the good pertaining to its own nature."[65] This orientation, ultimately rooted in the self, as it is for Aristotle, is elevated, but not destroyed, for Aquinas. Pope goes on to write, "Thomas's interpretation of charity fol-lowed from the fundamental theological axiom that grace perfects, and does not destroy, nature. One important implication of this principle is, in Thomas's theological perspective, that charity retains natural love, though the latter is given a new animating principle."[66] For Aquinas, nature *as such* is fundamentally good, and while sin distorts, and has distorted, our affections, the position of nature, strictly speaking, is not itself evil. While it is true that nature is incapable of catapulting the hu-man being to her supernatural end in glory, Aquinas simply does not believe that nature is as ruined as Kierkegaard and his Lutheran tradi-tion would have us believe.

For Kierkegaard, nature, or "the natural man" (*naturlige Menneske*) is so damaged by sin, prior to the advent of Christian faith in the in-dividual, that it has, in some sense, turned in on itself in an effort to become something other than what God would have it be (*SUD,* 20). The actions of this distorted self belong to the "rubric" of sin, even if particular actions of this self seem above reproach.[67] This seems to be why Anti-Climacus approvingly cites the dictum that "the virtues of the pagans [are] glittering vices" (SUD, 46). Indeed, for Kierkegaard, again following Luther's work on reason, the "natural man" will regard Christianity as epistemologically suspect and even treacherous.[68] For Anti-Climacus and Kierkegaard,[69] there are only two rubrics, faith and despair, which Kierkegaard also calls sin (SUD, 105). This means that if there is any despair to be found in the self, the self is fundamentally in a bad relation to God. Prior to rooting out despair in faith, the self may have been inclined in this or that direction and even chosen this or that relationship in which to engage, but these arose from within a self that was already disordered at its root.[70] Consequently, these prior inclinations and relationships must be subject to a radical scrutiny when the proper God-relationship is established. There can be no strictly theoretical judgment in advance on whether they are to be absorbed by Christian love or to be abandoned because of it, which is why Kierkegaard is so insistent on the collision between the merely human and the Christian conceptions of love. This also seems to be why Kierkegaard explains that "the love-relationship as such can be the sacrifice that is required" (WL, 130).

In saying that Kierkegaard has a more negative conception of nature than does Aquinas, I do not mean to resurrect the old canard that Kierkegaard repudiates erotic love and friendship. The foregoing should have made it clear that he does not. Rather, erotic love and friendship flourish in the context of neighbor-love, where they are given their status as genuine love-relationships. Evans writes, "Special relations are not to be abolished, but purged of what Kierkegaard calls the 'selfishness' present in them." Still, it is important to note, as Evans does, that "Kierkegaard is not as clear as he could be about what this entails for actual human life."[71] I submit that he is not as clear as one might wish because he simply cannot be; prior to the advent of Christian love in the human being, the ordering that already existed can only have been fundamentally sinful because it arose from a self that was fundamentally sinful. God may reaffirm some or all of these relationships upon the advent of Christian love (and no doubt God's mercy plays some role here), but if this does take place, it will not be based on a conviction that this ordering was already in some sense good. This is because true love is always Christian love, for Kierkegaard, and "it is God who in every case will determine what is love" (WL, 126). The ordering of love prior to the advent of Christian love in a Kierkegaardian framework can only be thought a sinful ordering, not because its outward manifestations were necessarily wrong, but because their inward origin was disordered.

It might seem to suggest a different view when Kierkegaard claims that the "need of love" is deeply rooted in human nature (WL, 154).[72] Indeed, Kierkegaard shows how deeply it is rooted by noting how the perfect Christ needed friends (WL, 155). However, Evans, in discussing natural love, goes on to write, "The natural needs and desires that form the foundation of preferential loves are not things 'that human beings gave themselves' . . . They came from the Creator and thus cannot be inherently bad, and thus should not be abolished."[73] However, expanding the passage on which Evans comments gives us some room to question his approach. Kierkegaard writes:

> No, just because Christianity is truly spirit, it understands by the sensuous something quite different from what is simply called the sensuous nature, and it has been no more scandalized by a drive human beings have indeed not given to themselves than it has wanted to forbid people to eat and drink. By the sensuous, the flesh, Christianity understands selfishness. . . . Therefore, self-love is sensuousness. Christianity has misgivings about erotic love and friendship simply because preferential love in passion or passionate preference is actually another form of self-love. (WL, 52–53)

Now here the "sensuous nature" is human beings' benign tendency to desire erotic love-relationships. Since Christianity is not a kind of Gnosticism, the sensuous aspect of our being is not repudiated. "The sensuous," by contrast, is "selfishness" and ultimately "self-love." But now if Kierkegaard's trouble with Aristotle's conception of love is that it never "discovers alterity," as Evans puts it,[74] because it is based on improper self-love, then a relationship that does not yet have neighbor-love at its foundation will necessarily be disordered. It will come from a more Lutheran "nature" in the sense of human beings left to their own distorted devices, rather than from a supernaturally equipped human nature that is ready to love in Kierkegaard's sense.

But if this is so, then where do the drives that we have not given ourselves come from? In the case of Christ, Adam and Eve prior to the Fall, and even redeemed human beings, this is easy to answer: they come from the properly ordered (or repaired) self that God has given to us, which fittingly desires to live the blessed life of love. Ferreira claims that this need of love is "ineradicably human"[75] for Kierkegaard, but even if she is right about this, it does not follow that the unfallen human nature and the fallen human nature must crave to love and be loved *for the same reason*. For Kierkegaard, it is relatively easy to see why human nature, in a properly ordered relationship to God who is love, would feel a need to love human beings, who have kinship with God (whom they also love, if they belong to the rubric of faith). It might seem difficult for my view of Kierkegaard to explain why the fallen human nature has a need to love and be loved. But this is not true. Aristotle himself can provide us with such reasons. First, for Aristotle, a vicious person wishes to keep company with others because he wishes to be distracted from the fact that his actions are disordered.[76] The second reason is more telling, though. Since Aristotle's "perfect friendship" is still based on what Kierkegaard considers to be improper self-love, a good reason to love for Aristotle can still be a bad reason to love for Kierkegaard. For Kierkegaard the very orientation of Aristotelian love is selfish in the bad sense because all such friendships are rooted in self-love. So it should be no surprise that a sinful nature, even considered as an Aristotelian nature, would feel a need for friends: friends are the "greatest of external goods"[77] and *I want them*. Without neighbor-love, which is based on the love of God, at their foundation, all love-relationships are simply forms of improper self-love, which is to say that they are not real love at all, for Kierkegaard.[78] To make the point clearer, suppose, on Kierkegaard's terms, that Bob and Sue have a relationship that an Aristotelian would consider an instance of virtuous people in love but that does not have neighbor-love at its foundation.[79] Suppose that later in time these people come to love God more than themselves and to love their neighbors as themselves, so that Bob loves Sue (his wife) and Sue loves Bob (her husband), but this erotic love is secondary to the primary neighbor-love between the two. I believe that Kierkegaard's view of this is as follows: only in a rough sense can we say that this so-called natural love-relationship was transformed into a deeper love-relationship. Clearly, the relata are in some sense the same (we are still dealing with Bob and Sue), but in fact what has occurred is that the relationship has gone from being one of disordered self-love to being one of neighbor-love (the *only* kind of love for Kierkegaard) and thus from being something that is not love to something that is.

I disagree with this view, which I take to be Kierkegaard's, but I think that Kierkegaard's Lutheranism and his radical repudiation of Aristotle require this view. In the next section, I will describe what the Thomistic ordering of love looks like, along the way noting its apparent divergences from Kierkegaard's view.

The Order of Love in Aquinas

Aquinas's views on the ordering of love were clearly conceived of as a kind of expansion of the view on love's ordering to be found in Augustine. On this point, Augustine wrote, "There are, then, four kinds of things to be loved: first, that which is above us; second, ourselves; third, that which is equal to us; fourth, that which is below us."[80] Augustine himself goes on to argue that these categories contain God, ourselves, our neighbors, and our own bodies, respectively. Aquinas saw himself as giving a more precise rendering of what this traditional ordering amounted to. We have already seen that, for Aquinas, we ought to love God more than ourselves, and we will revisit this issue in the next section. The next aspect of the ordering of love that calls for our attention is the claim that we ought to love ourselves more than our neighbors. From a Kierkegaardian standpoint, this sounds disastrous. Not only does it seem decidedly against Kierkegaard's view, it sounds as if it compromises Christ's own command that we love our neighbors as ourselves. Ferreira explicitly contrasts Kierkegaard's perspective with Aquinas's on this point, noting "the Thomistic tradition's refusal in Roman Catholicism to read the love commandment as a requirement that we love others as much as we love ourselves."[81] While there are indeed contrasts to be made on this front, there is a larger story on this point that should be told.

When Aquinas argues that we should love ourselves more than we should love our neighbors, we must be very careful to understand what he means, and we should do this first by understanding two things that he does *not* mean. First, Aquinas does not mean that we wish ourselves "everlasting happiness," while we do not wish this for others, since he clearly does insist that we should will "everlasting happiness" for all human beings, and this also means, for Aquinas, that we are to *love* all human beings.[82] Second, Aquinas also does not mean that we should love ourselves more than others in a way that would suggest that we have no duty to sacrifice life and limb for their sake. On this point, Susan C. Selner-Wright very helpfully writes:

> One may ask, however, whether this conclusion is not in conflict with Jesus' teaching, "Greater love hath no man than this, that he lay down his life for his friends" (Jn 15:13). Does this teaching not direct us to love others more than ourselves? Thomas answers that we must distinguish between two aspects of ourselves, the spiritual and the corporeal, the soul and the body. It is the spiritual, the "inner man," which we are to love above all others except God. . . . Loving our neighbor, then, can never legitimately cause us to endanger our own spiritual welfare, the "inner man," but it may well lead us to risk our bodies for our neighbors.[83]

What Aquinas means in having us love ourselves more than our neighbors is thus to be distinguished from any sense in which we, in a cowardly way, exempt ourselves from acting in the service of the good of others because we love our *bodies* more than we love them.[84] What Aquinas means, rather, is that there must be a sense in which we hold some paramount principles so dear that we are unwilling to violate them even for the good of another. Selner-Wright writes, "Charity may dictate that we go to heaven early for our friends, but it can never dictate that we go to hell for them."[85]

I know of no passage where Kierkegaard considers this issue directly, but one might wonder what effect it would have on his thought, were he to explicitly embrace the view that I should *not* love my own soul more than another's soul. One area where this issue strikes me as a point of interest for Kierkegaard is in relation to H.H.'s essay, "Does a Human Being Have the Right to Let Himself Be Put to Death for the Truth?" H.H. struggles with this question because he realizes that those who kill a martyr will have the martyr's proverbial blood on their hands and that martyr's not-so-proverbial death on their consciences (*WA*, 50–89). He answers that, in relation to a transcendent truth such as Christianity, the martyr can die, but only at the hands of non-Christians (*WA*, 86). He claims this because "the strongest expression of absolute superiority over others still is and remains: to let them become guilty of one's death—for the truth" (*WA*, 84). The conflict is between one's duty to the truth and one's duty to one's fellow human beings. H.H. writes, "Do I then have the right to do this, or does a human being have the right for the sake of the truth to allow others to become guilty of a murder? *Is my duty to the truth* of such a nature, or *does my duty to my fellow human beings* rather bid me to yield a little? How far does my duty to the truth reach, and how far my duty toward others?" (*WA,* 68, emphasis original). According to H.H., to allow one's duty to the truth to take precedence over one's duty to others in allowing them to have a murder on their consciences is to presume that one has a very firm and unclouded grip on absolute truth (*WA,* 86). The apostles and martyrs are justified, therefore, because their conviction of the truth of Christianity was quite firm and clear, especially when compared with the falsity of paganism. One dare not, H.H. claims, presume such a grasp of absolute truth as to make one's fellow Christians guilty of one's death in this way (*WA,* 86).

The interesting thing for Aquinas here is that it is precisely an expression of virtue to love one's soul more than one's neighbor. Aquinas writes, "A man ought to bear bodily injury for his friend's sake, and precisely in so doing he loves himself more as regards his spiritual mind, because it pertains to the perfection of virtue, which is a good of the mind. In spiritual matters, however, man ought not to suffer injury by sinning, in order to free his neighbor from sin."[86] A question that Aquinas would no doubt put to H.H. on this point would be whether the duty to the truth that the Christian discharges in her martyrdom at the hands of non-Christians is a duty that she has no personal stake in obeying. If she has such a stake, is it not an expression of preference for her own soul over against those of her assailants? On this point, Aquinas writes, "Man, *out of charity,* ought to love himself more than his neighbor: in sign whereof, a man ought not to give way to any evil of sin, which counteracts his share of happiness, not even that he may free his neighbor from sin."[87] That is, it is precisely an expression of the Divine Wisdom that a person should not sacrifice his share in eternal happiness even when his doing so will result in the staining of his assailant's conscience. On the other hand, if we say that our Christian martyr has no personal stake in obeying, then this may be belied by other Kierkegaardian texts that allow us to will the good out of a hope for an eternal happiness (*UDVS,* 49), and tell us that we are to cling to the highest [good] even if everyone else should let go (*WL,* 27).

Aquinas does not think that we should love ourselves more than others because greed is an evolutionary necessity, but because *God wills* that our first-person perspective should help us to sort out our commitments to virtue and deep happiness. The natural impulses of a creature are instances of the Divine Wisdom working within us. On this point, Christopher Toner writes, of Aquinas's position, "the will must ultimately be ruled by the common good that God wills for the universe."[88] On H.H.'s logic, if we are not allowed to assert "superiority" over others in allowing them to become guilty of our own deaths, we are ultimately left to an immanent worldview where we cannot even envisage living and dying for a transcendent truth in martyrdom. This is because there would be nothing to place our duty to the truth over and above our duty to our fellow human beings, as H.H. would put it.

Supposing, then, that we should love God and ourselves more than our neighbors (in this more nuanced way); how should we love our neighbors? Is there a principle that would explain why we should love others with varying degrees of love? If so, what principle should we use to decide how they are to be loved? Whom should we love more, those who are more ethically praiseworthy or should we love those who are closer to us by family relationships?

Aquinas argued that nature itself provides the principle that explains our varied but ordered love for others. As Pope writes, "In the natural world, inner tendencies accord with external actions suited to the natures of things; so also in human life the inner affections, whether of grace or nature, correspond with the external actions that they produce. The order of charity requires not only greater beneficence but also more intense affection toward those nearest to the agent."[89] We can have a good will toward all (benevolence), but our situation in the natural world does not permit us to act in beneficent ways to all.[90] This fact explains what Aquinas would do with Kierkegaard's famous desert island case (*WL*, 21). I cannot perform beneficent acts to all, but I can wish good to all, and this is the sense in which I can love, even on a desert island. For Aquinas, we also cannot love all with an equal intensity of affection, so some will be loved more intensely than others, and this is because they are nearer to us in some quite ordinary way (such as familial ties).

However, there is also another principle that complicates matters a bit. Aquinas thinks that we should love better (i.e., more virtuous) people more than inferior (i.e., more vicious) people. This is because we wish a greater good to the better person, namely, a fuller share of eternal happiness in God.[91] However, Aquinas insists that there are three reasons why we still love those who are closest to us more, or at any rate, more intensely, than those who are better people and distant from us. The first reason, he argues, is that we may love better people by wishing them a greater good, but the intensity of our love arises from ourselves and our natural relations, and so we wish the appropriate good to our kith and kin more intensely. The second reason has to do with the fact that "some neighbors are connected with us by their natural origin, a connection that cannot be severed, since that origin makes them to be what they are."[92] By contrast, virtue "can come and go," and so it is possible to wish a better good, namely, a greater share of everlasting happiness, to a person who is actually closer to oneself, *precisely because one also wishes for that person to become more virtuous.*[93] The third reason that we should love those who are nearest to us more than those who are better people is that there are simply more ways in which we love those who are nearest to us. What Aquinas means here is that, on the one hand, we love those who are better people simply because they are closer to God. He writes, "The object of charity's love is God, and man is the lover. Therefore . . . we should wish a greater good to one who is nearer to God."[94] On the other hand, this is the only connection we have with better people *as such*. With those who are nearer to us we are more likely to have a variety of connections. Aquinas later writes that "in matters pertaining to nature we should love our kindred most, in matters concerning relations between citizens, we should prefer our fellow-citizens, and on the battlefield our fellow-soldiers."[95] Since the friendship of nature, or kin, is more fundamental, and other relations can "supervene" upon it, there are, especially in a less-transient society than our contemporary one, likely to be more connections we have with our kith and kin than with better people as such (e.g., civic friendships can supervene on family ties if we live in the same locale as our families).[96] Accordingly, we are to love those who are nearest to us more intensely than those who are better people.

Aquinas goes on to argue for various distinctions between various persons in the order of love, based, in part, on the nearness of the person to the agent of charity. Some of these conclusions are based on an outdated Aristotelian conception of biology,[97] but the basic framework for Aquinas's ordering of love is an important challenge to Kierkegaard's view of love as unconditional and non-preferential. In the next section I will argue that, despite these significant dissimilarities, there are some possibilities for partial reconciliation between Kierkegaard's and Aquinas's views of love.

The Arrow of Love and the Arrow of Nature: A Partial Reconciliation

We have seen enough in the preceding section to suspect that the divides between Kierkegaard and Aquinas on the order of love will not admit of any complete reconciliation. This is, in part, because Kierkegaard's suspicion of self-love runs very deep in his thought.[98] By contrast, Aquinas has the usual Aristotelian appreciation for the importance of self-love in his thought, and yet it is precisely Aristotle's view of love that Kierkegaard singles out as objectionable. For similar reasons, Carlos Steel has written, of Aquinas's treatment of preferential love, "Whoever is attracted by the radicalism of someone like Kierkegaard will find nothing to admire here."[99] What kind of reconciliation, if any, might be possible here? To begin an investigation into such possibilities, I want to take a fresh look at self-love in the historic, and then contemporary, Catholic tradition to see what potential might exist in Aquinas for discussion with Kierkegaard along these lines.

The most historically significant magisterial decision on the issue of self-love occurred over four centuries after Aquinas's death. In 1699 Pope Innocent XII undertook to resolve a dispute between two bishops, Jacques Bossuet and François Fénelon. Innocent XII issued a brief that condemned some propositions from Fénelon's work (which, it should be noted, need not carry with it an endorsement of any or all of Bossuet's views). It is perhaps best to simply quote two of the relevant condemned propositions:

1. There is an habitual state of the love of God, which is pure charity and without any admixture of the motive of one's personal interest. Neither fear of punishment nor desire of reward any longer has a share in it. God is no longer loved for the sake of merit, nor because of one's own perfection, nor because of the happiness to be found in loving Him. . . .
5. In the same state of holy indifference we wish nothing for ourselves, all for God. We do not wish that we be perfect and happy for self interest, but we wish all perfection and happiness only in so far as it pleases God to bring it about that we wish for these states by the impression of his grace.[100]

After delineating five different positions on the pure love of God, which he sees Innocent XII as rejecting, Edward Collins Vacek then turns to a sixth position, which he believes is an adequate way to understand the Catholic tradition on this point. This sixth position "affirms a pure love of God, but also permits an eros love of God for the sake of our own happiness, as long as the latter love remains subordinate."[101] Indeed, as Vacek helpfully points out, a traditional act of contrition in the Catholic tradition reads, "I am sorry for my sins because I dread the loss of heaven and the pains of hell, but most of all because they offend you, my God."[102] Vacek points out that many advocates of such a position hold that God uses our naturally strong desires for God because of our own happiness and gradually tutors them so that they become purer forms of love for God. The personal interest does not drop out entirely, for Vacek and the Catholic tradition, nor should it. Vacek writes, "The condemnation can be understood to affirm that there is some sense in which we can and must include ourselves and our interests within Christian life. . . . Within that context, both other-directed agape and eros have their place. The wisdom of the Church, I think, resisted Fénelon's purist position."[103]

In this view, there is some mixture of self-love that is always present in our love for others and God, but self-love can be more or less dominant at any one time, and it should, at any rate, be subordinate to a purer form of love. In criticizing Fénelon on this point, Robert M. Adams writes, "I do not think there is necessarily anything wrong with wanting, for its own sake, to *enjoy* loving God, so long as one's interest in the subjective pleasure is subsidiary to one's desire for the objective relationship."[104] We simply cannot fail to care at all what our attitude toward God, our highest good, would be, as Fénelon seemed to encourage us to do. As Adams points out, this would be a manifestation not of love for God, but of something "much more impersonal."[105]

The suggestion that eros and agape should not be understood as radically separate from one another has caught the eye of Pope Benedict XVI. Perhaps surprisingly, there are some interesting points of contact with Kierkegaard's work in the encyclical *Deus Caritas Est*. Benedict recognizes that we are dealing with a command to love God and love the neighbor, "Since God has first loved us . . . , love is now no longer a mere 'command'; it is the response to the gift of love with which God draws near to us."[106] For all his denigration of self-love, Kierkegaard clearly sees a sense in which love has everything to do with human happiness. On this point, Kierkegaard has a fanciful incarnation of the apostolic author of 1 John say, "The commandment is that you shall love, but ah, if you will understand yourself and life, then it seems that it should not need to be commanded, because to love people is the only thing worth living for, and without this love you are not really living" (WL, 375).

Benedict goes on, however, to argue that a strict distinction between agape and eros is ultimately untenable. On this point, Benedict writes, "Were this antithesis to be taken to extremes, the essence of Christianity would be detached from the vital relations fundamental to human existence, and would become a world apart, admirable perhaps, but decisively cut off from the complex fabric of human life."[107] We have already seen that Kierkegaard's account is not detached in this way. Should we see in this conflict a point for Kierkegaard against Benedict, or for Kierkegaard against Kierkegaard? That is, if the separation between agape and eros were quite rigid, as it sometimes seems to be in Kierkegaard's work, does the intense involvement we have seen in Kierkegaard work to invalidate Benedict's inference that a distinction between eros and agape entails detachment? Or, alternatively, does Kierkegaard's conception of love as intensely involved show that the depth of his conception of love belies his "official position" that erotic love and Christian love are quite distinct? I will be arguing that the second option is the correct one.

According to Benedict, eros cannot live without agape and agape cannot live without eros. He notes that eros, properly understood, begins as a "fascination for the great promise of happiness," it comes "increasingly" to "seek the happiness of the other."[108] One important reason for this is that "I cannot possess Christ just for myself."[109] Similarly, Kierkegaard writes, "you are not to have it [the highest good; God] selfishly for yourself, since what you can have only for yourself alone is never the highest" (WL, 27). Benedict further notes that there is a "communion of will" between God and human beings, "based on the realization that God is in fact more deeply present to me than I am to myself."[110] There is ample continuity here with Kierkegaard, who appears to agree with Benedict in the view that God is closer to me than I am to myself. There also seems to be a real unity of the Christian's will with God's will in Kierkegaard's thought (M, 272–73).[111]

These similarities on the question of the relationship of the human being to God suggest a reexamination of a point on which we have seen that Kierkegaard and Aquinas agree, namely, that we should love God more than ourselves. Indeed, when Francis de Sales espouses this Thomistic doctrine, he explicitly notes that this claim that "love for God . . . preexists all love for ourselves" is the very point at which he differs from Aristotle.[112] Kierkegaard, however, distances himself from Aristotle by arguing against the latter's claim that love is based on self-love. In this context, Aquinas appears as a kind of midpoint between Kierkegaard and Aristotle. This is, in effect, how the late Avery Cardinal Dulles regards him. Dulles writes:

> Taking his departure from Aristotle, he held that everything seeks its own good, but he added that God was the common good of the whole universe and that human beings, by their spiritual nature, were open to union with God. "Just because every creature belongs to God naturally by everything it is," wrote St. Thomas, "it follows that by the very movement of its nature a man or an angel must love God more than itself." Human beings, in particular, are made in the image of God and thus tend to the divine likeness as their own perfection. St. Thomas, then, while remaining fundamentally in the Aristotelian tradition, escaped the trap of egocentrism.[113]

Aquinas can escape the charge of egocentrism because he holds that we do and should desire truly common goods over merely private goods, precisely because they are common goods.[114] Indeed, this is part of Aquinas's interpretation of the apostolic dictum (1 Cor 13:5) on which Kierkegaard reflects in his discourse, "Love Does Not Seek Its Own" (WL, 264–79).[115] It is natural for us to love God as the common good, but the love of God that comes from infused charity moves further and further away from a selfish love, though it is never divorced from the happiness it has in God. Aquinas writes, "That a man wishes to *enjoy* God pertains to that love of God which is love of concupiscence. Now we love God with the love of friendship more than with the love of concupiscence, because the Divine good is greater *in itself* than *our share* of good in enjoying Him."[116]

In my view, the whole dialectical movement toward eternal happiness is itself a movement of love for God in Kierkegaard.[117] This claim, paired with the fact that we are to love God more than ourselves, means that the love for God in Kierkegaard is, in the deepest sense, a kind of eros.[118] When the individual is redeemed, there is a kind of friendship with God that is established by the indwelling of God in one's "innermost being" (*WL*, 9–10). It is from this that Christian love for the neighbor, or agapic love, arises. In Kierkegaard's Christian love, we love God more than we love ourselves. Indeed, God, as the highest, and common, good of all human beings, must be loved. However, we do and should cling to this, our highest good, even if everyone else should give it up (*WL*, 27). In a similar vein, the Thomist philosopher Josef Pieper writes, "That love, insofar as it is real love, does not seek its own remains an inviolable truth. But the lover, assuming that he is disinterested and not calculating, does after all attain his own, the reward of love. And this reward, in its turn and in view of human nature, cannot be a matter of indifference to him."[119] This, I believe, means that the eros for God and agapic love that Christians have for one another, on Kierkegaard's scheme, should, and ultimately really do, merge.

What we have seen thus far is that Kierkegaard's concept of love has our unconditional love for the neighbor arising out of our love for God, over and above the love we have for ourselves. It is this love that wrests Kierkegaard and Aquinas away from egocentrism. If it were not for this, our love for the neighbor would be out of a simple, and selfish, preoccupation with our beatitude (since for both thinkers our love for the neighbor arises out of our love for God). We have a love for God that can be and become purer and more refined by grace. That we should have a share in this love is not a matter of indifference to us. It is this love, when primed by Christian love, or Christian charity, that extends to the neighbor in agape, which is, at least in part, a benevolent willing of good to all.

Why, then, does Aquinas permit the ordering of love on the basis of the particular neighbor's distance from the self? The answer is that this is what is natural to human beings, and this means, at least partly, that it is not a simple choice of theirs.[120] This predisposition is, rather, part of the nature of human beings, which nature is given to them as an expression of the Divine Wisdom. That is why I love God more than I love myself, it is why I love my soul more than I love my neighbor, and it is why I love my neighbor more than I love my body: because that is precisely what God's wisdom ordained. Kierkegaard can go along with this up to a point. Christian love, or charity, is for both of these thinkers an expression of what Aquinas would call the Divine Wisdom. But for Aquinas, and the Catholic tradition that in large measure follows him on this point, the human animal, just as with all other creatures, has desires and loves that belong to the creature's very being. If grace is to perfect nature, it must perfect, and not destroy, the natural human self. As we have seen, for Kierkegaard, the self is either sinful or faithful. For Kierkegaard and Luther, nature is run through with sin and thus is not an intermediate position as it is for Aquinas. For Kierkegaard, our love-relationships can "materially coincide" with Christian love, but they become genuinely love for the first time when primed by Christian love. For Aquinas, our natural love-relationships were always love-relationships, but they are elevated, crowned, and perfected, rather than created, by Christian love. This means, accordingly, that the real difference between Kierkegaard and Aquinas on the question of love is not the concept of *preference* but the concept of *nature*.

In my view, however, the difference between the two, at least on the issue of love, is not really so great. This is for two reasons. First, I see no obvious reason why Kierkegaard's account of love and Aquinas's would actually issue in different actions in any one case of an individual in need. It is not at all clear that Aquinas's conception of love is any less self-sacrificing than Kierkegaard's, and Kierkegaard has the individual hold firmly to her principles, regardless of resistance from others, as does Aquinas. The second reason is a bit more detailed. Kierkegaard insists that Christian love should not dwell on itself, but should get to the business of loving. Otherwise, it is like an arrow that, in order to consider its progress, stops in midair, instantly falling to the ground (*WL,* 182), thereby nullifying whatever progress had been made. Thomistic nature is itself like this arrow. It is shot toward happiness, yes, but more, it is shot toward God as the common and highest good of all. Pieper writes, "One who comprehends man to the depths of his soul as *creatura* simultaneously knows that in the act of being created we are—without being asked and without even the possibility of being asked—shot toward our destination like an arrow. Therefore, a kind of gravitational impulse governs our desire for happiness. Nor can we have any power over this impulse because we ourselves *are* it."[121] Kierkegaard and Aquinas can, at bottom, agree that we are the impulses toward deep happiness in God that God himself intends. As a part of this happiness that we also will, we will the good of others in love. The theological underpinnings of this path can admit of some dispute. The fact of it cannot, for a Christian.

‡

Kierkegaard's concept of love not only can withstand charges of abstraction, but can even model the virtues of other accounts that suppose themselves superior to Kierkegaard's. In considering Aquinas's views on the order of love, readers of Kierkegaard have less reason for affront than might at first be supposed. Aquinas may insist that one should love oneself more than one's neighbor, but what he means is that one should love one's soul more than the neighbor's soul, and one's body decidedly less. What this really amounts to is the claim that one should be willing to sacrifice life and limb for the neighbor, but should not, perversely, attempt to swap one's eternal destiny in heaven for another's in hell (which would be especially strange given our epistemic limitations in that regard). It is by no means clear that Kierkegaard's considered view is at variance with a subtler understanding of Aquinas on this point.

Indeed, the Catholic tradition's retention of certain virtues of self-love should not be deplored as if selfishness were there seen as the only, or even the best, motivation for love of God and neighbor, as it is neither. Kierkegaard and Aquinas, as a representative of the Catholic tradition on this point, can come to partial agreements on some of these matters once their real commitments with regard to the role of the self in love are understood. Where they will differ is with respect to Aquinas's order of love. However, grounded as the ordering is in a love for God that exceeds one's love for oneself, the order is seen to really rest on Aquinas's conception of nature. Kierkegaard does not share Aquinas's conception of nature, but whether and how far it would change the essence of his thought is an interesting question. Such disputes may have their roots in denominational divides in which I dare not claim neutrality. What cuts across denominational boundaries in this respect is Jesus' question, from which none of us will be exempt, namely, "what have you done for the least of these?"[122]

FOUR

The Catholic Moment?
Apostolic Authority in Kierkegaard
and the Catholic Tradition

A Catholic poet should be an apostle by being first of all a poet, not
try to be a poet by being first of all an apostle. For if he presents
himself to people as a poet, he is going to be judged as a poet
and if he is not a good one his apostolate will be ridiculed.

THOMAS MERTON

The Catholic conception of authority is one at which many in our age
bristle. The hierarchy in the Church is a source of scandal to many, and
Luther's leveling of this hierarchy in his famous doctrine of the priesthood of all believers is often warmly received.[1] Curiously, this is one area
where Kierkegaard's reception of Luther is not clearly favorable. Indeed,
many have suggested that Kierkegaard's concept of apostolic authority
brings him close to Catholicism. I argue that this is in part the case, but
that it is perhaps better understood as Kierkegaard's resolving of an am-
biguity in Luther. Kierkegaard saw the opportunity for a purer gospel in
Luther, but he also saw corruption and a movement toward secularism,
especially in Luther's doctrine of the universal priesthood.

Writers on Kierkegaard from Walter Lowrie to Frederick Copleston
have been among the many to claim that Kierkegaard's conception of
the apostle is a movement toward Catholicism.[2] Given the attention
this topic has received, I would be remiss not to include an inquiry into
the topic in a book devoted to a dialogue between Kierkegaard and the
Catholic tradition. In the present chapter, we will reflect on the way

in which God might make known certain supernatural truths or doctrines that are binding on those to whom such messages are delivered, whether that delivery should be firsthand or secondhand. I will begin by explaining, in the first part, just what role the apostle might play in Kierkegaard's larger religious thought. The three subsequent sections will focus on the question of how close Kierkegaard's concept of the apostle, perhaps most clearly articulated in the essay by H.H.,[3] "The Difference between a Genius and an Apostle," brings him to Catholicism (and also to his own Lutheran tradition, which was, of course, itself a response to Catholicism).

The Apostle in Kierkegaard's Thought

In *The Point of View for My Work as an Author*, Kierkegaard notes that he is neither an apostle nor a teacher, but only a fellow pupil (*PV*, 78–79). Accordingly, Kierkegaard denies having any apostolic authority and conceives of his authorship as using something quite different in an effort to expose the inadequate Christian credentials of his age. Thus, while Kierkegaard's task is neither to upbraid Christians nor to preach Christian doctrine directly, he understands his role as a "genius" and a "poet" (*WA*, 235; *PV*, 235) to be that of "deceiving" others into the truth. For as Kierkegaard writes, there are two kinds of deception: one can deceive out of the truth, and one can deceive into the truth (*PV*, 53). What does the latter sort of poet do? Kierkegaard writes, "What, then, does it mean 'to deceive'? It means that one does not begin *directly* with what one wishes to communicate but begins by taking the other's delusion at face value. . . . One does not begin in this way: It is Christianity that I am proclaiming, and you are living in purely esthetic categories. No, one begins this way: Let us talk about the esthetic" (*PV*, 54). Why use this kind of "indirect communication"? Because "direct communication presupposes that the recipient's ability to receive is entirely in order, but here that is simply not the case" (*PV*, 54).

Thus, Kierkegaard's pseudonymous works approach the spheres of existence in a very particular way. *Either/Or*, part 1, for instance, begins by allowing the aesthete, A, to articulate his own life-view, and to allow the reader to delight in it long enough to see that it is ultimately in despair. Judge William then follows in *Either/Or*, part 2, and counsels A to despair of the aesthetic view of life, and leap into the ethical, where one receives a self (*EO*, 2:213–14). The ethical is different from the aesthetic because one no longer delights (as in the aesthetic sphere) in the "interesting" from afar, but has due concern for one's life and has not lost one's soul in speculation, as Johannes Climacus would claim that Hegel and the Hegelians had.

It is in this context that the possibility of an eternal happiness (in light of one's finitude and temporality) is raised. This brings on the moments of Religiousness A, which is the religiousness one can acquire without a specifically divine revelation.[4] Here one tries to sustain a relationship to an eternal happiness, but in the attempt discovers that one cannot, with her whole life, satisfactorily sustain the relationship because the very act of beginning to relate to an eternal happiness presupposes a moment before the attempt, in which time the whole person was not related to an eternal happiness (*CUP*, 526). For Climacus, this is meant to preclude an individual's ability to establish his or her own God-relationship. Here one not only must maintain hope in the "absurd" entry of the god (*Guden*) into time, but must also maintain hope in the forgiveness of sins. The entry of God into time is the signifying of the sphere of the transcendent religion, what Climacus variously calls Religiousness B or Christianity.[5] Accordingly, "immanence" and "transcendence" in the context of this discussion do not simply refer to whether God should be thought of as residing within the individual or without, but more than that, they refer to an individual's efforts to relate to God on his or her own (immanence) and the knowledge that those efforts are doomed to failure and that only God can intervene, by special assistance, to save an individual from outside (transcendence).

Now, as H.H. tells us, "*in the sphere of immanence, authority is utterly unthinkable, or it can be thought only as transitory*" (*WA*, 99, emphasis original). On this point, H.H. writes, "As a subject I am to honor and obey the king with undivided soul, but I am permitted to be built up religiously by the thought that essentially I am a citizen of heaven and that if I ever meet his departed majesty there I shall not be bound in subservient obedience to him" (*WA*, 100). Governments may be better or worse, but whatever earthly authority they carry is transitory. In the sphere of immanence (as we understand it here), the individual is assigned to him or herself and can only attempt to persuade others. Such an individual would have no special divine gift that would allow him or her to communicate with authority; rather, within immanence, an individual relies on his or her own efforts and talents to either persuade or coerce (in one form or another) an individual to obey. It is quite exceptional for an individual to be specially chosen to communicate with authority on this view.

Accordingly, no one "matures into" an apostle. One can only be called, directly by God, to exercise direct communication in an authoritative way. In this vein, H.H. writes:

> An apostle is not born; an apostle is a man[6] who is called and appointed by God and sent by him on a mission. An apostle does not develop in such a way that he gradually becomes what he is. . . . Prior to becoming an apostle, there is no potential possibility; every human being is essentially equally close to becoming that. An apostle can never come to himself in such a way that he becomes aware of his apostolic calling as an element in his own life-development. The apostolic calling is a paradoxical fact that in the first and the last moment of his life stands paradoxically outside his personal identity as the specific person he is. (*WA*, 95)

One does not become more intelligent for being an apostle (*WA*, 95), but is simply entrusted with the ability to communicate directly and with divine authority.

In contrast to the method Kierkegaard uses in his authorship, indirect communication, the apostle can use direct communication. About the need for both, Kierkegaard writes, "Yet the communication of the essentially Christian must end finally in 'witnessing.' The maieutic cannot be the final form, because, Christianly understood, the truth doth not lie in the subject (as Socrates understood it), but in a revelation which must be proclaimed" (*JP*, 2:1957 / *SKP*, IX A 221). Just as Kierkegaard argues that people need to be "deceived into the truth" when the ability of the various recipients to receive direct communication is not yet entirely in order, when they have been "deceived" sufficiently to the point where their ability to receive is in order, then a direct communication must come forward. Accordingly, on the normal run of Kierkegaard's thought, as sketched out briefly above, an apostle can communicate directly all he or she might wish to an individual, but if that individual is dialectically unprepared for direct communication (that is, the individual is, for instance, still embroiled in the aesthetic sphere), that direct communication will simply fall, as it were, on deaf ears. However, when the appropriate point is reached, nothing but direct communication will do.

There is, however, another issue worth our attention. If we grant that the individual to whom the apostle communicates directly does not simply "jump" stages in the dialectic when he or she is not sufficiently prepared to receive the direct communication, what then about the apostle, whom presumably God calls to the task of administering divine authority? H.H. notes that every human being "is essentially equally close" to becoming an apostle (WA, 95). Perhaps this could be explained by noting, as Climacus does, that the apostle's situation is "qualitatively different from that of others" (CUP, 453). Thus, we might explain that, as the divine call to apostolic mission is qualitatively and not quantitatively different from the lot of others, everyone who has not yet been called to such a task is equally (that is, infinitely) far away from such a call. But this interpretation seems belied by the fact that individuals on the normal run of things need to make dialectical progress in order to be *prepared* for a direct communication, which, one would have thought, God's call to embark upon an apostolic ministry would be.[7] Now, H.H. does make it clear that there is no implanted potentiality in an apostle when he or she is born that simply flowers into his or her apostolicity. Apostles, on this view, do not have an additional moment in the dialectic that others lack. There is no Religiousness C (or D)[8] that those burdened with apostolic authority have that the rest of us do not. But all of this simply forces the question, if the case of the apostle is so exceptional, must the apostle be subject to the normal dialectical considerations?

In order to answer this question, let us briefly look at what Climacus has to say about the apostle. First, we might note, as before, that "the paradox is that the direct relation is higher for the apostle, but this is not the case for others" (CUP, 605). It appears that, on Climacus's view, this direct relation of the apostle extends both to God and to others. Now, if the direct relation to God is paradoxically higher in the case of the apostle (that is, in the moment of the apostolic call, and presumably thereafter) than the indirect, then we might well assume that God can "empower" (WA, 241; JP, 1:187 / SKP, X-2 A 119) the individual to communicate a revelation directly, regardless of his or her dialectical position on the path to Christian faith. A paradigm case would seem to be the Apostle Paul, who, Luke goes out of his way to tell us, at the time of his conversion was "still breathing murderous threats against the disciples of the Lord" (Acts 9:1) as he began the journey to Damascus, along the road to which he would be called to begin his apostolic ministry. Surely it is plausible to simply suggest that a man who was engaged in such murderous plots had not yet learned all the maieutic lessons that indirect communication might have afforded him. Another case, perhaps an even clearer one, would be the case of the prophet Jonah, whose reluctance to preach to Nineveh nearly boiled over into ultimate defiance, but who finally did obey and preached to Nineveh the need for repentance. In these cases, it seems quite possible that God calls individuals to communicate directly, regardless of their positions with respect to the religious dialectic.

Accordingly, Kierkegaard writes, "How, after all, can a *divine* doctrine enter into the world? By God's empowering a few individuals and overpowering them, as it were, to such a degree that at every moment throughout a life they are willing to act, to endure, to suffer everything for this doctrine" (*WA*, 241; *JP*, 1:187 / *SKP*, X-2 A 119, emphasis original). God empowers, even overpowers, certain individuals for the task of direct communication. Yet, Kierkegaard does not want, thereby, to compromise their freedom. In fact, in an entry on the extraordinary (which is similar to but should not be identified with the apostle), Kierkegaard writes, "If Christ had called to me and said, 'You shall be my chosen instrument, I shall—glad tiding!—show you what you shall come to suffer for my name's sake'—then I would have implored that I might be free, etc." (*JP*, 1:1087 / *SKP*, X-4 A 518). Accordingly, some individuals can initially resist.

In fact, it would appear that some individuals can outright defy the call to communicate directly *with authority*. The Pharisees are the paradigm case for Kierkegaard here. He writes, "True authority is present when the truth is the cause. The reason the Pharisees spoke without authority, *although they were indeed authorized teachers,* was precisely that their talk, like their lives, was in the finite power of seventeen concerns" (*WA*, 211; *JP*, 1:183 / *SKP*, VIII-1 A 416, emphasis mine). Earlier in the same entry, Kierkegaard writes:

Authority does not mean to be a king or to be an emperor or general, to have the power of arms, to be a bishop,[9] or to be a policeman, but it means by a firm and conscious resolution to be willing to sacrifice everything, one's life, for one's cause; it means to articulate a cause in such a way that a person is in identity with himself about needing nothing and fearing nothing. This recklessness of infinity is authority.

The significance of these claims is hard to overestimate. A Pharisee can effectively relinquish what would otherwise be his authority because of his being in the "finite power of seventeen concerns." Further, despite Kierkegaard's respect for ordination, even a bishop must pair this with the "recklessness of infinity." This suggests that the authority gained by ordination or episcopal consecration is not genuinely divine or apostolic authority, at least not unless it is exercised together with the unconditional obedience and recklessness of infinity. Thus, if a genuine divine call were not matched with unconditional obedience and resolution, Kierkegaard would seem to have it that the resulting communication would not be actually administered with *authority* at all.

Using an example, H.H. writes, "When someone who has the authority to say it says to a person, 'Go!' and when someone who does not have the authority says, 'Go!' the utterance (Go!) and its content are identical; evaluated esthetically, it is, if you like, equally well spoken, but the authority makes the difference" (*WA*, 98–99). We are simply not to evaluate things putatively said with authority according to any aesthetic criterion. On this point, H.H. writes, "The son is willing to obey on the basis of the father's profundity and brilliance, and on that basis he simply cannot obey him, because his critical attitude with regard to whether the command is profound and brilliant undermines the obedience" (*WA*, 104). While H.H. here notes two aesthetic criteria that cannot be evaluated if obedience is not to be undermined, note that he does not include any other criteria here. Nothing is said to prohibit a critical attitude with regard to the unconditional obedience of the father to God; only a critical attitude with regard to whether the command is profound and brilliant is prohibited.[10] For if authority can be had only in one's unconditional obedience (even supposing the necessary divine "authorization"), and, as H.H. emphatically states, *"The divine authority is what is qualitatively decisive"* (*WA*, 96), then it would appear that one is not responsible for obedience when the teaching is not delivered with authority, even if delivered by the one who would otherwise be authorized. Accordingly, on the view that seems to be taking shape at the hands of Climacus, Kierkegaard, and H.H., authority is divinely commissioned, but fragile, and to preserve it is a task that is assigned to the divinely commissioned apostle, and one at which he or she can fail.

Now, of course, this claim does not change the fact that authority comes from outside an individual; authority remains something transcendent, and given from God (*WA,* 99). Single-minded devotion to the doctrine one teaches is not a sufficient condition for authority, but the question we are asking here is whether it is a necessary condition for it, and if the Pharisees effectively relinquish their authority by disobedience and double-mindedness, then true devotion may well be a necessary condition for "apostolic" authority.

Kierkegaard and Luther on Religious Authority

Before launching into a discussion of Kierkegaard's relation to Catholicism on the matter of authority, it is important to remember that no thinker appears in a historical vacuum and that Kierkegaard himself belongs to a theological tradition whose storied relationship to Catholicism is even better known (or at any rate, more frequently discussed), namely, the Lutheran tradition.

Much has been written about Kierkegaard's relation to Martin Luther, which, while in many ways appreciative, is by no means one of uncritical acceptance.[11] The most interesting remark, from the point of view of Kierkegaard's relationship to Catholicism on our subject in this chapter, is that Kierkegaard insisted that the Reformation, particularly under Luther, was really best understood as a "corrective" rather than as a new and decisive change to the Church. Now, this is not to suggest that Kierkegaard believes that Luther should simply have remained a faithful (if critical) Catholic.[12] Rather, Kierkegaard makes it clear that Luther played an indispensable role in repudiating the pope's authority. He writes, "The same thing happened to Catholicism as happened to the entire globe. Another Copernicus (Luther) came along who discovered that Rome is not the center about which everything revolves but a point on the periphery" (*JN,* 1:259 / DD: 166). Thus, in Kierkegaard's view, neither Protestantism nor Catholicism is self-sufficient. He writes:

> Are not Catholicism and Protestantism actually related to one another as a building which cannot stand is related to buttresses which cannot stand alone, but the entire structure is able to stand, even very stable and

secure, when the building and the buttresses together give it stability. . . . In other words, is not Protestantism (or the Lutheran principle) really a corrective, and has not a great confusion been brought about by making this normative in Protestantism? (*JP*, 3:3617 / *SKP*, XI-2 A 305)

Kierkegaard also regularly contrasts Catholicism's accentuation of Christ as prototype, the result of which he takes to be a kind of meritoriousness in being a Christian, with Protestantism's (and especially Luther's) accentuation of Christ as redeemer and gift, the result of which he takes to be nothing short of spiritual laziness and ultimately secularism.[13] Both of these approaches have their problems. In fact, Kierkegaard claims that Luther is the "very opposite of 'the apostle.'" This is because the apostle brings forth Christianity in God's interest, where Luther has ultimately brought forth Christianity in "man's interest" (*JP*, 3:2556 / *SKP*, XI-2 A 266).

This, I think, signals where Kierkegaard sees himself as departing from his master, Luther.[14] Luther, in extending the priesthood to all believers and denying its special "character," went too far in catering to the tastes of the many.[15] No doubt one part of what might be troubling to Kierkegaard about Luther's view of the ministry here is that Luther claims that no one should be set over a congregation as priest without the congregation having first elected the priest to such a post.[16] In contrast, there does not appear to be anything democratic about apostolic authority in Kierkegaard's view. Kierkegaard writes:

> Luther was perfectly right in smashing the egotism of the clergy domineeringly wanting to be the intermediate authority; but, O, he had very poor knowledge of mankind if he could think that it was possible for all of us to become priests, that the only way of doing it in the world was— and this is what happened—for priests to become landlords—and all of us priests. There should be a clergy as the middle term. The clergy should be rigorously Christian, should express the most strenuous demands of Christianity, at least approximately, for otherwise the whole thing is destroyed and everything become secularism through and through, which is the actual case. Draconian laws amount to nothing, and the magnificent sublimity that we are all priests—leads to the tragic nonsense we see before us. (*JP*, 3:3153 / *SKP*, X-3 A 267)

This is not to say, of course, that Luther has no concept whatever of special responsibilities that are best undertaken by a priest. He reinterprets

Christ's entrusting of the "keys of the kingdom" to Peter (which is so important for the Catholic understanding of the teaching authority of the apostles, and their successors the bishops), but he does not, of course, jettison it entirely.[17] Nor, importantly, does Luther take the administration of a sacrament by a wicked (or "papist") priest to be reason to disregard it.[18] This question, particularly as it pertained to rebaptism, loomed large in the Donatist controversy (see below), but Luther does not appear to worry about whether the Roman Church has a true baptism.[19]

Kierkegaard may have thought with some reason that Luther's own thought on certain matters wavered a bit (as did Kierkegaard's own assessment of Luther).[20] Despite his toleration for "papist" baptisms, Luther takes a different tack on ordination and the persistence of its effects in the face of priestly sin. He writes:

> For what purpose were you consecrated, if you did not have a true faith, if you were consecrated contrary to every ordinance and intention of Christ—as a priest for your own sacrifice, as a priest for a special work, and not as a priest for the communal church. . . . Then in fact you have been consecrated contrary to Christ's intention to do everything that opposes him. But if you have been consecrated in opposition to Christ's intention, then your consecration is certainly false, anti-Christian, and altogether meaningless. For that reason also you have surely not effected conversion, but you have sacrificed, received and worshiped mere bread and wine and have charged others to worship them.[21]

Here Luther seems to waver a bit on whether priests who have celebrated a private Mass ("contrary to Christ's intention") have actually administered a valid sacrament (even outside a private Mass). This appears to be in contrast to his earlier acceptance of baptisms administered by such priests.

For Kierkegaard, this perceived contrast might well be a sign of something deeper, since, as we have seen, Kierkegaard appears to hold that disobedience relinquishes authority. Yet, for Kierkegaard, Christian obedience always entails worldly conflict. For Kierkegaard, Luther himself did "incalculable harm by not becoming a martyr. . . . Furthermore, he gave birth to the confusion of being a reformer with the help of politics" (*JP*, 3:2546 / *SKP*, XI-1 A 61).[22] Thus, the very concept of a Magisterial Reformation, in which Luther was engaged, appears to be, for Kierkegaard, a near contradiction in terms. Why is this? Because the reformer is, no doubt, entrusted with a divine commission to return the Church of

Christ to its narrow way. But the call to do this with authority may very well be, for Kierkegaard, an apostolic commission, and presupposes the double danger, that of internal conflict as well as external conflict with the established order. In Kierkegaard's later thought, the "witness to the truth" must "always be distinguishable by heterogeneity with this world" (*M*, 10), and such a witness getting along well in the world is "not only a monstrosity but an impossibility, like a bird that is in addition a fish, or an iron tool that in addition has the oddity of being made of wood" (*M*, 11). The result is that one's Christian and apostolic credentials are in serious jeopardy when one is not persecuted, and especially when one's Reformation receives wide acclaim from citizen and ruler alike.[23]

Kierkegaard makes it clear that his own view of clerical authority (that of the pastor) includes ordination as a necessary condition, in addition to the requirement that the message be delivered with authority (*JP*, 3:3477 / *SKP*, VIII-1 A 434). So the ordination carries with it (as, on this view, any apostolic commission would) the requirement that one arrange one's life in accordance with the teaching one proclaims. Without this obedience, Kierkegaard insists, the result will be that there is no Christianity, because there are no Christians (*JP*, 3:3170 / *SKP*, X-5 A 10). Kierkegaard appears to see a kind of middle ground between Christian rigor and subservience to "the public" in Luther. Since he rejects the latter, my suggestion is that Kierkegaard's thought be seen as an intensification of the former.

Kierkegaardian and Catholic "Apostles": Some Similarities

Having examined the role for the apostle in Kierkegaard's thought (in light of his relationship to Luther) we shall now ask whether we might be inclined to view Kierkegaard's understanding of the apostle as a turn in the direction of Catholicism. In order to do this, we shall further examine H.H.'s discussion of the apostle, placing it alongside Catholic documents and certain writings of the Church Fathers. Then, we shall examine the results of the comparisons that have been drawn, and ask whether the understanding of the apostle and apostolic authority in the writings of Kierkegaard and his pseudonyms matches up at all with the understanding of those topics in the Catholic tradition.

Before embarking on this portion of the argument, however, it is best to consider briefly a question about the Catholic view of apostles.[24] On the one hand, the Catholic tradition tends to restrict the "apostles" to those twelve apostles whom Jesus directly appointed. Thus, the "apostolic age" closed, for Catholicism, roughly speaking, near the end of the first century.[25] The *Catechism* explains it this way: "In the office of the apostles there is one aspect that cannot be transmitted: to be the chosen witnesses of the Lord's Resurrection and so the foundation stones of the Church. But their office also has a permanent aspect."[26] Thus, while the present-day bishops are seen as "successors of the apostles," they are not apostles in the strictest sense.[27]

What does it mean, then, when the pope (as he does often enough) issues an "apostolic blessing" or an "apostolic exhortation?" Gerald O'Collins and Mario Farrugia explain this by saying that there are three aspects to revelation in the Catholic tradition, namely, foundational revelation, dependent revelation, and eschatological (or final) revelation.[28] Final revelation is God's definitive self-revelation at the end of history, and so need not concern us much here. Foundational revelation, however, is confined to the apostolic age and includes the apostles' experience of Christ, their writing of the New Testament, and so forth. Dependent revelation, however, is not confined to the apostolic age, but depends upon the foundational revelation, and refers to God's "living and enlightening voice speaking now and calling human beings to respond, also here and now, with faith."[29] While the current pope is surely not an apostle in the strict historical sense, his ministry is nevertheless apostolic in a clear sense, since his role is to guide the Church to a faithful understanding of foundational revelation. To see this, consider the language used in the bull *Ineffabilis Deus,* which defined, in a way that the Catholic tradition generally regards as infallible, the Immaculate Conception of the Blessed Virgin Mary, alongside the language used by H.H. to describe how a Kierkegaardian apostle might call upon the obedience of a disciple:

> Wherefore, if any should presume to think in their hearts otherwise than as it has been defined by Us, which God avert, let them know and understand that they are condemned . . . have suffered shipwreck in regard to faith, and have revolted from the unity of the Church. . . .[30]

> I cannot, I dare not compel you to obey, but through the relationship of your conscience to God, I make you eternally responsible for your relationship to this doctrine by my having proclaimed it as revealed to me and therefore by having proclaimed it with divine authority. (*WA*, 97)

I submit that there are relevant similarities between the use of present-day papal authority (which nothing prevents us from calling apostolic) and Kierkegaard's own conception of apostolic authority.

Returning to the context for our Kierkegaardian inquiry, while we have noted that there is a role for both indirect and direct communication, until now we have largely viewed these roles as separate, imagining that the apostle communicates directly and that Kierkegaard and most of his pseudonyms (the geniuses) are in the business of communicating indirectly. But, as Dunning aptly points out, "the fact that an apostle or someone who is the exception (*extraordinarius*) submits to authority in no way means that such a person cannot also be reflective."[31] The effect of this is to say that while the apostle and the genius are conceptually different, one who is an apostle can also engage in indirect communication.

In order to see something about how the two might overlap, let us first consider *For Self-Examination,* in which Kierkegaard comments on the story of the Prophet Nathan and King David, where the prophet relates the parable of the rich man who owned much livestock and who stole the one little lamb of a poor man. Kierkegaard writes:

> I imagine that David listened attentively and thereupon declared his judgment, did not, of course, intrude his personality (subjectivity) but impersonally (objectively) evaluated this charming little work . . . in short, expressed his opinion the way we cultured people today tend to judge a sermon for the cultured—that is, a sermon that is itself also objective. Then the prophet says to him, "Thou art the man." See, the tale the prophet told was a story, but this "Thou art the man"—this was another story—this was the transition to the subjective. (*FSE*, 38)

The way Kierkegaard presents the story is not exactly the way the biblical text presents the story (see 2 Sm 12:1–8), but I see no reason why we can't, in the attempt to understand the story, help ourselves to a bit of both accounts.

In this connection, Hugh Pyper writes, "Nathan is the bearer of the authoritative word of God. We are not told that God supplies him with any form of words, however. There is nothing to indicate that, having received the divine revelation, he did not go off and himself compose an elegant short story as the best means of carrying out his commission."[32] This is an interesting way to approach the story, and it allows us to see how the commission to communicate directly can be executed in many different ways, especially for different individuals.[33] Yet how should we judge Nathan's success if this account were true? Kierkegaard's account has Nathan grow so frustrated with the objectivity of David (almost as if his somewhat indirect story either had failed or was certainly not working as quickly as expected), that he must finally add the direct and authoritative punch: "Thou art the man" (*FSE*, 39).[34] By contrast, the biblical text tells us that David "grew very angry" with the rich man in the story (2 Sm 12:5). Here we can combine the biblical account with Kierkegaard's version and see that David might well have had his sympathies roused with the character in the story, but in much the same way as that happens in a theater. We can almost picture David saying, as 2 Samuel 5 has it, "As the Lord lives, this man merits death!" and then revert to the theater critic in him and say, "Speaking of your little story, Nathan, it's really quite something."

At this point, in order to get hold of the spectator whose emotions have been roused against a villain, but only in the distanced way our emotions are roused against a villain in a theater, Nathan summons his authority by shifting the arena from a fictitious one to a very real and personal one. As Pyper notes,[35] David could of course simply turn Nathan's implicit rebuke aside, but he doesn't. Nathan forces him to consider his own life as an instance of the villainy against which his sympathies have been roused. This is the ethical point of view, where, as Climacus has it, one becomes infinitely interested in, what would be, for David, his standing before God. The direct communication comes when David sees Nathan, whom his conscience cannot deny is a duly appointed prophet of the Lord, revealing his sinful condition to him and his need for repentance as a matter of authority.

What the episode with the prophet Nathan should show us, then, is that there is an art to direct communication, and a burden, not only to suffer for the truth, but also for the communicator to enable his or her listeners to be in a position to receive the message (which may involve some maieutic carefulness). In a related connection with respect to the apostle, H.H. writes, "I am not to listen to Paul because he is brilliant or matchlessly brilliant, but I am to submit to Paul because he has divine authority; *and in any case it must become Paul's responsibility to see to it that he produces this impression,* whether anyone submits to his authority or not" (*WA,* 96, emphasis mine). Thus the apostle is burdened not only with the task of unconditional obedience (without which he or she appears to forfeit his or her apostolic authority, on this view), but also with the burden of working relentlessly to assure that his or her listeners are disposed to hear the authoritative proclamation.

Now Kierkegaard thinks of himself as a genius and not an apostle. He thus envisions himself as offering a bit of dialectical preparation for the eventual reception of an authoritative proclamation. However, if the apostle is charged with the responsibility to produce the impression of divine authority, then he or she ultimately must work tirelessly to see to it that the message is received in the proper authoritative light.[36] The apostle not only must deliver God's word, but must also engage in what maieutic work is necessary to see that it gets a hearing. Little wonder, then, that James 3:1 warns us that not many of us should become teachers!

In sharing part of H.H.'s conception of the burden of discharging one's apostolic authority, Pope St. Gregory the Great, in distinguished historical company,[37] wrote a work known as *Regula Pastoralis,* or *Pastoral Care,* on the occasion of his having been elected to the office of the papacy in 590 upon the death of Pope Pelagius II. The occasion for the treatise was not simply his election to the papacy, but also his deep sorrow upon having been so elected, and a letter, apparently from Archbishop John of Ravenna, which gave Gregory some trouble for his reluctance to assume the office. In the treatise, one of Gregory's chief aims is to detail the burden and responsibility of the priesthood, such that one might understand his reluctance to undertake the high office to which he had been elected.

In *Pastoral Care,* part 3, by far the longest of four parts to the work, is almost entirely devoted to giving instructions about how the priest must minister to roughly seventy-two (thirty-six sets of two, such as "men and women, young and old, poor and rich," etc.) characteristics that parishioners might have that issue in as many unique needs. Following an analogy he uses of how a skillful harpist plays with a variety of strokes the various strings of the harp to eventually produce a beautiful melody, Gregory writes, "Hence, too, every teacher, in order to edify all in the one virtue of charity, must touch the hearts of his hearers by using one and the same doctrine, but not by giving to all one and the same exhortation."[38] Gregory's insight in the case of Nathan and David is also quite interesting for our purposes. He writes:

> But at times, in taking to task the powerful of this world, they are first to be dealt with by drawing divers comparisons in a case ostensibly concerning someone else. Then, when they give a right judgment on what apparently is another's case, they are to be taken to task regarding their own guilt by a suitable procedure. . . . Thus it was that Nathan the Prophet, come to chide the king, to all appearance asked his judgment in the case of a poor man against a rich man. . . . For a short while he concealed the person whom he was aiming at, and then at once struck him when he had convicted him. His stroke would, perhaps, have had less force, if he had chosen to castigate the sin directly the moment he began to speak. . . . He, therefore, concealed the surgeon's knife under his coat, but drawing it out suddenly, pierced the wound, that the sick man might feel the knife before he saw it, for if he had first seen it, he might have refused to feel it.[39]

Here Gregory, like Kierkegaard, recognizes the value of concealing the direct exercise of authority for a bit, noticing that certain dialectical concerns are at issue and that the likelihood that David will grieve and repent over his sin is greatly reduced by a simple direct report of the sin.

This is also borne out in Gregory's understanding of St. Paul's various admonishments. He writes, "When admonishing Timothy, he says: *Reprove, entreat, rebuke, in all patience and doctrine.* But when admonishing Titus, he says: *These things speak, and exhort, and rebuke with all authority.*"[40] To explain the reason for such differing pieces of advice, Gregory writes, "Is it not that he sees Titus endowed with too meek a spirit, and Timothy with a little too zealous one?"[41] Here, Gregory sees Paul as encouraging both meekness and sternness in Timothy and Titus, in which each seem to be respectively deficient. No doubt this has everything to do with approaching those under one's care from where they are, and according to what they need. This parallels Kierkegaard's insistence that the true teacher first finds the other person where he or she is (*PV*, 45–47).[42]

Part 1 of *Pastoral Care* is devoted to showing not only why a certain reluctance is permissible but rather is even praiseworthy in assuming such an important sacerdotal office as the one to which Gregory had then been elected.[43] Nevertheless, if one knows that he has the appropriate calling and abilities, he must take the post, since, "whosoever does not care to assist others by the favours which he has received, is reprobated by Holy Church."[44] This is especially true for those ministers who preach the doctrine of the Church, but do nothing to alleviate the external sufferings of those to whom they preach. To this effect, Gregory writes, "Doctrine taught does not penetrate the minds of the needy, if a compassionate heart does not commend it to the hearts of hearers."[45]

Gregory even suggests that the (would-be) listeners are justified in being averse to the teaching of a priest who is insensitive to their physical needs.[46] These elements of responsibility to one's calling and the harmful effects of a pastor's sinful life seem to find a prima facie parallel to Kierkegaard's pseudonymous and signed work related to the apostle. What we have seen in this section is that there is a good deal of commonality between Kierkegaard and important representatives of the Catholic tradition with respect to the way the authority is discharged by prophetic and apostolic representatives. In the next section, we will consider in what ways there may be a certain contrast between Kierkegaard's apostle and the Catholic view on that topic.

Kierkegaard's Apostle and Donatism

While Gregory allows us to glimpse some similarities to Catholicism with the account we receive at the hands of H.H. and Kierkegaard with respect to how one entrusted with apostolic authority discharges that authority, there also appear to be some important differences. For while indirect communication and direct communication are both necessary and useful, there is still only one sort of person, an apostle, who can communicate directly and with authority. Yet, in order for an apostle to retain her or his authority, it would seem, from the point of view of Kierkegaard and H.H., that he or she must render unconditional obedience and suffer for the doctrine and his or her preaching of it.

H.H. makes it clear that "the doctrine communicated to him [i.e., the apostle] is not a task given to him to cogitate about; it is not given to him for his own sake" (*WA*, 106). Accordingly, the apostle's life is lived for the sake of others. H.H. writes further that "even if an apostle is never persecuted, his sacrificial life consists essentially in this: 'that he, himself poor, only makes others rich.' . . . Spiritually understood, he is like the busy housewife who herself, in order to prepare food for the many mouths, scarcely has time to eat" (*WA*, 106). Pursuing the apostolic ministry with such single-minded devotion seems to be a sine qua non for the binding proclamation of revelation, for Kierkegaard and H.H.

This has not been the case for the larger Catholic tradition.[47] At times, as in the writings of Gregory, as we have seen, the failure of priests to minister to the external needs of the parish is cited as partial justification for the parish's turning a deaf ear to whatever the priest directly communicates. Yet, this condition is never claimed to be an effective relinquishing of the priestly (or apostolic) authority entrusted to such clerics, as Kierkegaard seemed to assert with respect to the teaching authority of the Pharisees.

The distinction between these two viewpoints might be examined a bit more closely in connection with the ancient Christian schism known as Donatism. While a variety of factors contributed to the origin of the sect, the theological claim with which it was virtually identified by the likes of Augustine was that, as J. N. D. Kelly puts it, "the validity of the sacraments . . . depended on the worthiness of the minister."[48] The group arose in opposition to the ordination of Caecilian as bishop of Carthage. The reason for such opposition was that, in the midst of earlier persecution, one of those charged with the ordination of Caecilian had surrendered copies of the Scriptures to the Romans. Such a sacrament of ordination, claimed the Donatists, could not be seen as valid when administered (in part) by one who had allegedly defiled himself by placing his obedience to the secular authorities over and above his obedience to God. The rigorism behind this view led the Donatists to rebaptize people whose only baptism had been in the Catholic Church that they considered evil, as well as to an enthusiasm for martyrdom that showed an undervaluing of this earthly life. They held (what appear to be necessary conditions for) a true bishop to be one who is "predestined to salvation, ever the gospel on his lips and martyrdom in his heart."[49]

Augustine, in writing against this schism, takes it so seriously because he regards it as having dire ecclesiological consequences. This is so because the Donatists insisted that their church was (as they thought, to its credit) without "spot or wrinkle or any such thing."[50] But this strikes at the heart of Augustine's idea (and indeed the Catholic idea) of the Church, for the Church, on this view, is a community of people struggling to live the Christian life, some of whom may in fact be grave sinners who will not gain their ultimate beatitude. On this point, Augustine writes, "How can you separate yourselves by a wicked crime from Catholic unity, as from the Lord's threshing floor, which, until the time of winnowing, must needs contain both the grain which is to be gathered into the barn and the chaff which is to be consumed in the fire?"[51] This Augustinian notion of the Church bears considerable similarity to the notion of the Church Militant we receive from Anti-Climacus in *Practice in Christianity* (*PC*, 221).[52]

Now, it would be inexcusable forthwith to attribute the Donatist ecclesiology to Kierkegaard, and even more so to his Lutheran tradition.[53] Yet, even if Kierkegaard and his religious pseudonyms agree on significant portions of a more generally Christian and even Catholic ecclesiology, the Donatist controversy still raises questions for Kierkegaard's understanding of the apostle. For Catholic clergy are ordained as ministers of word and sacrament, and the status of a sacrament, administered at the hands and by the mouth of a sinful priest, is what was at issue for the likes of Augustine in the Donatist controversy. For Augustine's part, Donatists who returned to the Catholic faith, after having been baptized originally by the Donatists, were readmitted to the Catholic Church without rebaptism, showing that the Church regarded a heretical or schismatic priest as able to give a valid baptism.[54] Further, as Augustine described numerous hardships inflicted upon the Catholic community by the Donatists, he recounted the suffering of one bishop, who apparently had his hands and tongue cut off.[55] This would seem to suggest that the Donatists took the membership of the bishop in a rival church to result in his profanation of the sacraments and, perhaps, illegitimate administration of them. It might also suggest, though, that the Donatists believed that this bishop no longer possessed the *authority* to administer a proper sacrament and, perhaps, to preach the Gospel.

It is here that the robust conception of authority in the person of the apostle that we are given from Kierkegaard and his pseudonyms has a double force. For while only a very special individual (who is divinely authorized) is equipped to execute judgments and preach the Gospel with authority, the question is whether the rigorism involved in this concept of the apostle brings Kierkegaard and his religious pseudonyms toward

Catholicism, or so far in the direction of Catholicism that it actually looks more like the rigorism of Donatism, against which Catholicism opted for a more moderate view. Recall that Luther himself seemed to Kierkegaard to be "muddle-headed" and perhaps to waver between returning to the original gospel and enthroning "the public." In order to resolve Luther's confusion, Kierkegaard looks to have turned in a more decidedly rigorist direction, which may bring him closer to Donatism.

It must be granted that nothing in the foregoing has discussed Kierkegaard's pseudonymous or signed views concerning the status of the minister of various sacraments. But it must also be admitted that we simply do not get a lot of anything that would qualify as dogmatic theology from Kierkegaard on that score.[56] What we do get, however, is a view on the divine authority of the apostle that seems to make the authorized teacher who forfeits his or her authority not only unfit to give an authoritative proclamation, but *unable* to do so.[57] It seems to me to be an open question as to whether Kierkegaard would draw this further in the direction of the sacraments.[58]

Whatever Kierkegaard would in fact have said about what conditions needed to be met in order for the minister of a sacrament to validly administer it, he certainly had significant resources at his disposal to escape theological traps of a Donatist sort.[59] For instance, H.H. writes, in narrating how Paul might appeal to his divine authority, "you must consider that what I say has been entrusted to me by a revelation; so it is God himself or the Lord Jesus Christ who is speaking" (*WA,* 96–97). Here, H.H. clearly recognizes that all divinely authoritative proclamations come not so much from the apostle as from Jesus Christ himself, to recall (from another context) a phrase from St. Francis de Sales, "immediately and at the same time mediately."[60] In recognizing this model of apostolic authority, one would seem to have little further to go to claim that the unconditional obedience in other aspects of one's life might be, if not a matter of indifference, at least not a logically indispensable sine qua non with respect to whether one can utter a proclamation with divine authority. Yet, as we have seen, this does not seem to be Kierkegaard's larger view on the matter.

While we have noted that Gregory indicates that parishioners are for the most part justified in turning a deaf ear to their pastor when that pastor does not show appropriate concern for their external needs, he never (to my knowledge) claims, as Kierkegaard seems close to doing, that such authority itself is lost through factors having to do with one's unconditional fidelity to the message he relates. On the one hand, this view finds a superficial resonance with Pope John Paul II's 2003 apostolic exhortation, *Pastores Gregis,* in which we read, "Objective sanctification, which by Christ's work is present in the sacrament through the communication of the Holy Spirit, needs to coincide with subjective sanctification, in which the Bishop, by the help of grace, must continuously progress through the exercise of his ministry."[61] Yet, in tones that seem to echo Kierkegaard's denunciation of the Pharisees, he goes on to cite Gregory the Great's lamentation concerning his *own* ability to administer his apostolic authority. Gregory writes:

> After having laid upon my heart the burden of the pastoral office, my spirit has become incapable of frequent recollection, because it remains divided among many things. . . . And so with my mind pulled and torn, forced to think of so many things, when can it recollect itself and concentrate totally on preaching, without withdrawing from the ministry of proclaiming the word? . . . The life of the watchman must always be on high and on guard.[62]

No doubt Kierkegaard would agree that one charged with apostolic authority "must always be on high and on guard" against the "seventeen concerns" of the Pharisees (*WA,* 211; *JP,* 1:183 / *SKP,* VIII-1 A 416). Yet John Paul II does not mean to suggest that Gregory's apostolic authority is imperiled by his administrative struggles, and not even in the strict sense, by his moral struggles.

While John Paul II strongly emphasizes the need for a bishop's living what he teaches, he nonetheless distinguishes between a kind of authoritativeness that can be lost when a bishop does not live what he teaches and a kind of authority that cannot. He writes, "The witness of his life becomes for a Bishop a new basis for authority alongside the objective basis received in Episcopal consecration. 'Authority' is thus joined by 'authoritativeness.' Both are necessary. The former in fact gives rise to the objective requirement that the faithful should assent to the authentic teaching of the Bishop; the latter helps them to put their trust in his message."[63] On this view, then, the faithful are called to assent to the teaching of the bishop. No doubt the fidelity of the bishop to the teaching that he himself proclaims is altogether helpful in fostering such obedience (and the consequences for disobedience are sometimes softened when he is not faithful). But the authority of the bishop springs from his episcopal consecration, not from his living a single-minded and spiritually pious life.

Kierkegaard would, of course, agree that the initial apostolic call must come from outside, since apostolic authority comes from God and not from one's self. But the Catholic faithful are not in a position to withhold their "religious assent" to the teaching of a bishop until it is ascertained whether or not he is single-mindedly devoted to the doctrine that he preaches.[64] There are moments where the same seems to be the case with respect to Kierkegaard's apostle, and these may well be Catholic moments.[65] But there are also moments, as we have seen, where Kierkegaard seems to make the administration of authority depend on the worthiness of the apostolic minister. These moments are not so much Catholic as Donatist.

I finish this section by briefly discussing the troubling shifts for orthodox Christians in Kierkegaard's late writings. As we have already seen, there are many elements in Kierkegaard's thought on authority that align well with the historic Christian faith, and, indeed, the Catholic Church. There are also rigorist and Donatist elements that I believe were disproportionately brought to the fore in some of Kierkegaard's later writings.[66] In chapter 8 we will discuss some of the ways in which Kierkegaard can tend toward anti-ecclesiastical extremes, despite the fact that I, along with others, do not believe that the passages in which these views come forward represent his considered (or best) views. My own view comes closest to Michael Plekon's view, that Kierkegaard remains a theologian of the Church, even if some of his statements, by their vehemence, tend toward troubling extremes.[67] One such statement can be found in one of Kierkegaard's articles titled, "A Genius / A Christian." There, Kierkegaard writes:

> The thesis may well be posited: Christianity has not actually entered the world; it never went any further than the prototype and at most the apostles. But these were already proclaiming it so powerfully along the lines of propagation that already here the dubiousness begins. It is one thing to work for propagation in such a way that one uninterruptedly, early and late, proclaims the doctrine to all; it is something else to be too hasty in allowing people by the hundreds and thousands to take the name Christian and pass as followers of Jesus Christ. (*M,* 181)[68]

Here, Kierkegaard is contrasting the way Christ taught Christianity and the way that the apostles, notably Peter (after whose speech, we are told in Acts 2:41, some three thousand were baptized and began to devote themselves to the teaching of the apostles) proclaimed the Christian Gospel. Accordingly, Christ managed "only eleven" followers in three years of ministry, and yet "one apostle in one day," gains three thousand (*M*, 181). Kierkegaard writes, "Either the follower is greater than the Master, or the truth is that the apostle is a bit too hasty in striking a bargain, a bit too hasty about propagation; thus the dubiousness already begins here" (*M*, 181). The dubiousness, we are told, consists in the fact that the apostles effectively replaced the picture of Christ as prototype (the imitation of whom results in persecution and suffering) with a milder picture of Christ as redeemer (*M*, 182).[69] This resulted in more converts, but Christianity had, so we are told, been distorted.

Now here we have a duly appointed apostle (to whom the keys of the kingdom of heaven had been entrusted),[70] who baptizes a mass of no less than three thousand, and comes in for heavy criticism (from Kierkegaard) for having compromised the message of Christianity. Surely, on Kierkegaard's view of the matter, this apostle is not, at that particular moment, exercising single-minded devotion, and unconditional obedience, with all the recklessness of infinity to the teaching that he preaches. And with that, I think, we are in a position to ask Kierkegaard (though I believe not to answer for him) a particularly vexing question for his understanding of the authority of the apostle to administer sacraments (and, ultimately, to preach the word). Were the baptisms of the three thousand converts, when Peter supposedly got a bit ahead of himself and began to exchange the prototype for the redeemer, validly administered? It is, of course, no trifling matter that, for Catholicism, this is tantamount to asking, "were their sins remitted or not?"[71]

‡

A dialectical role for the apostle emerges from Kierkegaard's writings (pseudonymous and signed). Particularly with reference to H.H.'s essay, "On the Difference between a Genius and an Apostle," the indirect "genius" often lays the foundation for the divinely commissioned "apostle" to preach with authority. Both are necessary, and in the most practically effective cases, both are combined in a person who possesses apostolic authority. Yet authority, for Kierkegaard, emerges as a fragile commodity that one must preserve with single-minded devotion, unconditional obedience, and a certain recklessness. With respect to his own Lutheran tradition, Kierkegaard sees a worldliness in Luther (and what he sometimes calls "the Lutheran principle") that he appears to resolve in the direction of a rigorism that requires unconditional obedience of a priest or minister. Failing such obedient preservation, the one who communicates directly seems to effectively relinquish his or her claim to apostolic authority.

Aspects of this overall picture resonate clearly with the Catholic tradition's understanding of the proper role of pastoral care in the writings of Pope St. Gregory the Great, and even Pope John Paul II. For the Catholic tradition has often recognized that different sorts of sinners need to be approached in different sorts of ways to heal their troubled souls and commune with Christ. But the Catholic Church has also emphasized, in opposition to the Donatist schism, that the authority to administer the sacraments of God's grace and to preach the gospel is decisively communicated by episcopal and priestly ordination in such a way that, for the good of the community that the priest serves, the faithful meet with Christ's own authority in the priest and bishop, regardless of whatever failings of devotion may attend the minister. There are times when Kierkegaard and his pseudonyms seem close to agreeing. Yet, there are other moments when Kierkegaard's own rigorist conception of what constitutes obedience and authentic Christian preaching is brought to bear on those who possess an apostolic commission to suggest that their failure to meet such standards is an effective relinquishing of their authority. For this reason, the most we are licensed to say about Kierkegaard's conception of the apostle and apostolic authority is that there are indeed Catholic moments in it.

PART TWO

Sin, Justification, and Community

FIVE

Must All Be Saved?
A Kierkegaardian-Catholic Response
to Theological Universalism

That God could create beings free in relation to himself is the cross which
philosophy could not bear but upon which it has remained hanging.

KIERKEGAARD

Once again we are hit with the weirdness of it all: we get an
inkling of an inner contradiction in sin, we feel its absurdity.

JOSEF PIEPER

In my experience, many people who react strongly to what they perceive
to be authoritarianism in the Catholic tradition are often surprised to
learn that the tone of its theologians and even of its popes on the issues
of hell and damnation has been quite gentle of late. Indeed, as we shall
see in what follows here, it appears to be an open question for contemporary Catholicism whether anyone, even Judas, Christ's own betrayer, is
or will be finally lost. Thus, while an individual's own pursuit of holiness
in the Catholic tradition can be rigorous and demanding, theologians
often urge a policy of compassion on the question of whether anyone
else will be finally lost in hell. This impulse in the Catholic tradition,
exhibited in an interesting way by the Catholic theologian Hans Urs
von Balthasar, harmonizes very well with Kierkegaard's own thought.[1]
Indeed, Balthasar returns, again and again, to this idea in Kierkegaard,

that an individual should be rigorous with herself and lenient with others.[2]

However compassionate Kierkegaard's approach to such questions may be, his larger reception has been similarly enigmatic. On the one hand, his rescue of "New Testament Christianity" often endears him to traditional Christians. At the same time, Kierkegaard's polemical attack on the Christianity of his day was so vociferous that he crept close to direct criticism of the New Testament apostolic community itself.[3] Some are inspired by his harsh critique of so-called Christendom but wish he had seen through to a rejection of Christianity, or at any rate, to a much more critical stance with regard to traditional Christianity. This mixed reception situates Kierkegaard's thought at an interesting place between traditionalism and secularism, or perhaps religious liberalism. I think that this interesting place is where Kierkegaard intended himself to be seen. In this chapter, however, I will use the resources of Kierkegaard's writings, along with some help from the Catholic intellectual tradition, to provide a response to one tenet sometimes associated with religious liberalism, namely the strong doctrine of universal salvation, or, alternatively, strong theological universalism.

The question of universal salvation has been a topic of great interest of late in the Catholic tradition, as it has been in philosophical and theological circles generally. In many ways, this question came to a head in Catholic circles with Hans Urs von Balthasar's book *Dare We Hope "That All Men Be Saved"*? Although Balthasar's position received a good deal of animated discussion,[4] I think that his position on the isolated issue of whether all human individuals might possibly end up in heaven is one tenable option for Catholics in the contemporary Church.[5] I will be calling this position, as I understand it, Cautiously Moderate Theism (CMT). I believe that both Kierkegaard and Balthasar hold versions of this position, and I think they can be mutually reinforcing in its defense.

This is the most cooperative chapter in this book. In many ways, it is also why Luther does not play any central role in this chapter.[6] This issue does not clearly divide the Protestant and Catholic traditions, although related issues in succeeding chapters will. I say this not because I wish to resort to polemics in foregoing or subsequent chapters, but because there are differences in many other issues between the Catholic tradition and Kierkegaard, and the dialogue on these points should not ignore the differences. However, I believe that on the present question, Kierkegaard and the Catholic tradition have not only a largely harmonious vision, but a common foe, namely, strong theological universalism.

Kierkegaard appears to think that the possibility of eternal damnation, a person's supernatural punishment, can reach the ears of human beings only through an authoritative proclamation (on which, see the previous chapter). Indeed, Anti-Climacus appears to advance this very claim (*PC*, 229). In addition, Kierkegaard himself regarded the doctrine of eternal damnation as a doctrine that was revealed to Christianity and that would seem "ludicrous" to the world (*WL*, 196). Accordingly, we would never discover the danger of eternal damnation without apostolic authority's proclamation of it. In this chapter, I discuss the relevance of many of Kierkegaard's pseudonymous and signed views on despair and how they relate to what turns out to be a kind of Kierkegaardian vision of hell, or damnation. That Kierkegaard should believe in some such thing as eternal damnation and have a certain understanding of it becomes important in the following chapter when I will discuss Kierkegaard's rejection of the Council of Trent's claim that the fear of eternal punishment can be a just motive for repentance.

Turning our attention to the question of how we can think of eternity and God's will for us with respect to it, we should consider that in one of Kierkegaard's journal entries, he writes, "They argue about whether God intends the salvation of all or only some—almost forgetting the far more important theme: You, O God, intend my salvation; would that I myself might intend it also" (*JP*, 4:4920 / *SKP*, X-1 A 516). This entry reflects Kierkegaard's frequent refusals to answer metaphysical questions about the immortality of the soul, as well as doctrinal questions such as the one here, having to do with God's universal or only limited salvific will. The passage, like so much of Kierkegaard's writings, in effect says, "Stop working on metaphysical questions and start working on yourself!" Now I do not for a moment wish to obscure this well-documented fact about Kierkegaard's intentions. But let us not forget another point worthy of note, namely, that the fact that Kierkegaard often cautions his readers about their losing themselves in abstract questions at the expense of their spiritual health does not mean that he lacks beliefs about the answers to those questions. The point is not to profess agnosticism about theological or philosophical truths but to direct one's spiritual attention in the right direction.

In like manner, while readers of Kierkegaard who are inspired by his approach in this regard should have an appropriate concern for the spiritual attentiveness of individuals, they nonetheless may have a belief about whether what I will call strong theological universalism, that is, the view that all human individuals *must* gain salvation, is true or false, and I want to show here that they can assemble good reasons to believe the latter (on the assumption that they can already provide adequate justification of one sort or another for belief in the theistic underpinning of that view). I also believe that on this matter, Kierkegaard's quite considerable resources can be strengthened when they are used in tandem with the resources of the Catholic intellectual tradition.[7]

On Theological Universalism

Before we get to our Kierkegaardian response to universalism, let us have a brief look at universalism itself. Let us call Strong Universalism (SU) the view that, owing perhaps to some perceived contradiction between God's mercy and the affliction of an eternal punishment, hell not only *is* empty (or lacks human inhabitants) but *in principle must* be empty (or lack human inhabitants).[8] It is important to note that the impulse according to which people might endorse this view has a good bit going for it. Not only do traditional, and in particular, Christian, theists believe that God desires the salvation of all (see esp. 1 Tm 2:4), but most traditional theists believe that God is sovereign and that he has the power to bring about whatever he wishes for the world, with only the restriction—which, as Aquinas argued, is hardly a restriction at all—that God's choice be logically (or absolutely) possible.[9]

Indeed, the desire that hell lack human inhabitants often makes an appearance in the Catholic tradition, which has always endorsed, at the very least, hell as a possible destiny.[10] For instance, in the Catholic tradition, one of the regular prayers of the Rosary finishes its plea to Jesus with, "draw all souls to heaven, especially those who are most in need of your mercy."[11] Yet it is just as much a part of that tradition that it is at least possible that some souls are not finally led to heaven.[12] The desire that no one suffer eternal torment is a worthy desire, and the desire seems to belong (in some sense) to God as well. Accordingly, the questions, "if God loves us so much, how could he wish to send anyone to eternal torment?" or better, "how could God's fervent desire for the salvation of all be frustrated?" are, after all, good questions. Hell, unlike purgatory, is a *final* destination. Once one is in hell, it is impossible for one to leave. Evidently, individuals in hell don't offer petitions for their release, or, if they do, those petitions are denied by God. Aren't these facts inconsistent with a loving God?

According to SU, these facts are inconsistent with a loving God. Although the contemporary literature on the topic of hell, and often, by consequence, universalism, is vast, I shall focus primarily on one particular representative Christian philosopher, Thomas Talbott, who has championed universalism by denying that various forms of theism that endorse the doctrine of everlasting punishment in hell are logically consistent. Talbott claims that four propositions should be held by anyone whom he will call a theist.[13] These are

(1) God exists.
(2) God is both omniscient and omnipotent.
(3) God loves every created person.
(4) Evil exists.

A person he calls a Conservative Theist (CT), however, holds to an additional proposition, which Talbott takes to be inconsistent with the above four. That proposition is

(5) God will irrevocably reject some persons and subject those persons to everlasting punishment.

Talbott distinguishes this position from what he calls Moderately Conservative Theism (MCT), which endorses, not (5), but (5'), where (5') is:

(5') Some persons will, despite God's best efforts to save them, finally reject God and separate themselves from God forever.

Talbott thinks that the conjunction of (5) with (1)–(4) is inconsistent, as is, on his view, the conjunction of (5') with (1)–(4). By contrast, his (5"), which together with (1)–(4) entails universalism (or what he, explicitly acknowledging his bias, calls "Biblical Theism"), is, supposedly, consistent. That proposition is

(5") All persons will eventually be reconciled to God and will therefore experience everlasting happiness.[14]

Two things, it seems to me, are immediately worthy of note about (5″). The first, as Michael J. Murray has noted, is that it is not identical to what Murray has called "naïve universalism," the view that "upon death all persons are instantly transformed by God in such a way that they fully desire communion with God and are thus fit for enjoying the beatific vision forever."[15] Rather, Talbott's universalism is consistent with, and even suggests, not hell, but a sort of purgatory. *Eventually* all persons will be reconciled to God. Probably some, but presumably many, are not in a position to enter into full communion with God upon their deaths.

The second thing worthy of note is that Talbott here gives no intermediate option between (5′) and (5″). But there certainly are such options, and one such proposition requires only a possibility operator in front of (5′). So let's call it by that name.

> ◊(5′) *Possibly,* some (human) persons[16] will, despite God's best efforts to save them, finally reject God and separate themselves from God forever.

In addition to this proposition, I want to make it clear that the view of which I undertake to give a partial defense also holds some version of this proposition:

> ◊(5″) *Possibly,* all (human) persons will eventually be reconciled to God and will therefore experience everlasting happiness.

I will be calling any person who endorses both ◊(5′) and ◊(5″) together with (1)–(4) a Cautiously Moderate Theist (CMT).[17] As I have noted, I believe that Kierkegaard and Balthasar both endorse a version of CMT.[18] We should note, however, that the introduction of an intermediate position is in no way a *response* to Talbott, since he clearly thinks that ◊(5′) is just as inconsistent as (5′).

To see why, let's first consider his response to the suggestion that people choose hell and, accordingly, damn themselves. Talbott writes:

> What could it possibly mean to say that some sinners are trying as hard as they can to damn themselves? . . . The picture I get is something like this. Though a sinner, Belial, has learned, perhaps through bitter experience, that evil is always destructive, always contrary to his own interest as well as to the interest of others; and though he sees clearly that God is the ultimate source of all happiness and that disobedience can produce

only greater and greater misery in his own life as well as in the life of others, Belial *freely* chooses eternal misery (or perhaps eternal oblivion) for himself nonetheless. The question that immediately arises here is: What could possibly qualify as a motive for such a choice? As long as any ignorance, or deception, or bondage to desire remains, it is open to God to transform a sinner without interfering with human freedom; but once all ignorance and deception and bondage to desire is removed, so that a person is truly "free" to choose, there can no longer be any motive for choosing eternal misery for oneself.[19]

Although the passage about Belial is supposed to show how deeply incoherent the suggestion of someone's damning herself is, Talbott does not rest his whole case on this point.

Next, he argues, there are two conditions under which we feel justified in interfering with the freedom of others. Talbott claims that these are (a) we feel justified in preventing one person from doing irreparable harm to another (giving an example of a father's reporting his son's murderous plot to the police for the sake of the intended victim) and (b) we feel justified in preventing a person from doing irreparable harm to herself (giving an example of a father's physically overpowering his daughter in an effort to prevent her from committing suicide).[20] Citing faulty inferences from these claims, he notes that "even if a loving God can sometimes permit murder, he could never permit one person to destroy the very possibility of future happiness in another; and even if he can sometimes permit suicide, he could never permit his loved ones to destroy the very possibility of future happiness in themselves."[21] This is meant to suggest that while freedom is better than coercion, God might prefer coercion to damnation.

Further, anyone's perfect happiness in heaven is taken by Talbott to be incompatible with anyone else's suffering everlasting torment. He writes, using his daughter as an example, "If I love my own daughter as myself, her damnation would be an intolerable loss to me and would undermine the very possibility of my own happiness. . . . And if supremely worthwhile happiness requires that I learn to love my enemies even as I love my own daughter, then the damnation of a single person is incompatible with such happiness in me."[22] These, then, are Talbott's main lines of argument against the view that it is possible for some individuals to damn themselves, and I will try to address each in turn. First, there could be no possible motivation for the free decision to damn oneself; second, God prefers merciful coercion to human voluntary damnation; and third, the eternal suffering or misery of anyone is incompatible with the eternal happiness of another.

A Kierkegaardian Conception of God: Against Conservative Theism

Turning now to our Kierkegaardian account, let us first notice that, in his works, Kierkegaard seems to share Talbott's rejection of Conservative Theism. For however clearly God is an objective reality for Kierkegaard, he nevertheless holds that a relationship to God is foundational for the human self.[23] This means that Kierkegaard rejects the view that God is an "external" object. Accordingly, we should not think of God as a tyrannical judge, sentencing individuals to hell for failing to acquire certain belief states, or even for having flouted one (or more) too many divine decrees. Johannes Climacus is explicit about this in *Concluding Unscientific Postscript*. He writes, "God is not something external, as is a wife, whom I can ask whether she is now satisfied with me . . . God is not something external, but is the infinite itself, is not something external that quarrels with me when I do wrong but the infinite itself that does not need scolding words, but whose vengeance is terrible—the vengeance that God does not exist for me at all, even though I pray" (*CUP*, 162–63). To think of God as an external person of this sort involves an existentially pernicious misunderstanding of God's relationship to humans, for Kierkegaard. In fact, Kierkegaard and his pseudonyms seem to be of one voice in repeatedly denying that God is a person in the "external" sense.[24]

Now, just as Kierkegaard scorns purely doctrinal questions whose answers do not result in spiritual upbuilding for the individual, so he warns us against trying to learn about God in the abstract, because, according to him, God is not an external object. What it seems Kierkegaard and his pseudonymous authors mean by this is that God ought not to be treated as an external object, whose approval needs to be sought for some *other* purpose. Climacus further writes of the wellspring in each person where God is said to reside (*CUP*, 183). Yet, it becomes clear that, for Kierkegaard, because of sin the person cannot reach that wellspring. Yet, the wellspring metaphor is again invoked in *Works of Love*, where redemption from this predicament has been found in Christ, who, by coming into time, made it possible for us to commune with God again. Here, however, God is love, and love is God. This appears to be what Kierkegaard means in saying that God is not a person or an object in the external sense. Kierkegaard writes:

> Love's hidden life is in the innermost being, unfathomable, and then in turn is in an unfathomable connectedness with all existence. Just as the quiet lake originates deep down in hidden springs no eye has seen, so also does a person's love originate even more deeply in God's love. If there were no gushing spring at the bottom, *if God were not love, then there would be neither the little lake nor a human being's love.* (WL, 10, emphasis mine)

I take it that part of the reason Kierkegaard is so intent on attacking the view that God is an external person is that this view disqualifies God from being love itself.[25] One of Kierkegaard's favorite ways of referring to the Christian requirement is "the unconditioned,"[26] and it is fair to say that many of the demanding claims that Kierkegaard's Christian love makes on us are made because Kierkegaard thinks this is the only way that love can be genuinely unconditional. As I read Kierkegaard, he here takes it that if God is not the same as love in the strongest sense, then there is no love, and out the window go the first and second great commandments, and with them all the law and prophets. On his view, Christianity itself seems to hang in the balance. To a similar effect, Kierkegaard writes, "This business of a friend in heaven is a sentimentality which has made a thorough mess of Christianity" (*JP* 2:1285 / *SKP,* X-3 A 200).

Kierkegaard links the fact that God is not a person in the external sense with human freedom as well. He writes, "God is not in the external, palpable sense a power who, face to face with me, asserts his rights. . . . But to repeat, God is not an external, palpable power who bangs the table in front of me when I want to alter his will and says: No, stop! No, in this sense it is almost as if he did not exist. It is left up to me" (*JP,* 2:1273 / *SKP,* X-5 A 13). For Kierkegaard, it is not as if God stands, over against a human being, demands that his will be done, and, failing compliance, damns a human being to hell. Rather, God is unconditional love, and without participation in this love, a human being does not live the blessed life. God constantly extends his very self to us, and yet we can refuse this gift. Kierkegaard writes, "Precisely because God cannot be an object for man, since God is subject, for this very reason the reverse shows itself to be absolute: when one denies God, he does God no harm but destroys himself; when one mocks God, he mocks himself" (*JP*, 2:1349 / *SKP*, VII-1 A 201). Another passage, however, complicates things, when Kierkegaard claims that it is "the wrath of God to permit a human being to walk as an animal whom he does not call" (*JP*, 2:1367 / *SKP*, IX A 75). How can Kierkegaard dispute God's external presence as an executor of wrath and at the same time affirm divine wrath in refusing to "call" some people?

It has been argued, and I think correctly, that Kierkegaard belongs in the Arminian camp with respect to grace and salvation, rejecting the Calvinist position because he believes it to make God the cause of sin.[27] In contrast to the classical Calvinist position, the Arminian position holds that God predestines some people to salvation, but does it having foreseen the kinds of lives that they would live (or faith that they would have, given sufficient grace). Classical Calvinism (along with Thomism), by contrast, holds that God predestines without regard to foreseen merit or faith.[28] Indeed, in Catholic circles, this debate might be recast as that between the Thomists and the Molinists.[29] On the Arminian or Molinist account, accordingly, God fails to offer salvation to some, but that is because he knows that they would freely reject it.[30]

But why not go beyond this question to a rejection of predestination altogether? Kierkegaard did, after all, write that the notion of predestination must be regarded as a "thoroughgoing abortion" (*JP*, 2:1230 / *SKP*, I A 5). Yet, let us notice that, for Kierkegaard, God is eternal love, and as truly eternal, he does not change. Thus, God knows the fate of all human individuals, as all time is laid bare before him. Existence is a system for God, but not for us, as we live in time and not eternity (*CUP*, 118). Accordingly, "before the world began" God "knew" the fate of all human individuals, and God creates them with this knowledge, that they will choose the particular fate that he knows they will choose. This is the sense of conditional predestination. In fact, because eternity is so radically different than time for Kierkegaard, there is actually no divine sense to be made of words such as "before" and the past tense involved in "knew," but this is how they appear from our existential perspective. This appears to be what Kierkegaard means in saying that "only that person is saved from despair who is *eternally* saved from despair" (*WL*, 42).

What remains is to understand what Kierkegaard means in saying that God's wrath is the permitting of a human being whom God does not call to walk as an animal, especially given what that would mean for human freedom in *The Sickness unto Death*. Yet, it would seem that, in order for that to be true, God must select some individuals who will not receive his truly efficacious grace, which seems to risk a retrogression into Conservative Theism, and ultimately into unconditional predestination, which Kierkegaard seems clearly to reject. Accordingly, I turn to the topic of human freedom in Kierkegaard.

A Kierkegaardian Conception of Human Freedom

Here is the problem for which Kierkegaard's account of freedom needs to provide a solution: On the one hand, Kierkegaard denies that God damns anyone to hell for disobedience as if he were an "external" person. Yet, on the other hand, he claims that God's wrath is such that it permits those whom God does not call to "walk as . . . animal[s]." This seems to imply that God does stand as an external power demanding obedience, since presumably this is the reason that certain individuals are not called. How can we provide a solution to this? Kierkegaard begins to provide some resources for this in the pseudonymous text *The Sickness unto Death*.

In that text, Kierkegaard's pseudonym, Anti-Climacus, claims that despair, which is, at its root, a human being's defiant resolve to remain separated from God, is the ruin of a human being. Yet, on the other hand, the fact that a human being *can* despair is a great dignity to the human being. Anti-Climacus writes:

> Is despair an excellence or a defect? Purely dialectically, it is both. . . .
> The possibility of this sickness is man's superiority over the animal, and this superiority distinguishes him in quite another way than does his erect walk, for it indicates infinite erectness or sublimity, that he is spirit. The possibility of this sickness is man's superiority over the animal; to be aware of this sickness is the Christian's superiority over the natural man; to be cured of this sickness is the Christian's blessedness. (*SUD*, 14–15)

What might Anti-Climacus mean here? One thing that it seems he means is that the possibility that a human being possesses of ruining herself spiritually is actually a dignity to her, one that is lacking in the so-called brute animals. Now a human being, Anti-Climacus says, is like a house (*SUD*, 43). There is a basement, a first and a second floor. A human being who, as most (we are told) do, chooses to live in the basement, lives in only sensate categories having to do with pleasure and the pursuit thereof. This results in almost no distinction between human beings and brute animals. But the possibility of despair indicates that a human being is in transition, is intended to be something more, namely, spirit. What does this mean?

First, let us notice that Anti-Climacus distinguishes despair from a common sickness like a cold by noting that while someone might possibly choose to go outside in the rain having good reason to believe that she would catch cold if she did so, once she has thus voluntarily contracted the cold, she at no further point in the illness is bringing that illness upon herself. On the other hand, the person in despair is always bringing the despair upon herself. Anti-Climacus writes, "Every actual moment of despair is traceable to possibility; every moment he is in despair, he *is bringing* it upon himself" (*SUD*, 17). Now, despair has certain levels, and the most intense despair, the devil's despair, is to know precisely what one's blessedness is and to reject it. All despair is traceable to this form of despair, though the less "intense" despairs occur when people pretend that they are not in despair, and hide their condition from themselves. Thus, if we can figure out what is meant by this most intense form of despair (defiance),[31] we will have understood despair at its most fundamental level, the other types arising from self-deception.

Perhaps the most philosophically interesting commentary Anti-Climacus gives us on what despair is occurs in part 2 of *The Sickness unto Death,* where he distinguishes despair, or sin, from ignorance, which he associates with Socrates. Socrates, in the early Socratic dialogues at least, claimed that no one could believe something to be bad and yet pursue it. Thus, all actions that are bad or wrong result in some way from ignorance about what is good or right. In the *Protagoras,* Plato has Socrates say, "Now, no one goes willingly toward the bad or what he believes to be bad; neither is it in human nature, so it seems, to want to go toward what one believes to be bad instead of to the good. And when he is forced to choose between one of two bad things, no one will choose the greater [i.e., the worse] if he is able to choose the lesser [i.e., the better]."[32] Anti-Climacus will have none of this. Assuming (rightly, it would seem) that ignorance is thus Socrates' explanation for the Christian doctrine of sin, he writes, "If sin is ignorance, then sin really does not exist. . . . If sin is being ignorant of what is right and therefore doing wrong, then sin does not exist" (*SUD,* 89).[33]

Why is it the case that if sin is ignorance, then sin does not exist? In order to briefly examine this, let us define sin as the conscious rejection of the good for which an individual is genuinely blameworthy. Now it would seem to be a necessary condition for an individual's being genuinely blameworthy for an action that the action not have its ultimate cause in the ignorance of the subject.[34] Accordingly, if the subject rejected the good for the reason that she could not accurately understand what it was, then she is not fully blameworthy for this rejection, because she lacks the conscious defiance that is, on this view, at the root of all despair. The objection that this choice has no rational motivation, and is thus incomprehensible, far from being treated as an objection, is *embraced* as foundational to the doctrine of sin, for Anti-Climacus and Kierkegaard.[35] Anti-Climacus and Kierkegaard are radical and uncompromising on this point, and it is hard to overestimate the ramifications of this point in Kierkegaard's larger thought.

Jerry L. Walls attempts to use Anti-Climacus's work here in an effort to combat Talbott's universalism.[36] But it seems to me that he appropriates just enough of Anti-Climacus's work to vitiate his own analysis. Walls writes:

> What all these cases show us, I want to emphasize, is that hell may afford its inhabitants a kind of gratification which motivates the choice to go there. In each case the choice of evil is somehow justified or rationalized. In each case there is an echo of Satan's claim that hell is better than heaven. That belief is what finally justifies and makes intelligible the choice of hell. . . . Hell cannot truly be heaven, or be better than heaven, any more than evil can be good. But this lesson may be finally lost on those who persist in justifying their choice of evil by calling it good.[37]

Walls here construes the choice of hell as justified or rationalized by one's conception of it as somehow good, noting that the gratification involved in hell motivates the choice to go there.

Anti-Climacus might respond that the first could be true, but not the second. When we speak of rationalizing one's choice, we sometimes mean that, *after* we performed a certain action, we tell ourselves a soothing story about why we did it. If this is all we mean by rationalizing one's choice of hell, then Anti-Climacus may accept it, since we lie to ourselves in a host of ways, according to him, especially about why, in the past, we chose evil. But the desire for perceived gratification in hell that outweighs the perceived gratification of heaven cannot be, according to Anti-Climacus, what actually motivates the choice of hell. If this were the case, then the ultimate sin of the damned issues from a false set of information.[38] Walls's unfortunate construal of heaven's superior goodness as a *lesson that is lost* on the damned seems to fall prey to this objection.

Despair, then, is, at its root, inexplicable, but Anti-Climacus rejects the covert assumption that Talbott and his detractors seem to accept, namely, the assumption that no inexplicable or irrational choice can be blameworthy.[39] Now, to simply reject this could, of course, seem like a cheater's way out. But Kierkegaard does not believe that it is. In discussing what he takes to be a fault in Kant's discussion of radical evil, he writes,

> It is customary to say something like this: To say that we cannot understand this and that does not satisfy scholarship and science, which insist upon comprehending. Here is the error. We must say the very opposite, that if *human* scholarship and science refuse to acknowledge that there is something they cannot understand, or, more accurately, something that they clearly understand that they cannot understand, then everything is confused. (*JP*, 3:3089 / *SKP*, VIII A 11)

The point of this seems to be that Kierkegaard wishes to reply to those who cannot find a motivation for the choice of hell and thus reject its very possibility, that they themselves are unwilling to acknowledge the limits of their own understanding, or at least, that they fail to appreciate what he thinks are the disastrous consequences such a rejection would have for human freedom. If we apply this to Talbott, Anti-Climacus's position would seem to hold that Talbott's bewilderment at the case of the demonic Belial is ultimately the bewilderment that we should all feel at what Pieper calls the "craziness" of sin.[40] The fact that it is crazy, however, does not change the fact that it occurs.

If one thinks that a motivation, sufficient in the abstract, for any-one's making the same choice must be found for every action, then hu-man freedom essentially does not exist, Anti-Climacus would argue. If each sinful action is due in some part to an agent's ignorance or some other defect having to do with her motivational structure, then some accounting must be given for this earlier defect which caused this sin. If this does not terminate in some inexplicably deep ground of the agent, then it simply arises out of an ignorance for which the subject is not blameworthy. If the latter is the best we can do, then we have a world without sin, but also a world without the possibility of despair. Conse-quently, for Anti-Climacus, we would have a world with infinitely less human dignity. Further, according to Kierkegaard, this would seem to entail an unconditional doctrine of predestination, which, he thinks, makes God the cause of sin (see *JP*, 2:1302 / *SKP*, I A 2).

But let us consider those whose minds are already made up. Kier-kegaard writes, "Faith is essentially this—to hold fast to possibility" (*JP*, 2:1126 / *SKP*, IX A 311). Now, do the blessed in heaven hold fast to the pos-sibility of redemption? Yes and no. They do hold fast to it in the sense that they will never let it go, for they are finally and permanently redeemed. Yet, in another sense, they are not really holding fast to this possibility at all. This is because they cannot possibly *let go* of their blessedness. In one of his rare claims about the afterlife (*WL*, 194), Kierkegaard notes, "[Christianity] will be abolished in eternity, where it will cease to be *militant* [*stridende*]." In a curious Kierkegaardian mix, then, the blessed in heaven should have the passion and bliss of faith, but not the struggle. Perhaps, on earth, it is a dignity to be able to despair, but in heaven, to have chosen union with God in virtue of this earthly dignity is itself attaining a higher dignity, or moving out of the basement to the luxuri-ous second floor, to follow up on the house analogy. At this point, we'll need to go a bit beyond what Kierkegaard actually tells us to consider the damned in hell.

Do the damned in hell despair? Yes and no, it would seem. Anti-Climacus notes that one can try to obscure his despair all he wants, and yet,

> eternity will nevertheless make it manifest that his condition was de-spair and will nail him to himself so that his torment will still be that he cannot rid himself of his self, and it will become obvious that he was

just imagining that he had succeeded in doing so. Eternity is obliged to
do this, because to have a self, to be a self, is the greatest concession, an
infinite concession, given to man, but it is also eternity's claim upon him.
(*SUD*, 21)

That is, God intends the person to become spirit, as he is intended and
best suited to be, and yet one can decide, knowing precisely what he
ought to do,[41] that he will not become this self. He wishes to be something other than what he truly is. This is the situation of the damned
in hell, and hell is clearly a permanent state, for Anti-Climacus (one is
"nailed" to oneself). Yet, because it is a horribly permanent state, after
death, it is clear that one cannot be constantly bringing the spiritual
torture that is despair upon oneself, just as Anti-Climacus insists is true
of despair as we saw earlier. This is because in this sort of permanent
state, one has earlier chosen, but in view of this earlier choice has finally
contracted, the spiritual torture of hell, much as if one had voluntarily
contracted a cold that one is no longer bringing upon oneself. This appears to be the sense of Anti-Climacus's claim that eternity "nails" one to
oneself. Accordingly, just as the blessed in heaven experience the passion
and bliss of faith, but they are no longer struggling to acquire faith, so the
damned in hell must experience the pain and torture of despair, but this
is no longer because their defiant resolve is constantly bringing it upon
them, at least not in the same way in which such resolve was bringing it
upon them in their earthly life.

In this somewhat attenuated sense, then, the damned in hell do not
despair in the strict sense, because they are not bringing their despair
upon themselves. But then, in hell, it is not possible to despair in the
fullest sense. What this means, for Anti-Climacus, is that the damned
in hell have voluntarily chosen a lesser plane of existence; a lower dignity. Yet, this also has a disquieting corollary: the self, which *is freedom*
(*SUD*, 29), appears not to be free in hell, since it can no longer choose
to rest in God. This claim, however, seems contradicted by the fact that
the self is *nailed to itself,* and thus the self seems preserved, even if its
moral character should be "frozen." A related difficulty can be posed for
Kierkegaard's account of heavenly bliss, which we have just considered.
How should we reconcile this?

While it is beyond the scope of this chapter to enter into an independent philosophical dispute about whether all of Kierkegaard's com-

mitments are coherent, I want to suggest that some help can be solicited from the Catholic tradition in the person of St. Bernard of Clairvaux. Bernard articulated his conception of freedom in his treatise *On Grace and Free Choice*.[42] One of his concerns was with the blessed in heaven and the angels, who, on his view, could no longer sin. But there is a difficulty that Bernard spots, namely, that if one were to take away free choice, "there would be nothing to save."[43]

Out of a concern to preserve freedom in such circumstances, then, Bernard gives us his famous "three freedoms." For Bernard, the first freedom, the Freedom of Choice, is inseparable from human beings. Even sinful humans after the Fall possess it, and with no diminution whatsoever.[44] For Bernard, Freedom of Choice corresponds to the image of God that sin does not destroy, while the other two freedoms, Freedom of Counsel and Freedom of Pleasure, correspond to the likeness of God, which is lost through sin.[45] While Bernard emphasizes that Freedom of Choice is never lost, post-Fall sinful human beings nonetheless "cannot not sin."[46] The reason for this is that sin ruins the other freedoms, and Freedom of Counsel in particular shows the will, through the power of the intellect, what course of action is suitable to pursue. Without this freedom, which is absent in hell, and weakened in earthly life by sin, we are able to conceive partially of the good, but we are unable to select it for the right reason.[47] While Bernard appears to believe that the will can choose to obey or not to obey the intellect on this score, it is nonetheless unable to do either without Freedom of Counsel. As Bernard McGinn puts it, "Free choice is free for Bernard, but free only to sin."[48]

Bernard notices that true freedom must be more than simply the absence of external constraint, since if it were not, God, the angels, and the blessed in heaven would not be free.[49] Rather than being less free, they are *freer* than earthly human beings. Accordingly, Bernard insists that Freedom of Counsel and Freedom of Pleasure, while capable of being possessed in this life, can be possessed permanently and in their fullness only in the next life by human beings. He similarly claims that the damned in hell are also free, despite the fact that they can no longer choose the good, precisely because they no longer have the other two freedoms.[50] It would be interesting to know how Bernard would have received the statements of subsequent Catholic dogma on some of these questions, but his "three freedoms" have been influential in the

Catholic tradition. In the cooperative spirit of this chapter, I suggest that this account could prove of some use to Anti-Climacus in sorting out some of the problems that arise from his conception of freedom and the self. Although in Bernard's scheme, human beings would retain some degree of properly human freedom even in hell, their dignity is lessened. This loss of dignity is, I think, why Kierkegaard says that it is the "wrath of God" to allow those whom he does not call to "walk as animals."[51]

Yet, why does God "not call" these people? (*JP*, 2:1367 / *SKP*, IX A 75). The answer seems to be that God is eternal, and sees them in their steadfast defiance. Accordingly, he does not call them precisely because his call does not (and would not) reach them.[52] This, then, is our response to the criticism that God is construed as an external power who demands compliance and damns those who don't comply. By way of response, a Kierkegaardian God is eternal love, and fails to save only those who defiantly and irrationally do not want his salvation. Yet, we can do this, and this ability is an infinite dignity to us as humans. This is why one ought to concentrate on intending one's salvation just as God already intends it for us, as Kierkegaard says in the passage that began this chapter. Damnation is our no to God's yes. When one mocks God, accordingly, he mocks himself.

How shall we respond, then, to Talbott's other reasons for endorsing universalism? Kierkegaard's radical view of human freedom must be taken as an alternative to Talbott's claims about Belial's case of defiance (which for Kierkegaard, and many others, is a perfectly real possibility). Recall, then, that Talbott's second claim was that God prefers coercion of those he loves to their damnation. Yet, a Kierkegaardian could respond that the blessed life is the life of faith and/or love, where one experiences unity with God, who just is love. If this is what the bliss of heaven essentially is, then only on what Kierkegaard would see as an inadequate conception of the Christian afterlife could one claim that God could coerce someone into heaven. God can give someone all the earthly delights she might wish, but God can no more make someone love him than a mother can force a child to apologize to his sibling *with sincerity.*

Talbott's third objection was that the salvation of anyone is incompatible with the damnation of any person. In order to marshal the resources for a more adequate defense of CMT in the face of this and another objection, I will, in the next section, discuss the relevance of the Catholic intellectual tradition and Balthasar's contribution to the question of universalism.

The Catholic Tradition and Balthasar's Hope

While the position of CMT is purely logical in character, Balthasar's version of CMT, in effect, adds that (5"), the claim that all individuals find their ultimate beatitude, must be understood to be *epistemically possible* in *this world*. This is because Balthasar contends that we have a positive duty to *hope* for the eventual salvation of all human beings. On this point, Edward T. Oakes writes that Balthasar would agree with the passage from the *Catechism* that says that "the Church prays that no one should be lost."[53] Oakes goes on to add, "Balthasar would certainly agree, only adding that it is both a logical and psychological impossibility to pray for something for which there is antecedently no hope."[54]

Historically speaking, there have been some obstacles in the way of the Catholic tradition's endorsement of the idea that all humans might perhaps be saved.[55] Some may believe that Christian Scripture is the most serious obstacle, whereas others might think that Scripture positively settles the matter in favor of a Strong Universalism.[56] To these, Balthasar, after having listed off a range of biblical passages for each view, simply says, "We shall not try to press these biblically irreconcilable statements into a speculative system."[57] What I take him to mean in saying this is that to try to list off passages that sound universalist and passages that do not will not get us very far, and so the testimony of Scripture on this point should not be regarded as explicitly decisive for either view. I believe that this view on Scripture and the decidability of our question is substantially correct.

Turning, then, to other historical obstacles in the way of the Church's endorsement of the hope of salvation for all, the first most noteworthy Catholic obstacle seems to be that the Church has consistently maintained that if an individual should die in a state of mortal sin, then that individual should be destined for hell.[58] This is an obstacle because the proliferation of evil in our world makes it difficult to imagine that no one has died in a state of mortal sin. Mortal sin is defined by the Church as sin with respect to a suitably grave matter, committed with full knowledge and deliberate consent.[59] The trouble, as Pieper has noted, is "whether a specific human deed is a 'mortal' sin, a deliberate turning away from God—that is something no one can measure except, as we said, God Himself and, perhaps, one's own heart."[60] For reasons of this sort, many contemporary Catholic documents use language such as "grave" or "serious" to demarcate such offenses from venial or light ones. The effect of this is to concede that the matter of the sin is sufficiently grave for the relevant sin to count as mortal. Yet, without being able to inspect whether the necessary subjective conditions of full knowledge and deliberate consent are met, judgment is reserved on whether the sin is in fact mortal. Accordingly, the jump from the claim that *if* someone were to die in a state of mortal sin *then* she would find herself in hell to the claim that there actually *are* individuals in hell has been found an invalid inference in the contemporary Catholic tradition.

The second obstacle to the Church's endorsement of a hope of salvation for all has been the dogmatic claim that those outside the confines of the Church, a group which of course includes the great majority of human beings, are likewise destined to perdition.[61] The Catholic sources for the claim that "outside the Church there is no salvation" are nearly unimpeachable,[62] and so the Catholic Church has *reinterpreted* this patristic dictum, rather than reject it entirely.[63] Vatican II's *Lumen Gentium,* accordingly, details "various ways" in which non-Christians are related to the Church as the people of God.[64] Indeed, as we have seen, John Paul II argues that many have an "implicit" faith in Christ, in some cases despite explicit rejection of Christianity.[65] John Paul II also notes that "*In Christ the Church is a communion in many different ways,*" and that "besides formal membership in the Church, *the sphere of salvation* can also include *other forms of relation to the Church.*"[66] Now the aim here is not primarily to render a verdict on whether these claims are defensible or coherent (though I think they are), but to explain how the Catholic Church has made room for the consideration of a hope for wider salvation.

In what, then, does this hope consist? Balthasar sets up on one side the *apokatastasis* position that knows that all will be saved, and on the other side, the Augustinian position that knows that at least some will be damned.[67] Neither position, Balthasar argues, can be sustained. Citing Pieper, he argues that both are forms of hopelessness, and therefore vices in relation to the Christian virtue of hope. Pieper notes that there are two kinds of hopelessness: presumption and despair. The first is "a perverse anticipation of the fulfillment of hope," and the second is "a perverse anticipation of the nonfulfillment of hope."[68] Further, for Balthasar, we have a duty to hope for the salvation of all human beings.[69] Balthasar writes that one should never "say at some time to the Good Lord: 'Am I my brother's keeper?' Can a Christian allow himself to utter those murderous words? And which man is not my brother?"[70] Thus, Balthasar claims, we have good grounds for hope that all shall be saved, but we have no guarantee on this point. This strikes me as a helpful way to elucidate what I take to be Kierkegaard's quite similar point when he writes, "Blessed is the one who loves—he hopes all things. Even in the final moment he hopes for the possibility of good for the worst reprobate!" (*WL*, 260). Importantly, this constitutes an agreement between Kierkegaard and Balthasar that our Christian hope is generally too individualistic.[71]

Balthasar clearly sees Kierkegaard as a close ally on this point. Indeed, the passage from Kierkegaard to the effect that one should consider the issue of one's own salvation with fear and trembling, and trustfully believe in the future blessedness of everyone else, seems emblematic of his entire viewpoint.[72] In a very Kierkegaardian spirit, Balthasar counsels us against treating hell as an object for theological speculation, especially regarding who or how many are consigned there. He writes, "For at that moment everything is transformed: hell is no longer something that is ever mine but rather something that befalls 'the others', while I, praise God, have escaped it."[73] Hell is a state and not a place, for Balthasar.[74] Treating hell simply as an object about whose population one could speculate is inevitably to treat "others" as constituting its population, and never me. To treat hell this way is thus to bring about the inverse attitude of that toward which Kierkegaard urges us, and of which Balthasar heartily approves. Instead, we must see that hell is not an object that is "full" or "empty" of human individuals, but a possibility that is not "created" by God but in any case by the free individuals who choose it.[75] Balthasar writes, "It is therefore indispensable that every individual Christian be confronted, in the greatest seriousness, with the possibility of his becoming lost."[76] Thus despite our trustful hope in the salvation of all human beings, we must reckon with hell as a possible destiny for each individual, and most especially for *me*.[77]

Final Objections

I wish to close with two final worries that have been left substantially unaddressed by the preceding remarks. Before considering Talbott's final objection, that the damnation of anyone is incompatible with the salvation of anyone (because the latter would entail the kind of love that would regard anyone's damnation as an "intolerable loss"), I want to first consider a different objection. It is this: Perhaps it is right that we should admit it to be possible that someone choose a lesser dignity. Yet, if God is love, why not place the individual not in the traditional hell but in a state where the opportunity is always present to enter into oneness with God?[78] Even if she never does choose to do so, at least the opportunity is there. This actually inaugurates a fifth option between Talbott's universalism and CMT. The new option holds (1)–(4) and now a final proposition, namely,

(6) *Possibly,* some persons will, despite God's best efforts to save them, *continually* reject God, but nonetheless, God will always allow the option of salvation to remain open.

Let's call this Holding Pattern Theism,[79] since the individual who hasn't entered heaven is in a sort of holding pattern until she does (even if she never in fact does). How should or could we respond to this? I want to suggest, in what follows, that the answer may perhaps be sought in Kierkegaard's existentialism. Like Nietzsche, Kierkegaard would agree, though not in the same way, that "what is great in man is that he is a bridge and not an end."[80] This is the human dignity, that it has a necessary contribution to make in determining its eternal destiny.

But, to raise the issue in a more penetrating way, and in a more Catholic guise, it is clear that we human beings, with a "new initiative" of God's grace,[81] can recover from our garden-variety instances of willful rejection of God in this life (what the Catholic tradition calls mortal sin). So how plausible can it be to claim that there is one particular time at which an individual sinfully chooses, but this time *without hope of redemption,* her eternal (lesser) dignity? After all, God, who, as Talbott points out, faces "only logical limits," could surely give the person an extended deadline.[82] At first glance, nothing about the notion seems logically impossible. The picture the Holding Pattern Theist might have is this: an individual is on a bridge from a lesser place to a better place, and, even supposing (contra Talbott) that freedom is such a good that God would only have the individual *choose* the better place, why could God not simply see to it that the bridge remained functional, perhaps indefinitely, until the individual did choose the higher and better place (even if she never in fact did)?

To make this point, Buckareff and Plug introduce an imaginary character named Joe. They write:

> Consider Joe, an overweight smoker. Could Joe run a three-minute mile? Well, yes, if the sort of possibility is broad enough. The ability we are talking about is stronger than Joe's ability to run a three-minute mile. Rather, it is closer to the following case: Joe is in his upstairs office. Downstairs are all of the necessary ingredients to make iced tea. Joe knows this and he knows how to make iced tea from these ingredients. Joe thinks about making iced tea but decides against. Could Joe have made iced tea? Of course he can, no matter how narrowly we defined possibility. We are claiming that people have a similar level of ability with respect to accepting God's grace.[83]

This sort of example may be a formidable challenge for someone who believes that hell is primarily about everlasting punishment. But someone who believes (as I think both Kierkegaard and the Catholic tradition do) that heaven and hell are primarily about freedom and human dignity will consider the argument to commit the fallacy of weak analogy. For someone who truly chooses the lesser dignity of a defiant human (closer to the level of beast than spirit) is not on a bridge to a higher place; her earthly life is that bridge. If she genuinely chooses the lesser dignity of defiance, it is such a decisive change that the matter is more (but not exactly) like choosing a different species than choosing to go to another side of a bridge.

To supply some help on this point, I think it is important to consider what Balthasar calls the "self-consumptive" nature of evil. Balthasar writes, "Being a person always presupposes a positive relation to some fellow person, a form of sympathy or at least natural inclination and involvement. Precisely this, however, would no longer be predicable of a being that had, in its entirety, made a radical decision against God, or ab-solute love; thus, we would have to join J. Ratzinger in speaking of an 'un-person,' of the 'decomposition, the disintegration of being a person.'"[84] Balthasar means for this to apply to the devil, but there is no reason why it cannot shed light on the problem for human beings. C. S. Lewis[85] helps us to glimpse this in precisely the work whose view Buckareff and Plug mean to approximate, *The Great Divorce*.[86] In Lewis's antechamber to heaven we find a "silly, garrulous old woman who has got into a habit of grumbling." Lewis's guide, a fictional George MacDonald, says, "The question is whether she's a grumbler, or only a grumble. If there is still a real woman—even the least trace of one—still inside the grumbling, it can be brought to life again."[87] A similar source of aid can be found in Lewis's other probing work on the psychology of damnation, his novel *That Hideous Strength*. In that work, he writes:

> The last moments before damnation are not often so dramatic. Often the man knows with perfect clarity that some still possible action of his own will could yet save him. But he cannot make this knowledge real to himself. Some tiny habitual sensuality, some resentment too trivial to waste on a blue-bottle, the indulgence of some fatal lethargy, seems to him at that moment more important than the choice between total joy and total destruction. With eyes wide open, seeing that the endless ter-ror is just about to begin, and yet (for the moment) unable to feel terri-fied, he watches passively, not moving a finger for his own rescue, while the last links with joy and reason are severed, and drowsily sees the trap upon his soul. So full of sleep are they at the time when they leave the right way.[88]

These passages give us some sense of what a view might look like that would be capable of responding effectively to Holding Pattern The-ism. To do this, we need to recognize, as Anti-Climacus does, that sin begets more sin (*SUD*, 105–109). The idea behind this suggestion is that sin sinks one's very self further and further into evil and evil becomes harder and harder to break free of, even with the help of grace. There is nothing obviously incoherent about supposing that this process has a limit; in fact, it seems at least as intuitive that it should have a limit as that it should not. The suggestion that it might have such a limit has its origins as far back as Aristotle's distinction between brutishness and di-vinity, at the far reaches of virtue and vice,[89] where Aristotle cannot even imagine godlike people performing vicious actions or brutish people performing virtuous ones; the possibility has been closed off, precisely by the relevant agents. The point in response to Buckareff and Plug is then that the nature of sin makes their "escapism" too optimistic. This is no longer a case of Joe going downstairs to make iced tea. It is a case of burying oneself alive.

Thus, the claim that one's "holding pattern" *can* be definitively brought to a close appears defensible. Yet, how long must this holding pattern last? The answer, for Kierkegaard, is that the holding pattern is just, in general, this earthly life, and it lasts long enough to allow the person to gain a consciousness of herself before God, and to determine, in light of her finitude, how she stands with regard to the infinite. Mercifully, God does not annihilate those who reject him, but grants them the lower dignity that they despairingly want, with only the torturous reminder that it was their choice. None of this, however, prevents Anti-Climacus (Kierkegaard's highest pseudonym) from praying, in the very text in which he claims that this earthly life is just such a test (see *PC*, 183, 259–62), and in some of the most moving passages in the entire corpus, for Christ to do as he said he would (Jn 12:32), and draw all to himself.

Still, one might protest that some human beings do not live long enough for the case of "burying oneself alive" to be even relevant, and the traditional position (and indeed the Catholic position) holds that one's fate is sealed this side of earthly death.[90] In response to this objection, we should begin by pointing out that the genuine possibility of someone's definitively sealing his or her fate is already a fatal blow to Holding Pattern Theism, or Buckareff's and Plug's "escapism," because this means that the gate of salvation cannot always remain open because some people have *definitively closed it for themselves.* What the real issue is at this point is how God's providence might work things out so that there is no *injustice* in allowing some sufficient time and others insufficient time to seal their respective fates. In response to this new and independent worry, one might point out that some recent theological proposals have had it that a great deal is decided in the very instant of death itself.[91] But even if Holding Pattern Theism should modify its position so that adequate postmortem transformation can occur for *those individuals* whose fates are not decided prior to, or in the moment of, their deaths, this is no better off than the more traditional position I am defending as part of CMT. This is because in Holding Pattern Theism God will patiently await the person's transformation for *however long it takes*. But this is precisely what the traditional position of my CMT holds, only *however long it takes,* on that view, turns out to be just exactly how long a person's earthly life lasts, together with her decision on the point of death. The suggestion that this is implausible (I see no reason for attacking its logical *possibility*) can only draw on knowledge of what the instant of death is and is not like. Where this knowledge will come from is not clear to me. Thus, until we have an argument for why it is impossible for God to have created human beings in such a way that their earthly lives are adequate (though not temporally equivalent) spaces in which to allow the person to gain a consciousness of herself before God, the more traditional position I am defending remains intact.[92]

Talbott's final objection, namely, that anyone's damnation is incompatible with anyone's salvation, is, I think, the most difficult to adequately answer. This is how Balthasar seems to consider it, and it must be conceded, I think, that he does not fully answer it.[93] A preliminary Kierkegaardian response to this problem might have it that Talbott's view is out of line with what seems to be Kierkegaard's view of hell (although it is fair to say we never get a fully explicit doctrine to that effect). For the thing to notice about Kierkegaard's view here is that, when one voluntarily excludes oneself from reconciliation with God, one gets what one, albeit irrationally and despairingly, wants. The freedom in virtue of which one chooses hell could be sacrificed only at the cost of the infinite dignity that very freedom bestows on humans. Would one wish for the salvation of those who do not want salvation? This again misconstrues heaven as primarily a place into which one can be smuggled. Rather, given the highest dignity an earthly creature can have (which can only bring joy to a loved one in heaven), an individual in hell has chosen a life of lesser dignity than she might have had.

If God does will the good for his creatures (as Talbott insists), then a Kierkegaardian can insist that the good of human creatures is appropriately found in having the kind of dignity that results in their having a say about their eternal destiny. But the claim I want to make about this kind of dignity is that it cannot be endorsed without understanding that it comes with a cost. Freedom, of course, is not cheap, and if we prefer, as I think we should, the eternal dignity of our loved ones over against their being coerced into a state that we are assured is happiness, but seems to take little account of the unique dignity of the human individual (and thus her deepest happiness), then we must countenance the idea that such individuals may choose what is not ultimately in their best interests.

The trouble here is that Balthasar includes texts from many saints and profound thinkers that appear to endorse a hope for all so strong that its nonfulfillment would be disastrous. Here, however, we must turn around Balthasar's position on hope and say that we cannot fear (in the sense of working out our salvation in "fear and trembling") something that we antecedently know is impossible. That is, we cannot hope for something (universal salvation) if we know antecedently that it is impossible. Further, I cannot fear something (my damnation, which I am to approach with "fear and trembling" on Balthasar's view and Kierkegaard's) if I antecedently know that it is impossible. Since Talbott's third criticism targets precisely the logical compatibility of anyone's salvation with anyone's damnation, it must, I think, be rejected by both Kierkegaardians and contemporary Catholics. Of course, these are simply methodological points for these groups, and they do not provide a substantive response to Talbott.

But understanding that hell is not a place into which one is thrown helps us here. For it is the person's own free choice, issuing from her dignity, to enclose herself in this predicament. If, as we have seen in chapter 3, our love is a reflection of God's love, we need not fail to love those in hell. Indeed, our reflection of God's love is only heightened in heaven.[94] However, if our love is itself a reflection of God's love, then it must be tutored by the understanding that the manifestation of that love may require sacrifice. Just as Christ does not fail to recall the pains of his death in his own heavenly bliss, but understands that this was necessary for the great good of humanity's redemption, so human beings must appreciate the dignity of their fellow creatures and recognize that this dignity carries with it the risk that they will not choose their higher dignity.

In eternity, we will be able to approve, with God, of evil that God intended for good. But there is no obvious reason why every case of this must involve the evil temporally preceding the good, especially when the good willed entails the possibility of the evil result (the choice of lesser dignity that would not have been possible without the higher dignity of freedom). Thus, Talbott is right that the problem of hell is a particular variety of the problem of evil.[95] And so reckoning with one is reckoning with the other. According to the enterprise of theodicy, even God cannot do without some evil, supposing that the appropriate good of free creatures is chosen.[96] We have no idea how we can reckon with the evils of innocent suffering that are discussed in connection with the problem of evil, but Christians must rest assured that union with God will somehow put the matter at rest. Similarly, we have no idea how our present conception of love could tolerate the demotion in the very creaturely dignity of a loved one. But we must rest assured that union with God will somehow put the matter at rest. If we think that the latter transition is impossible, there seems no clear reason why the former should be possible, either. But God's ability to bring about the former transition is required of any adequate theodicy. Accordingly, it is because of the dignity granted human beings that they can, though they are never forced to, choose hell. This entails that while it is possible that all human individuals go to hell, it is also possible that none do. Accordingly, a Kierkegaardian-Catholic can assemble resources for a defense of her endorsement of CMT.

‡

In this chapter I have argued that Kierkegaard's texts, helpfully supplemented by resources in Balthasar and the Catholic tradition (and some others), provide reasons for rejecting what Talbott calls Conservative Theism, and also for rejecting Talbott's universalism, or Biblical Theism, as he calls it. The position for which I have suggested a Kierkegaardian and Catholic can thus provide a partial philosophical defense is Cautiously Moderate Theism, which affirms the possibility that some may reject God so decisively that faithful union with God may be forever precluded by this defiance. Nevertheless, this position does not claim that philosophically it can be decided (absent special revelation about the fates of certain individuals) whether any have in fact chosen this fate. I have nowhere attempted to argue that some individuals do in fact so decisively reject God that hell turns out not to be empty.

SIX

On Being Afraid of Hell:
Kierkegaard and Catholicism
on Imperfect Contrition

And you who feel so far removed from your God, what
else is your seeking God in repentance but loving God.

KIERKEGAARD

What can be more grievous than hell? Yet nothing
is more profitable than the fear of it; for the fear of
hell will bring us the crown of the kingdom.

ST. JOHN CHRYSOSTOM

An act of contrition is usually spoken aloud when a penitent confesses
in the Catholic sacrament of reconciliation, or penance. One particular
act of contrition reads:

O my God,
I am heartily sorry for having offended you,
and I detest all my sins,
because I dread the loss of heaven
and the pains of hell;
but most of all because they offend you, my God,
who are all good and deserving of all my love.
I firmly resolve, with the help of your grace,
to confess my sins, to do penance,
and to amend my life. Amen.[1]

Confessing one's sins out of love for God above all things is called contrition, or "perfect contrition" in the Catholic tradition. Confessing out of the fear of the damnation or for other reasons than the pure love of God is called attrition, or "imperfect contrition." The foregoing act clearly suggests that the former is better than the latter. Still, attrition is acceptable for the Catholic tradition, as a step in the right direction, and it is claimed to be purified in the "sphere" of the sacrament itself.[2]

Luther loudly protested this claim, writing, "This attrition they grant to the wicked and unbelieving, and thus abolish contrition altogether."[3] For Luther, as for Kierkegaard, there are only two ways, the way of faith and the way of unbelief.[4] The former leads to salvation, and the latter to damnation. Attrition seems, to Luther, to be an inadequate form of contrition, and not to proceed from genuine faith. Thus, it belongs to the category of unbelief, and promotion of the idea that attrition is sufficient can only lead penitents astray. Kierkegaard appears to accept this view, at least with regard to what seems to be his "official" position.[5]

In his work "An Occasional Discourse," which many readers may know as *Purity of Heart Is to Will One Thing,* Kierkegaard argues that to will the good out of fear of punishment, even eternal punishment, is being double-minded. It might seem, therefore, to be part and parcel of the *problem* in which the prospective penitent finds herself, and certainly not an antidote to it. As a Catholic, I take issue with that claim, it being among the teachings of my faith that to be imperfectly contrite out of a fear of hell (together with the renunciation of the desire for sin and the hope for pardon) is not a symptom of sin but is rather "a gift of God and an impulse of the Holy Spirit."[6] Furthermore, *as a Kierkegaardian* (of one sort or another) I want to take issue with this claim, since it seems to me that the larger Kierkegaardian religious dialectic forces us to admit that there must be more to Kierkegaard's story.

Now perfect contrition is motivated by a pure love of God and is often claimed to be sufficient, even apart from the sacrament of reconciliation, to forgive venial sins, or those sins that are not as serious or involve something less than full and deliberate consent. The former sort of contrition (i.e., imperfect), which primarily concerns us here, is only one that desires to change its ways on the basis of its fear of eternal punishment and God as punisher. On this, we might consider Karl Rahner's words: "In practice these two theoretically distinguishable kinds of contrition coexist, though one or the other may emerge more strongly in our consciousness at a particular time."[7] Kierkegaard's official position would seem to disallow this coexistence. I argue that Kierkegaard's own argument in "An Occasional Discourse," after being examined in the light of the Catholic tradition and his own larger religious dialectic, suggests a reexamination of his position, which will bring Kierkegaard and Catholicism closer than one might initially suspect.

Kierkegaard's Argument in "An Occasional Discourse"

To begin this discourse, Kierkegaard is at pains to explain how repentance is not to be considered to belong to one particular period of life. Deploring the notion that young people ought to be allowed to live dissolute lives for a time while they, so to speak, "get it out of their systems," he urges that there is no age at which repentance is any more or less appropriate than at any other age (*UDVS*, 9). Since the eternal applies at all times and all places, no human being, whether young or old, is exempt from the demands it places upon him or her. He writes, "We dare not say of repentance and regret that it has its time, that there is a time to be carefree and a time to be crushed in repentance" (*UDVS*, 13).

Kierkegaard goes on to make a distinction between the temporal life and the eternal in a human being. The former has it that old age is the "eleventh hour," but the eternal has it that "the call to find the road again by seeking God in the confession of sins is always at the eleventh hour ... repentance and regret belong to the eternal in a human being, and thus every time repentance comprehends the guilt it comprehends that it is in the eleventh hour" (*UDVS*, 15). In fact, this sense that one must repent "at the eleventh hour" is so important that Kierkegaard claims that "the person who repents at any other hour of the day repents temporally" (*UDVS*, 15). This suggests that a repentance directly brought on by temporal factors, such as old age, would not be a genuine repentance, since it would take place only in temporality's eleventh hour, and not in the eleventh hour of eternity.

Notwithstanding his belief that one must always repent at the eleventh hour, Kierkegaard understands quite clearly (as indeed does the Catholic tradition) that there must be time allowed for what is commonly called an "examination of conscience."[8] On the one hand, eternity demands that repentance should take place "at once," and yet, since a human being lives in time, the eternal understands that neither impatience nor momentary repentance bears spiritual fruit (*UDVS,* 16). One must prepare for the confession of sins since, "one cannot *confess* without this unity with oneself" (*UDVS,* 20).[9] Accordingly, preparation is not only allowed but required. Unity with oneself, however, cannot be achieved when one is double-minded in any way, since double-mindedness is always a kind of despair and "everyone in despair has two wills" (*UDVS,* 30). Thus, the catalogue of types of double-mindedness with which Kierkegaard goes on to present us is intended to be a catalogue not only of types of despair, but of hindrances to a proper confession.

The first type of double-mindedness that must be renounced, according to Kierkegaard, is willing the good for the sake of the reward. The all-important premise in this argument is that "the good is one thing; the reward is something else," thus the person who wills the good for the sake of the reward is double-minded, since she in fact wills two things (*UDVS,* 37). At this point, Kierkegaard helps himself to Plato's *Republic,* and to the question there over whether a person who wishes to be just might be willing to be perceived as being unjust, and punished accordingly.[10] Glaucon's famous example from the *Republic* asks us to separate the good from the reward as far as possible (notwithstanding the fact that justice is ultimately taken to be its own reward), and to ask whether we would still will "the good" as Kierkegaard has it. When we are talking about things such as money, reputation, and in general extrinsic goods, this account seems clearly to highlight Kierkegaard's point. But Kierkegaard himself reminds us that "The reward we are speaking of here is the world's reward, because the reward that God has eternally joined together with the good has nothing dubious about it and is also adequately sure. Neither things present nor things to come, neither heights nor depths, neither angels nor devils will be able to separate it from the good" (*UDVS,* 37). Accordingly, Kierkegaard wishes to differentiate between willing the good out of concern for a worldly reward (which is impermissible because double-minded) and willing the good out of a concern for an eternal reward, which appears to be permissible.

The reason for this is that some rewards are externally related to the activity for which they constitute a reward and others are internally related to such an activity, as Kierkegaard seems to think is the case with the reward that God has eternally joined to willing the good. Jeremy D. B. Walker calls the former heterogeneous rewards and the latter homogeneous rewards. He gives the examples of "running fast and winning races" and "studying counterpoint and coming to appreciate sixteenth-century music" as examples of homogeneous rewards, and "running fast and winning silver cups" as an example of a heterogeneous reward.[11] Here, the idea is that some activities have within themselves certain rewards intrinsically. I am perfectly permitted in this view to spend more time with a relative because I wish to develop a better relationship with her. The enhancement of the relationship may be a reward, but it is internally related to the activity. I am not permitted to spend more time with my relative for the reason that I wish to be included in her will, because this reward is extrinsic to the activity itself, and therefore constitutes a second thing I will, resulting in "double-mindedness."

Kierkegaard makes it clear that "the good is its own reward, yes, that is eternally certain. There is nothing more certain; it is not more certain that there is a God, because this is one and the same" (*UDVS*, 39). Thus, the reward that comes as part and parcel of willing the good is an internal and thus homogeneous reward. There does not appear to be any indication that willing the good for the sake of *this* reward involves one in despairing double-mindedness. In fact, Kierkegaard consciously distances himself from making such claims, by making a distinction between the world's reward and the reward that God "internally and eternally" adds to the good, and then explicitly claiming that the second but not the first is homogeneous with the good (*UDVS*, 41).

The crucial premise in the matter of the one who willed the good for the sake of the reward is similar to the crucial premise in Kierkegaard's argument that the one who wills the good out of fear of punishment does not will the good in truth, namely, that "the good is one thing, punishment something else" (*UDVS*, 44). Accordingly, Kierkegaard recognizes that the question of willing for the sake of reward and for the sake of punishment are in reality, as we might say, two sides of the same coin, since "avoiding an evil is a gain of the same kind as acquiring an advantage" (*UDVS*, 44). In what does the double-mindedness consist? Despite the parallels, here the answer is a bit more nuanced than the one we received in the previous case. The trouble, as Kierkegaard points out, is that the conditional nature of the willing indicates that our willing of the good is only contingent upon our having avoided a certain punishment. But if the condition were stricken from the willing, so would be the willing of the good. As many have noticed, in a deeply Kantian text, this point resounds with the influences of Kant's discussion of hypothetical imperatives.[12] Our actions and our will cannot be genuinely good if they are based simply on our incentives, in which case we either want something or want to avoid it. Rather, they must be based simply on the good as such. So, the willing of the good must be unconditional; it must have, as we say, no strings attached. To apply the terminology of Walker's analysis here, in willing out of fear of punishment, a person fears something that is only externally and conditionally connected with what she wishes to avoid, and so fears a punishment that is, we might say, heterogeneous with respect to it.

Kierkegaard next distinguishes two kinds of the fear of punishment. The first is simply the defiant refusal to fear what one *should* fear, "the sanctity of shame, God in heaven, the command of duty, the voice of conscience, eternity's responsibility" (*UDVS*, 45–46). Instead, one fears the minor punishments that are intended as "medicine" that will rehabilitate one so that one can again will the good in truth. These are neither fearful nor harmful. Kierkegaard goes on to say that if a person were to fear the simple shame of being *caught* in an error (presumably as opposed to a deeper moral guilt), then she is not escaping the error at all, but being "led in to something more corrupting" (*UDVS*, 45). This is actually our second form of willing the good out of fear of punishment. In this version, which Kierkegaard says is an "even more pernicious sickness," one fears "*what a person should not fear and ought not to fear*" (*UDVS*, 46). Here, the person carefully, and in moderation, attempts to avoid the form of the punishment that she fears, not by being virtuous, but simply by cowardly seeking to be nothing more than "safe" from the disapproving glances of her fellows. Here one thinks one can avoid contamination with evil simply by refraining from performing such actions because there is always the chance that one could get caught. But this very attitude is itself a sickness, and "even more pernicious" because one vainly thinks one is safe. At any rate, in neither of our two cases of willing the good out of fear of punishment does one really fear what one ought to fear, or, indeed will the good in truth.

In these instances, one *should* (but of course does not) "fear doing wrong, but if he has done wrong, then, if he actually wills one thing and wills the good in truth, he must even desire to be punished so that the punishment can heal him just as the medicine heals the sick" (*UDVS,* 45). But in this case where one does not accept the punishment that is meant to be remedial, he protests loudly against the punishment that he justly deserves, even though he knows that this punishment will help to bring about his health. In this way, fearing the punishment is conceiving of the medicine (punishment) as itself a sickness, just as a child refuses beneficial medicine for the reason that it has a nasty taste. Accordingly, "all double-mindedness that wills the good only out of fear of punishment is ultimately recognizable by this: that it regards the punishment as a sickness" (*UDVS,* 47).

But one might object: surely some punishments *are* sicknesses. Certainly excessive punishment might be a "sickness" of this kind, to the extent that it is excessive. But even more to the point, the eternal punishment of hell is traditionally held to be one of infinite duration. In the case of a temporal punishment, one might regard it as the *antidote* so that one might be subsequently brought to health. In this case, it would seem to be nothing but despair and double-mindedness to protest against being cured of one's *real* ailment. But in the case of the traditional doctrine of hell (or, at any rate, and for our purposes, the Catholic doctrine of hell)[13] the punishments of the damned are thought to extend for eternity and therefore to be, in principle, irremediable. Here the analogy of a sick child refusing to take her medicine would seem to break down, because hell is not an eschatological training ground, as, in a certain sense, purgatory is.[14] Hell does not appear to be a medicine at all; it simply appears to be the most dreadful (because irremediable) sickness. Perhaps the fear of hell is not the only, or even the best, reason for willing the good, but what is wrong with a will that does the good out of a fear of *this* punishment? Is this, too, a form of double-mindedness?

Indeed it is, says Kierkegaard. He writes, "*By punishment someone perhaps thinks of* what is seldom mentioned these days, *the punishment of eternity,* and it might seem that the person who wills the good out of fear of punishment is not double-minded, since he assigns the punishment to eternity, thus to the same place where the good has its home.

And yet he does not will the good; he wills it only out of fear of punishment" (*UDVS*, 47). Again, for Kierkegaard, the reason for why this is double-minded is related to the conditional nature of the willing. The problem has to do with the fact that *if* there were no punishment, the person would not will the good at all. Here Kierkegaard has us imagine someone who could convince another that eternity's punishment was a fiction. Then the person would abandon her willing of the good because the condition on which the good was willed was stricken from the will *for her* (*UDVS*, 47).

What else can be said for or about this claim, that the person who wills the good out of fear of *eternal* punishment is double-minded, on Kierkegaard's behalf? Kierkegaard argues that the fear of punishment (all of this continues to be within the scope of the discussion of *eternal* punishment) "has an erroneous conception of the good," and the good does not let itself be deceived, nor does it tolerate any "alien helper" (*UDVS*, 48). Were we only to imagine, as Kierkegaard does, one person to whom the *reward or the good* beckons, and to compare this person to another who willed the good only out of fear of punishment, would it not be positively bizarre to find them spiritually in the same place, when all is said and done? (*UDVS*, 49).

It may seem that way, but before we too quickly agree, let us ask just why both the reward and the good are acceptable as sources of encouragement. Kierkegaard attempts to distinguish the encouragement of the good (or its reward) from the discouragement fear offers from doing anything other than the good. He tells us that the good and the (internal) reward work together in helping a person will the good, much as a mother helps her young child to walk alone by giving her child to understand that she is supporting the child with her arms, while all the while the child walks safely to her on his own (*UDVS*, 49). Hence, the reward of eternal happiness, which is what is explicitly mentioned in this connection, can serve as an encouragement to willing one thing. Why, then, is fear of eternal damnation, its apparent correlate, such a bad thing? Fear, we are told, is different, in that it "has no encouragement," and that, as opposed to the loving mother who beckons the child forward, fear "continually pushes the child over." "It will," Kierkegaard writes, "help him forward, but not as the loving mother's beckoning does, because it is fear itself that weighs upon him so he cannot move from the spot. It will lead him to the goal, and yet it is fear itself that makes the goal fearful to him" (*UDVS,* 50). Why would Kierkegaard claim that fear is continually "pushing the child over" and that "fear itself makes the goal fearful to him?" If anything, it would seem that fear makes the punishment, and not the goal, fearful.

Kierkegaard, however, explains that the person who wills the good out of fear of punishment "*is continually doing what he does not really will*" because the pleasure involved is the lowest kind of sensate pleasure, namely, one that consists in avoiding something "only by way of a contrast" (*UDVS,* 50). In this case, to follow up on Kierkegaard's example, perhaps the child walks alone to the refuge of the mother's arms, but remains there only to avoid something worse, or until something better comes along. The goal is fearful to this person because it is not the best that could be imagined; it is only better than what is being denied, for the same reason that the absence of pleasure is fearful, but certainly less fearful than the presence of pain.

In this way, the person in question is making a heterogeneous distinction between the good and the punishment, as Kierkegaard tells us, but someone who wills the good in truth "understands that the punishment exists only on account of the transgressions; he devoutly understands that the punishment is like everything else that befalls the one who loves God—a helping hand" (*UDVS,* 50). In an important passage for what follows, Kierkegaard writes, "The double-minded person stands at the crossroads; then two visions appear, the good and the dreaded shape of punishment. To him the two are not homogeneous, for it is undeniable that the punishment God in his wisdom has attached to every transgression is a good, but it is only that when it is received with gratitude, not when it is only feared as an evil" (*UDVS,* 56). Thus, the fear of the punishment of eternity and the good that is willed *are* homogeneous, but to the double-minded person they do not *seem* that way. Accordingly, for Kierkegaard, the person who wills the good out of fear of eternal punishment remains double-minded and therefore remains in despair. We will have occasion to subject some of these claims to closer analysis in the rest of the chapter. For now, let us turn to investigate the Catholic tradition to see why the fear of eternal punishment in that tradition is not continually pushing us down but is rather an important vehicle to forgiveness and beatitude.

Imperfect Contrition in the Catholic Tradition

As we noted earlier, the Catholic tradition shares with Kierkegaard the insistence that the penitent prepare herself by means of an examination of conscience. Pope John Paul II, in his 1984 apostolic exhortation *Reconciliatio et Paenitentia* (*Reconciliation and Penance*) notes, "an indispensable condition [for sacramental confession] is the rectitude and clarity of the *penitent's conscience*."[15] This is to be a "sincere and calm comparison" with the interior moral law, in which it becomes clear that sin has introduced a "division" into the conscience of the penitent. Thus, an examination of conscience is not to be an "anxious psychological introspection."[16] Accordingly, the "unity with oneself" that we saw Kierkegaard requiring is not what is at stake. In fact, Kierkegaard and Catholicism appear to be, if not of one voice, then sufficiently similar in this respect to warrant our assertion that both regard double-mindedness to be an impediment to making a proper confession.

Therefore, the real crux of the matter lies not in whether double-mindedness is a bad thing (which all seem pleased to grant), but rather in what *constitutes* double-mindedness. Specifically, it lies in whether willing the good (in this case, making confession, which, we will grant for the sake of argument, is a good thing) out of fear of eternal punishment is double-minded. The most definitive source on this question in the Catholic tradition is the Council of Trent. In chapter four of the fourteenth session, the council first declares the necessity of contrition ("a sorrow of the soul and a detestation of sin committed, with the determination of not sinning in the future"), which includes (1) "trust in the divine mercy," (2) "the desire of performing the other things that are required to receive this sacrament correctly [i.e., penance]," (3) "cessation from sin," (4) "the resolution and a beginning of a new life," and (5) "hatred of the old [life]."[17] The council then goes on to write:

> That imperfect contrition which is called attrition since it commonly arises either from the consideration of the baseness of sin, or from the fear of hell and its punishments, if it renounces the desire of sinning with the hope of pardon, the Synod declares, not only does it not make a person a hypocrite and a greater sinner, but is even a gift of God and an impulse of the Holy Spirit, not indeed, as already dwelling in the penitent, but only moving him, assisted by which the penitent prepares for

himself a way unto justice. And though without the sacrament of penance it cannot *per se* lead the sinner to justification, nevertheless it does dispose him to obtain the grace of God in the sacrament of penance.[18]

What is the target here? The view that is anathematized in canon 5 seems to line up with this passage in setting its sights on those who would say that imperfect contrition (as already described) "is not a true and beneficial sorrow, does not prepare for grace, but makes man a hypocrite and a greater sinner."[19]

Some have attributed this condemned view to Luther,[20] though I know of no text where Luther commits himself to precisely that view. Luther does hold that "the person who believes that he can obtain grace by doing what is in him adds sin to sin so that he becomes doubly guilty."[21] The trouble here is that any sense in which we regard our own efforts to produce contrition as securing the grace we seek is to plunge further into the search for righteousness through works, because it makes contrition a work. This seems to be Luther's contention in the following passage from "The Sacrament of Penance."

> You should not be debating in the first place whether or not your contrition is sufficient. Rather you should be assured of this, that after all your efforts, your contrition is not sufficient.[22] This is why you must cast yourself upon the grace of God, hear his sufficiently sure word in the sacrament, accept it in free and joyful faith, and never doubt that you have come to grace—not by your own merits or contrition, but by his gracious and divine mercy. . . . After that be contrite all the more and render satisfaction as well as you can.[23]

The interesting thing about this view is that *no* contrition is sufficient for forgiveness, sacramental or otherwise. But if no contrition is sufficient for forgiveness of sins, then certainly it would seem to follow that *imperfect* contrition is not sufficient, at least not in this way. To draw on some of our earlier discussions, perhaps Luther sees attrition as a work of the natural human being, but if the natural human being is condemned in unbelief, then attrition can be of no use, and relying on it is a further sin. On the other hand, if the human being is on the "way" of faith, then God's grace will be at work in her and will hardly stoop to produce a second-best attrition. This is not to say that for Catholicism, attrition or contrition could be produced simply through a human being's natural capacities, since grace would already be at work in such a person.[24] Nonetheless, if Luther holds the view under discussion, it appears to be condemned by the Tridentine decree.

Still, there are many debates about the nature of contrition (understood in this instance as a wider category under which attrition falls) that the Council of Trent did *not* answer. Richard M. Gula notes that "Trent left unresolved the theological problem of the relationship between the acts of the penitent and the action of the Church in the forgiveness of sins."[25] Specifically, Trent only stated that attrition *disposes* one to receive sacramental forgiveness. It did not dogmatically establish, for example, when one is restored to a state of grace (prior to or in the moment of priestly absolution), and how and when the attrite person becomes perfectly contrite.[26] However, for some time, the teaching of the attritionists (those who say that attrition suffices for forgiveness of sins in the sacrament) has been the common teaching.[27]

John Paul II, in *Reconciliatio et Paenitentia,* appears to endorse this view when he writes of the sacrament of penance that it "perfects attrition."[28] He goes on to say, "Of course, in order to approach the Sacrament of Penance it is sufficient to have *attrition,* or imperfect repentance, due more to fear than to love. But in the sphere of the Sacrament, the penitent, under the action of the grace that he receives, *'ex attrito fit contritus* [from an attrite person to a contrite person],' since penance really operates in the person who is well disposed to conversion in love."[29] John Paul II here cites an important claim, a form of which is originally attributed to William of Auvergne,[30] to the effect that an attrite person can be changed into a contrite person through the sacrament of penance. As we have noted, neither Trent nor any other dogmatic source definitively established just *how* this takes place, but surely if the Tridentine chapter and canon we have seen are supposed to establish anything, they are supposed to establish that attrition is not despair. Rather, it is a gift from God that can, along with the sacrament to which it is connected, eventually result in the forgiveness of sins and reconciliation with God. Thus, in the Catholic view, it is not part and parcel of the *problem* of despair. It is part and parcel of the *solution* to it.

Having seen that the traditional Catholic view has it that attrition is a good thing, and that, as John Paul II confirmed, it leads to contrition, we might now look briefly at a point we raised earlier about the relationship between the two. The very point seems to be implicit in John Paul II's description of attrition as being "due more to fear than to love." However, as we shall note below, for the Catholic tradition, the distinction is not merely a matter of emphasis or intensity, but of the motives from which the sorrow for sin arises. It is, of course, difficult to say when one's sorrow over sin is due to love. For my part, I feel sure that I can discern times when I entered the confessional being driven more by fear than by love. Other times, the sacrament feels more like the celebration that the *Catechism* calls it.[31] But most times, when I enter the confessional, I feel driven by elements of both fear and love. I am perfectly happy to recognize the truth of the theoretical distinction between attrition and contrition, but it is not clear to me that I have ever entered the confessional without some mixture of the two. On this point, Karl Rahner writes:

> Traditional theology has expended a great deal of needless energy to distinguish between complete contrition on the basis of the love of God and an incomplete contrition, which no doubt acquires an authentic distance from guilt based on motives of faith, but is not yet real love, only something moving toward it. This distinction may be theoretically correct. But it does not have much importance in actual practice. For whoever is really capable of turning away from guilt, whoever no longer culpably absolutizes a finite good, for such a person the real difficulty of loving God no longer exists; for, just as the heart of man cannot contain the fullness of its own love but must be ever-giving; so, too, the love of God which man is constantly receiving and by which man lives, is constantly giving Itself to man.[32]

One thing that is worthy of note about imperfect contrition, and that Rahner brings out here, is that it acts on "motives of faith." Despite the fact that it often fears hell, it is not like buying fire insurance, in the sense that when one buys fire insurance, one is simply "hedging one's bets," to protect one's assets in the unlikely event of a damaging fire. If imperfect contrition *were,* contrary to fact, like hedging one's bets, the attrite person might as well pray the Jewish *Shema,* the Islamic *Shahadah,* and the Shin Buddhist *Nembutsu,* along with her Act of Contrition. Attrition is not sorrow for sins "on the off chance" that there is a hell. Rather, it faithfully believes that hell does in fact await the unrepentant sinner, and, accordingly, repents. This is the meaning of St. John Chrysostom's praise of the fear of hell at the beginning of this chapter.

The relation to Kierkegaard's view should by now be fairly clear. Kierkegaard claims that willing the good out of fear of punishment, even if the punishment should be eternal, is double-minded and is therefore indicative of despair. The Catholic tradition, by contrast, claims that at least one instance, namely confession, of willing the good (in this case, reconciliation with God, sacramental or otherwise) out of fear of eternal punishment is not despairing, but is at minimum a gift of the Holy Spirit. Catholic thought tends to insist that sacramental confession can perfect attrition. How this transformation precisely occurs has not been defined. In what follows, I want to argue that portions of Kierkegaard's larger religious dialectic can be seen to offer an answer to this very question. This may bring Kierkegaard's work and the Catholic tradition closer than the text of "An Occasional Discourse" would immediately suggest.

Attrition to Contrition in Kierkegaard?

In this section, I argue that Kierkegaard's overall religious dialectic can be seen to contribute something in an effort to answer the question of how an attrite person becomes a contrite person. This might seem to be a strange endeavor, since Kierkegaard's heritage is profoundly influenced by Lutheran Christianity, and we have already seen Luther's very, well, *Lutheran* claim that no contrition is ever sufficient to obtain the gift of God's grace. In fact this, for Luther, is why we must cast ourselves upon the grace of God. Yet, is it not grace that enables a person to move through the stages of existence? Is not Kierkegaard's religious dialectic a search for God in repentance, which, according to Kierkegaard's claim in the quotation that begins this chapter, is the same as loving God, even if only in a preliminary way?

A clarification is also in order: for Catholicism, the normative value we sometimes give to terms such as "perfect" and "imperfect" can be misleading. There appears to be no reason in the Catholic tradition why one could not have both perfect contrition (contrition arising from a love of God above all things) and imperfect contrition (contrition arising from other motives such as fear of damnation) at the same time.

Kierkegaard's "official" position in "An Occasional Discourse," however, seems to reject imperfect contrition as such, regardless of what other motives might accompany it, and since one cannot be both in despair (with imperfect contrition) and faith at the same time, then for Kierkegaard there can be no mixing of the two.[33] Furthermore, while the "two kinds of sorrow" associated with imperfect and perfect contrition "are different not merely in degree but in nature,"[34] there is also a sense in which the Council of Trent makes it clear that the beginning of the love of God in the repentant sinner is not perfect love, but must rather be associated with imperfect contrition.[35] This appears to be what Aquinas called the love of concupiscence.[36] In chapter 3 we saw that an initial love for God (love of concupiscence) that is based on self-interest must be tutored so that the "love of friendship" develops, which loves God above all things, even the self, although it does not cease to love the self and to desire its reward in God. On this view, nothing prevents a person from having both attrition and (perfect) contrition at the same time, though one will spring from the interest the self has in gaining the reward of eternal beatitude or in avoiding damnation (here the love of concupiscence can come in), and one will spring from a love for God for God's sake and God's glory. Since eros and agape are not opposites, both attrition and contrition can be had at the same time, though one may rise to the surface more than another at any given time.

Few, if any, Christians would dispute the Lutheran claim that without God's grace we can never muster sufficient contrition to obtain forgiveness (to do so seems to push one into the heresy of Pelagianism), but neither Kierkegaard's view nor the view of the Catholic Church ever has us approaching redemption without some measure of grace already at work in our lives.[37] This is why Kierkegaard urges us to "go with God to God" (*UDVS*, 104). In that same passage, Kierkegaard goes on to say, "Continually take that one step more, that one step, which even the person who cannot move a limb can take, the one step that even the confined prisoner, even the chained prisoner whose foot is not free, can take—and in the decision you are with the good" (*UDVS*, 104). "Well said!" clamor Christians from all corners; just as Christ himself pardoned a dying prisoner on the cross (Lk 23:43), so also in one instant of decision for the good, one is with the good, in its kingdom. This same claim also parallels a peculiar remark made by Kierkegaard in his journals, which reads, "If you do not have faith, then at least believe that you will come to have faith—and then you do have faith" (*JP*, 2:1141 / *SKP*, X-3 A 536). Indeed, this seems to me to be the probable situation of our attrite penitent. With the hope for pardon, our penitent takes the step of which she is capable, psychologically driven by fear, and her resolution to sin no more is confirmed and perfected by God (indeed, in the Catholic view, this probably happens in the sacrament of penance). There is always a danger in anxiety, as Vigilius Haufniensis points out (*CA*, 154), but one can also be educated by it (*CA*, 155–62). The education the individual receives in the larger religious dialectic is similar, I argue, to a transformation of the person from being attrite to being contrite.

To see this, it is important to note first that the requirement of "unity with oneself," significant for both Kierkegaard and Catholicism, is not met by those who remain in the aesthetic sphere. A, Kierkegaard's aesthete, manages to show us this fairly well in his "Diapsalmata." A informs us there that he doesn't "feel like doing anything," citing among his examples, riding, walking, lying down, staying down, getting up again, and so forth. Feeling that this pretty well exhausts the options, he writes, "*Summa Summarum:* I don't feel like doing anything" (*EO*, 1:20). It seems clear that this individual lacks the constancy of spirit, or unity with oneself, that is necessary for a proper confession. He has not patiently and soberly understood himself, since he claims that he lacks "the patience to live" (*EO*, 1:25). The reflective aesthete, Johannes, also pursues "the interesting" in his relationships, but deplores the ethical since it is, by contrast, boring (*EO*, vol. 1, p. 1:367). His pursuits of pleasure are ultimately shipwrecked by existence because, in the words of *Stages on Life's Way*, "He could never become intoxicated, and when he had reached a certain point, he became more and more sober the more he drank" (*SLW*, 30).

Judge William claims to have achieved some of the unity that A lacks in the ethical stage of existence. By living a life that has an internal unity, he has chosen himself (*EO*, 2:214). But this self that he has chosen is in some sense not fully prepared for confession yet, because along with "unity with oneself," it is important to remember that Kierkegaard requires that confession take place at "the eleventh hour." Kierkegaard called old age the eleventh hour in the temporal sense, and death the final moment of that hour (*UDVS*, 15). Later in that same passage, Kierkegaard notes that "every time repentance comprehends the guilt it comprehends that it is in the eleventh hour." But Kierkegaard's religious dialectic has us coming to sin-consciousness only after having been revealed this condition by the god in time. Thus, we would be in a position to confess the real nature of our sinfulness only when the extent and depth of this sinfulness has been revealed to us in Religiousness B, or Climacus's Christianity.[38] All of this dovetails nicely with the requirement that confession take place at the eleventh hour.

Yet, there is another topic that is important in the development of Kierkegaard's dialectic here. This is the topic of eternal happiness, which is when we move decisively into the ethical-religious, or Religiousness A. The concern for eternal happiness plays a very significant role in the dialectic. In *Concluding Unscientific Postscript*, Climacus distinguishes the ethical (and we might include the ethical-religious) from faith by noting that "ethically the individual is simply and solely interested infinitely in his own actuality.—Faith's analogy to the ethical is the infinite interestedness by which the believer is absolutely different from an esthete and a thinker, but in turn is different from an ethicist by being infinitely interested in the actuality of another (for example, that the god actually has existed)" (*CUP*, 324). It is, however, *through* the concern for her actuality (in the issue of an eternal happiness) that the individual turns to the actuality of the god, because she cannot purchase the relation to an eternal happiness on her own. But if the concern for an eternal happiness is what got the dialectic moving into the religious in the first place, and what continues to fuel its movement, then the question of willing the good on the basis of the reward is particularly important.[39] In fact, it is because of this very issue that Climacus refuses to define an eternal happiness, namely, because our willing of it must not be separated from the God-relationship (the good) which is internally related to it, and therefore homogeneous with it (*CUP*, 392–93).

The eternal happiness that pushes us toward redemption in Christ cannot be defined in any normal sense, which means that it must remain unknown and yet somehow passionately desired. At this point, it is interesting to consider a signed work that Kierkegaard wrote a year prior to *Concluding Unscientific Postscript*, whose proper title is, interestingly enough, "On the Occasion of a Confession." In that discourse,

Kierkegaard writes, "In the world of freedom, where all striving indeed has its source and in which all striving has its life, there *wonder* appears on the road. Endeavor has various names, but that which is directed toward the unknown is directed toward God. That it is directed toward the unknown means that it is infinite" (*TDIO*, 20, italics mine). It does not seem too far a stretch to think that this dialectical progression is similar to the one Climacus is describing in the *Postscript*. But in that text, when sin-consciousness is revealed by the god in time, a person must choose to become a new creation, a new person in communion with God, or to be offended.[40] Now, what of her motivation in this case? Could it be that she is immediately overwhelmed with such explicit love of God for *who God is in himself* that she immediately desires to become the new creation that the forgiveness of her sins entails? This seems to me implausible and strange to think of even Kierkegaard contemplating. A comparison with the vision of the Council of Trent would strongly suggest that even yet we are dealing with an initial form of the love for God that is motivated at least partly by self-interest and a desire for beatitude and the avoidance of its contrary.

In fact, in "On the Occasion of a Confession," Kierkegaard goes on to discuss the transformation that occurs through wonder in ways that parallel the transformation from sinful self to new creation.[41] But if wonder is operative in this transition from sinful self to new creation, then it is interesting to see Kierkegaard discuss wonder in that text, saying, "Wonder, however, which is the beginning of all deeper understanding, is an *ambivalent* passion that in itself contains *fear and blessedness*" (*TDIO*, 24, italics mine). The question now becomes, if wonder is such a mixture, doesn't this mean that the desire for redemption has been dirtied a bit by fear?[42]

If we were to take the line of "An Occasional Discourse" as it seems at first glance, the answer would seem to be yes. However, on closer examination, it may not be quite so clear. Recall that the lynchpin of Kierkegaard's argument, to the effect that willing the good out of the fear of eternal punishment was double-minded, was that the good is one thing, the punishment another, suggesting that the punishment was heterogeneous with the good. Yet, all the while, Kierkegaard claims that "fear itself has an erroneous *conception* of the good" (*UDVS*, 48, emphasis mine). In what, then, does this error consist? What immediately comes to mind in this connection is Kierkegaard's claim that when two visions appear, namely, the good and the punishment, the double-minded person does not *perceive* them to be homogeneous, though every punishment that God attaches to sin is a good, but only when received with gratitude (*UDVS*, 56). However, the double-minded person *pays more attention* to the world's punishment (for instance, public humiliation) than to these divinely affixed punishments.

This suggests that the problem, for Kierkegaard, may be that a person not so much wills the good out of the fear of hell (in the sense of "An Occasional Discourse"), but wills the good out of the wrong *kind* of fear of hell. As we noticed earlier, according to Kierkegaard, the double-minded person here is continually doing what he does not really will. That is, the person does not really wish to be willing the good, only to be avoiding the (bad) punishment, and so the pleasure that he receives, on this model, is only the absence of the relevant pain. Kierkegaard goes on to say of this person, "*Neither does he relate the punishment to God and to the good;* on the contrary, in his conception the good is one thing, the punishment something entirely different" (*UDVS*, 50, emphasis original). As we saw earlier, Kierkegaard claims that the person who wills the good in truth will regard punishment as "a helping hand." But if the punishment in this case is eternal and irremediable, how is it *ever* going to be a "helping hand?"[43]

My suggestion is that the only way for this kind of punishment to really be a helping hand is if the correct conception of it can spur one on to willing the good in truth, and thus from beginning as an attrite penitent and becoming a contrite one. Although Kierkegaard never clearly develops a positive account of this in "An Occasional Discourse," my contention is that the dialectic itself is developing a positive account of it.[44] For when the individual is conscious of her sin and is faced with the choice between her sinful self and the new creation that she can become, she is certainly pushed forward by the encouragement of eternal happiness (which Kierkegaard does not call double-minded).[45] But she is also *concomitantly* repelled by the absence of the as yet "unknown" good that she has been seeking (which is God), and so fears the absence, together with the mixture of fear and blessedness she experiences at the prospect of an encounter with the eternal. Indeed, at this stage, both the desire for an eternal happiness and the fear of damnation arise at least partly from self-interest. As we saw Rahner noting in another connection, one of either of these two forms of motivation may emerge more or less strongly in the consciousness of the penitent from time to time.[46]

All of this raises the question: just what constitutes the fear of hell? The forms of double-mindedness connected with willing the good out of a fear of eternal punishment seem to have in common the fact that the person has some kind of erroneous conception of the good and of the punishment, and that the penitent does not connect the punishment to the good. But if hell itself *by definition* involves an appeal to God and the good, then our double-minded penitent does not even fear hell, strictly speaking, but only some rather vague idea about what it might be.[47] If hell is what the contemporary Catholic Church takes it to be, namely, a "state of definitive self-exclusion from communion with God and the blessed," whose "chief punishment is eternal separation from God, in whom alone man can possess the life and happiness for which he was created and for which he longs,"[48] then it is difficult to see how our dialectical wayfarer does not have a mixture of fear and blessedness when she journeys the path to redemption and reconciliation.

If this account is correct, then the double-mindedness is not so much from the fear of hell as it is from the disordered self that cannot approach a *genuine* fear of hell. Here I think we can recall the distinction between what John Paul II called an "anxious psychological introspection" that occurs in an improper examination of conscience, and a "sincere" and "calm" reflection about what hell really is. Psychologically, in this situation, it seems plausible that our double-minded penitent does not have the kind of faithful appreciation (and thus fear) of what hell is, but rather has an anxiously acquired desire to avoid any and all unpleasantries, especially the indistinct jumble of them that she imagines with the aid of "fire and brimstone" sermons.[49] This kind of anxiety does not educate, but can only issue in the kind of hedging of one's bets that is not real attrition. In contrast, a moderately careful survey of Religiousness A in the *Postscript* reveals that the self searching after eternal happiness does not, as Rahner puts it, culpably absolutize a finite good. It takes a kind of grace to move forward toward reconciliation, and ultimately, love. And yet, the fear of losing out on an eternal happiness and communion with God, which a baptized penitent can perhaps especially appreciate, can be a strong and merciful motivator.

A Final Objection

Before concluding, I wish to consider an important objection.[50] It is this: Suppose we grant that Kierkegaard could allow us to fear hell in a non-despairing way if, by the fear of hell, all we mean is the deprivation of eternal happiness in God's presence. In this way, the fear of hell is merely the logical equivalent of the hope for eternal happiness in God's presence (i.e., one fears hell precisely and *only* because it is not-communion-with-God, and one wants eternal happiness in communion with God). This is a formidable objection because, while it defends the fear of hell in a sense, it does so at a heavy cost to Catholicism. The reason for this is that if it were true that all the fear of hell in this context means is that one longs for the cessation of the absence of communion with God, this simply means that one longs only for not-not-communion-with-God, and this again is logically equivalent to longing for communion with God. Accordingly, the objection would have it that the only fear of hell (attrition) that is appropriate in a Kierkegaardian context is the kind of fear that is not really fear at all, but simply another *name* for the love of God connoted by *perfect* contrition. This would simply land us back where we started, since Catholicism claims that perfect contrition is really superior to (and therefore distinct from) attrition, but Kierkegaard would accept attrition only if it were logically identical to perfect contrition.

In response to this objection, I want to concede that Kierkegaard himself never explicitly accepts anything that would answer to the name of attrition. Nonetheless, I think there is a defense available to a "Catholic Kierkegaardian" on this point, and that Kierkegaard himself is not so very far away from a similar view as it might at first seem. However, the first thing to say to this objection from a Catholic viewpoint, it seems to me, is that the fact that it is difficult to imagine a penitent without both motivations of fear and (a form of) love does not mean that the motivations themselves are not distinct. Our dialectical wayfarer may be treading the path to reconciliation with God, and grace may have given her a motivation that is due primarily to a fear of hell and perhaps only Aquinas's love of concupiscence for God. On the other hand, God's grace may have inspired a penitent to approach her confession with a mature love for God above all things (the love of friendship) *and* with a certain amount of fear of the punishment that perhaps very few reflective Christians would lack. The first situation seems to be that of an attrite person who lacks perfect contrition at the moment under discussion. The second situation seems to be one where the person has both attrition and contrition.

However, it seems worthwhile to also consider a second response, since one might very well wonder whether the contrite (i.e., the second) person above does not really fear hell since perhaps she only detests the absence of the thing for which she longs, namely, communion with God. Further, Kierkegaard might wonder about how to combine contrition with attrition, since he might question how one could value and love God for God's sake while retaining aspects of one's self-interest. While much of this case has been made in chapter 3, Kierkegaard might still raise another interesting question, namely, even if we grant (as I think we should) that the love for God for God's sake (Aquinas's love of friendship) is compatible with aspects of the love of self-interest (Aquinas's love of concupiscence), how can we explain the psychological shift in a person's consciousness from love to fear and back again? Wouldn't the perfectly contrite person be singularly attentive and focused?

In response, we might argue that the unfortunate truth of the matter is that sin (venial as well as mortal, a distinction the Catholic tradition upholds) has cognitive consequences, among which we might perhaps number a diminished sense of appreciation for the life to which God has called one.[51] Kierkegaard may not accept the distinction between venial and mortal sins, but the next chapter will play host to some discussion of what he might mean by the "after-effects" of sin (*JP,* 1:411 / *SKP,* I A 6). If among these one could number cognitive consequences, then perhaps they could also result in a diminished appreciation of ultimate beatitude.[52] In fact, it seems plausible that the more that sin's cognitive consequences cloud an individual's conception of communion with God, the more prominent a role her fear of hell plays in her overall state of repentance. As we noted, there is no reason why a person could not have both attrition and contrition, and our penitent may indeed love God above all things (and thus have "perfect" contrition). However, she may do this less intensely than she would have without sin's interference, and the resulting cognitive cloudiness may make the fear of beatitude's loss more psychologically prominent in her mind.

A final problem arises here, however, because perfect contrition is supposed to be in some sense possible, both for those who are in a state of grace (with some measure of venial sin) and even for those in a state of mortal sin. There are two problems here. The first is that venial sins are thought to infect (nearly) all of humanity, so that no one can keep absolutely clear of them in this mortal life.[53] Here, it seems, we need a distinction. Perfect contrition is called perfect because of its source, namely, its arising from the love of God above all things. In this sense, perfect contrition does not admit of degree. On the other hand, can contrition, which is called perfect, be improved with regard to things such as its intensity and fervor? Here, the answer seems to be yes. On this point, the *Catechism of the Council of Trent* writes, "There are other dispositions which, although not essential to true and salutary penance, contribute to render contrition more perfect and complete in its kind, and which pastors will readily discover."[54] In the second sense, it seems, no one can have *perfect* contrition with regard to intensity and fervor, save perhaps Jesus and Mary, both of whom, according to the Catholic tradition, lack any sin over which to feel contrite.[55] In the first sense, perfect contrition (and here we are referring to perfect contrition as it is usually understood by the Catholic tradition) may be fairly common.[56] However, with regard to the intensity or fervor of our love for God from which our contrition may arise, our contrition, even our perfect contrition, may be "imperfect" in a sense. So the question of whether we can have an absolutely (that is, unsurpassably intense and fervent) perfect contrition will, in the ordinary run of things, receive a negative answer. Our answer to the first problem is now clear: when our contrition arises from love of God for God's own sake, it is "perfect," in the sense (the first sense above) that the contrition itself is "made" properly and from the right sort of motivation. All of us in whom God's grace is at work have an opportunity for "perfect" contrition, even though the intensity and fervor of this contrition may be partially diminished by our sinful state.

The second problem is that even mortal sinners, as noted, are supposed to have this "perfect" contrition available to them. However, mortal sin is said to "destroy" charity, or love in a human being's heart.[57] How can one muster contrition due to love for God above all things when one has destroyed that very love from within oneself? The answer here, I think, is to simply say that this is a desperate situation that requires God's unmerited grace, and so the *Catechism* claims that mortal sin "necessitates a new initiative of God's mercy."[58] When this new initiative begins in the heart of a person, and she consents to it, she is filled with a longing for God, the clarity of which may well be determined by the degree of openness she feels to this new initiative. Kierkegaard's reticence to talk about the *degree* of openness to this longing[59] does not prohibit him from discussing a similar longing for Holy Communion in the first of the *Discourses at the Communion on Fridays*.[60] There, Kierkegaard writes, "So also with longing. A person can ignore its call; he can change it into an impulse of the moment, into a whim that vanishes without a trace the next moment. He can resist it; he can prevent its deeper generation within him; he can let it die unused as a barren mood. But if you accept it with gratitude as a gift of God, it will indeed become a blessing to you" (*CD*, 254).[61] In this longing that God awakens in the soul of a communicant (or, presumably, a penitent as well), God can give the gift of a "new initiative" of grace.[62] Accordingly, there seems no reason why persons in a state of mortal sin could not have a "perfect" contrition due to love, since this is accomplished by God's grace, whose new initiative has begun in the penitent.

Again, however, a perfectly likely scenario is that our penitent is primarily motivated by despising her old life and what would be in many ways its eternal continuance in hell, and faithfully believes that liberation from it (whatever precisely that liberation looks like) awaits her in the sacrament of reconciliation. This is attrition, and the Catholic tradition has, for some time, deemed it sufficient to obtain the forgiveness of sins in sacramental confession. It may be that some people are contrite out of a pure love for God, so much so that for them the motivation of the avoidance of hell does not even make a psychological dent. Kierkegaard himself seems, especially in other texts, to appreciate that this is not the situation of most of us. He writes, in "On the Occasion of a Confession," "The person who was faithful over little, faithful on that day of distress when the accounting is made, faithful in understanding his debt, faithful in the stillness in which no reward beckons but the guilt becomes clear, faithful in the honesty that acknowledges everything, *even that this honesty is deficient,* faithful in penitent love, the *humble love whose claim is self-accusation*—he will certainly be placed over more" (*TDIO*, 37). For my part, on most days, the pull of desire for an eternal happiness, the push from fear of eternal separation from the ultimate reality of the universe, and the love for a gracious God, *combine* in my desire for reconciliation, and I hope that God will graciously crown and perfect my messy attrite heart. The rigorists have no need to fear; all of that presupposes that I've managed to surmount the aestheticism in which I regularly find myself. But I am unable to understand why a proper conception of hell and the related fear of it should be characterized as double-minded, and it remains unclear to me why Kierkegaard should hold this.

‡

Kierkegaard's account of double-mindedness in "An Occasional Discourse" can be reexamined with the help of the Catholic tradition and a look at Kierkegaard's larger religious dialectic. The Catholic tradition maintains that attrition (contrition out of a fear of hell) is a gift of God, rather than a symptom of despair, and that it will lead to perfect and loving contrition. However, one must be careful to understand that the anxious fear that does not appreciate the reality of hell lacks the sincerity (and singleness of mind) to make a proper confession, even in the Catholic tradition. Likewise, in Kierkegaard's religious dialectic one must first surmount the multiplicity of aestheticism, but one can then move forward toward communion with God. I submit that this is usually done with a mixture of fear of damnation, longing for eternal happiness, and a generous helping of grace. I think the account of the transition from the aesthetic sphere to Christian faith can form an interesting contribution to how the Catholic Church could explain the transition from attrition to contrition.

This means that the right kind of fear of hell can play an important role in the life of faith. Although Kierkegaard hardly develops a positive concept of the *right* kind of fear of hell in "An Occasional Discourse," his care in detailing the *wrong* kind of this fear allows us to imagine the kind that might win for us the crown of the kingdom. In any case, we must move forward in honesty and wonder, fear and blessedness. Kierkegaard presents the other alternative thus: "You say, 'What good can it do for me to set myself against the crowd as a single individual?' What good can it do?—Well, perhaps it can even help save your soul so that it doesn't go to hell! Or do you think that when God and eternity pronounce judgment this kind of talk can be of any good to you; do you not suspect that merely to risk such a lame excuse is guilt enough?"[63]

SEVEN

The Sickness unto Life: Justification in Kierkegaard and the Question of Purgatory

However, to reach the truth, one must go through every negativity, for the old legend about breaking a certain magic spell is truth: the piece has to be played through backwards or the spell is not broken.

ANTI-CLIMACUS

Just as a covered object left out in the sun cannot be penetrated by the sun's rays, in the same way, once the covering of the soul is removed, the soul opens itself fully to the rays of the sun.

ST. CATHERINE OF GENOA

In his essay "The Babylonian Captivity of the Church," Luther argued, among many other things, that penance was not the "second plank" after baptism (as the Catholic Church contends), but that the Christian's "whole life should be baptism."[1] The significance of this is easy to overlook. Since baptism, according to the Catholic tradition, cleanses the individual of original sin, actual sin, and any as yet accrued punishments for sin, Luther and the Catholic Church would agree that baptism signifies "full and complete justification."[2] Where the two would differ is when Luther would go on to claim that "when we rise from our sins or repent, we are merely returning to the power and the faith of baptism from which we fell."[3] This would mean that full and complete justification occurs not just at the instant of an individual's baptism, but also when an individual, in any numbers of ways, returns to the power of that original baptism. This is an instance of Luther's claim that because we are justified through the merits of Christ, and any justification is simply a return to our spiritual marriage with Christ, then the spotless merits of Christ belong to us.[4] For this reason, justification for Luther is, as the Lutheran World Federation has put it, "always complete."[5]

In this chapter, I want to consider Kierkegaard's view on the matter of the justification of the human person before God, in order to show that the question of purgatory can come into view within a Kierkegaardian framework. If the previous chapter was right in its contention that the mixture of fear and love in relation to God is the ordinary state of many penitents much of the time, then it will become pertinent to ask what becomes of the ordinary person when she dies. To this question, the Catholic tradition has answered with the doctrine of purgatory, according to which, such individuals are subject to a postmortem period of cleansing prior to entering fully into the presence of God.

I make no pretensions whatever that Kierkegaard is some kind of crypto-Catholic, but I do think that his unique theological viewpoint represents a balancing act of sorts between the classical Lutheran picture of a more or less forensic justification and the process of redemption that finds its home in Catholicism. Indeed, as Daphne Hampson has argued, Kierkegaard manages to unite differing strands and strengths of both the Lutheran and Catholic traditions, especially on the matter of the self and its justification.[6] Might this have an upshot for raising the question of purgatory?

Luther, of course, eventually rejected the notion of purgatory.[7] Yet, while Kierkegaard regards Luther as a "master" in a certain way, we have also seen that he nonetheless departs from his master at various points and does not hesitate to criticize him at others. We should thus expect that the foundations for Kierkegaard's rejection of purgatory are slightly clouded by his hybrid of the Lutheran and Catholic anthropologies. I argue that this is what we do find. In addition, I argue that the structure of Kierkegaard's thought, being a movement through the stages, provides us with a framework for asking the awkward question of what happens to the individual who has earnestly, but insufficiently, progressed through Kierkegaard's stages of existence at her death? Is she "nailed" to herself in eternal despair, as in *The Sickness unto Death,* or does she enter into the ranks of the blessed in the eternal rest where Christianity will "cease to be militant?"[8] Both alternatives, of course, look implausible to the Catholic eye, and this is essentially why the Catholic tradition has argued for the existence of purgatory.

While Kierkegaard himself almost never mentions the word "purgatory,"[9] I think the fact that he views himself as standing squarely in the Lutheran tradition gives us evidence enough to believe that he would not have received the idea very positively. Indeed, the structure of his thought would seem to militate against the doctrine of purgatory, since, as Hampson points out, the transition from the ethical is not smooth and easy, but one must rather witness the "collapse" of all of one's efforts in the ethical and see that they come to naught before there can be any question of the religious.[10] In addition, Anti-Climacus writes that there are "only two rubrics" in which a person lives her life, namely, faith or sin (*SUD,* 105). So viewed, it is difficult to see how anything other than an "all or nothing" approach to wholeness will prevail in a Kierkegaardian framework. All of this is simply to say that assembling Kierkegaardian resources for even raising the question of purgatory will take some doing. To argue that there are such resources is my task here; I will begin with a brief examination of a Catholic view of purgatory, and then go on to articulate what I take to be a standard Lutheran reason for why Kierkegaard would not receive the idea of purgatory very warmly. The subsequent sections argue that Kierkegaard's unique contribution complicates matters a bit and detail the reasons for why readers of Kierkegaard may want to look at this question with fresh eyes.

A Catholic View of Purgatory

The Catholic tradition furnishes us with the most developed Christian notion of purgatory, if for no other reason than that it has been officially taught within that tradition for over 750 years. Thus, before arguing that there are resources in Kierkegaard's thought for a concept of purgatory, it will be helpful to consult the Catholic tradition for an understanding of just what the concept is supposed to denote. In this connection, it is interesting to note that what takes place in purgatory, namely, the cleansing from sin and its effects, may by no means take place *only* in purgatory. On this point, St. Francis de Sales writes, "We agree that the blood of Our Redeemer is the true purgatory of souls; for in it are cleansed all the souls of the world. . . . Tribulations also are a purgatory. . . . Penance and contrition again form a certain purgatory. . . . It is well known that Baptism in which our sins are washed away can be again called a purgatory, as everything can be that serves to purge away our offences."[11] In this way, purgatory functions much like the Catholic view on the sacraments, where Christ, and in particular, Christ's Church, is the "universal sacrament of salvation," whereas particular sacraments are vessels through which this universal sacrament is accomplished in particular cases.[12] Likewise, all purgation occurs through "the blood of Our Redeemer," but for those who die imperfectly purified, there is a particular manifestation of the one purgation in postmortem cleansing that we refer to as "purgatory."

The doctrine of purgatory was first officially taught at the First Council of Lyons in 1245, and it was subsequently defined by the Councils of Florence and Trent (in 1439 and 1563, respectively).[13] Traditionally, the doctrine derives some of its biblical support, however thinly veiled, from such passages as 1 Corinthians 3:12–15, where we read:

> If anyone builds on this foundation [i.e., Jesus Christ] with gold, silver, precious stones, wood, hay, or straw, the work of each will come to light, for the Day will disclose it. It will be revealed with fire, and the fire [itself] will test the quality of each one's work. If the work stands that someone built upon the foundation, that person will receive a wage. But if someone's work is burned up, that one will suffer loss. The person will be saved, but only as through fire.

I invoke this passage not to debate over its biblical import, but to note the context in which the issues surrounding the topic of purgatory were to be debated. For instance, in Gregory the Great, wood, hay, and straw come to mean venial or light sins, whereas building upon the one foundation of Christ with such other materials as iron, bronze, or lead comes to mean precisely the kinds of mortal sins that the purgatorial fires will not take away.[14] Thus, those who build upon the one foundation of Christ, using, as it were, objects resistant to flame exhibit the hardness of heart for which the damned are punished, whereas those who have merely the wood, hay, or straw must go through the sort of cleansing that has an end and terminates in the Christian's entry into heaven. This is one reason for the purgatorial punishments, namely, the existence of venial sins that a person has committed prior to death.

Another reason for purgatory that has been offered by the Catholic Church is the existence of temporal punishments for sin. Sin has, as the *Catechism* states, a "double consequence."[15] Mortal sin deprives us of the beatific vision of heaven, which is an eternal punishment, but there is also a temporal punishment that goes along with the sin, which follows from the very nature of sin, according to the Church. Christ's sacrifice remits the eternal punishment, but the temporal punishment remains. St. Augustine was influential in the development of the doctrine along these lines, so much so that Jacques Le Goff has called him "the true father of purgatory."[16] In *City of God,* Augustine writes:

> Whether we suffer temporary punishments in this life only, or in the life after death, or in both, the sufferings precede that last, severe judgment. However, not all who suffer temporal punishment after death are doomed to the eternal pains that follow the last judgment. For, as I have said, what is not forgiven in this life is pardoned in the life to come, in the case of those who are not to suffer eternal punishment.[17]

While this notion has been understood in various ways throughout the history of the Church, the contemporary Catholic Church has it that this is a form of the view that sin is its own punishment. This is because sin always entails, by its very nature, "an unhealthy attachment to creatures,"[18] and the fullness of joy is to be found only in God. Sin, however, is really an inordinate kind of addiction to creaturely things,[19] and we know from similar experiences that the symptoms of addiction remain even after a person sincerely desires to eliminate the addiction.[20] Thus, we must be gradually weaned off our unhealthy addiction to creaturely things, and these temporal punishments are for our rehabilitation in this respect. These temporal punishments are also opportunities for a person who is already redeemed from the eternal punishment of hell to become a fully mature Christian. On this point, Peter C. Phan writes, "In this way, the 'temporal punishments' can be understood, not as something imposed from without onto the sinner, but as a required maturing process, more or less intense and painful."[21]

A closely related notion is the idea of acts of external penance, whereby a person does something quite positive to "help us acquire mastery over our instincts and freedom of heart."[22] In this way, there is naturally a penance attached to the committing of any actual sin, and this penance is to be done so that the sinner renews her soul and distances herself from the habit of performing the sin. Pope John Paul II explicitly denies that this penance should be understood as payment for sin; rather, he notes that these "acts of satisfaction . . . remind us that even after absolution there remains in the Christian a dark area due to the wound of sin, to the imperfection of love in repentance, to the weakening of the spiritual faculties. It is an area in which there still operates an infectious source of sin which must always be fought with mortification and penance. This is the meaning of the humble but sincere act of satisfaction."[23] Should an individual die without having done this penance, it would need to be undertaken in purgatory.

This purgative cleansing might actually be desired by the penitent. In fact, as C. S. Lewis, an Anglican who believed in purgatory, suggests, the pains of purgatory might themselves be voluntary. He rather famously wrote:

> Our souls demand Purgatory, don't they? Would it not break the heart if God said to us, "It is true, my son, that your breath smells and your rags drip with mud and slime, but we are charitable here, and no one will upbraid you with these things, nor draw away from you. Enter into the joy"? Should we not reply, "With submission, Sir, and if there is no objection, I'd rather be cleansed first." "It may hurt, you know."—"Even so, Sir."[24]

The question of whether the pains of purgatory are voluntary has been a rather protracted debate in the history of the Church.[25] Aquinas, for instance, claims that the pains of purgatory are involuntary in the sense that we do not wish for them to occur while they are occurring, but that they are voluntary in the sense that we wish to enter heaven, and understand that purification is necessary prior to our being able to do so.[26] St. Catherine of Genoa, however, comes a bit closer to the claim that purgatory is in some way voluntary when she writes, "the soul that has but the slightest imperfection would rather throw itself into a thousand hells than appear thus before the divine presence."[27]

While the existence of venial sins and temporal punishments for sins generally provide the theoretical framework in which the reality of purgatory came to be understood, in the development of this doctrine, theory, as is often the case, came much later than practice. Purgatory is thus an example of a doctrine where *lex orandi, lex credendi* (or, roughly, "the law of prayer is the law of belief") seems to have played a powerful role.[28] The "practice" in this case is that of praying for the dead, for which Catholics can find a certain amount of biblical warrant in 2 Maccabees 12:42–45. The practice of praying for the dead can also be attested in the very early third century, at least as early as the *Martyrdom of Saints Perpetua and Felicitas*.[29] There is a simple argument drawn from this idea, which is regularly cited in medieval and early modern Catholic sources as being a decisive argument for purgatory.[30] The argument is simply that it is pointless to pray for the damned in hell or the blessed in heaven (both of which have their lot for eternity), and so if prayer for the dead is salutary at all, it must be a service to those being purified prior to their entry into heavenly bliss.

In more contemporary Catholic theology, there has been a tendency to emphasize that aspect of the Tridentine decree on purgatory that exhorted the bishops to restrict the unhealthy and excessive discussion of subtle questions related to purgatory that do not "edify."[31] Having this in mind, the Congregation for the Doctrine of Faith writes,

> When dealing with man's situation after death, one must especially beware of arbitrary imaginative representations: excess of this kind is a major cause of the difficulties that Christian faith often encounters. Respect must however be given to the images employed in the Scriptures. Their profound meaning must be discerned, while avoiding the risk of overattenuating them, since this often empties of substance the realities designated by the images.[32]

That is, we must be on guard against overreaching with regard to what we can know about purgatory. The dogmatic sources on questions related to what occurs after death and the scriptural passages on which they rely are ultimately rather minimal. While we should be willing to consider the images of Scripture, we must be careful not to slavishly cling to an idiosyncratic understanding of them, since this would restrict the fuller meaning that could be discerned.

In such an effort to truly discern the relevant image in 1 Corinthians 3, and to rebut an interpretation that claims that the "as through fire" text does not lend biblical support for purgatory, then Joseph Ratzinger (now Benedict XVI) chides the interpreter, saying, "If one presupposes a naively objective concept of Purgatory then of course the text is silent. But if, conversely, we hold that Purgatory is understood . . . in terms of the Lord himself as the judging fire which transforms us and conforms us to his own glorified body, then we shall come to a very different conclusion."[33] Thus, Benedict parts ways with a naïvely substantialist view of purgatory and its images, in particular denying Tertullian's view of a "supra-worldly concentration camp,"[34] replacing them with a more psychologically nuanced understanding of the obstacles in the way of a full entry into union with God. We read:

> [Purgatory] does not replace grace by works, but allows the former to achieve its full victory precisely as grace. What actually saves us is the full assent of faith. But in most of us, that basic option is buried under a great deal of wood, hay and straw. . . . Man is the recipient of the divine mercy, yet this does not exonerate him from the need to be transformed. Encounter with the Lord *is* this transformation. It is the fire that burns away our dross and re-forms us to be vessels of eternal joy. This insight would contradict the doctrine of grace only if penance were the antithesis of grace and not its form, the gift of a gracious possibility.[35]

For Benedict, the encounter with Christ is the purifying fire, and even in purgatory, we are not without Christ. This is in line with John R. Sachs's claim when he writes, "Those in purgatory are not in some indefinite state 'between' heaven and hell. They have died in grace, having made a free and fundamental decision for God in their lives. For them purgatory is a final and sure path to heaven. It is not a 'second chance.'"[36] The essence of the contemporary theological turn on purgatory is thus that it tends to be absorbed more nearly into heaven,[37] so that the purgatorial punishments are given by the fire of God's love in which we are thereby educated to endure and, eventually, exult.

Purgatory has had, of late, something of a resurgence outside the Catholic Church. One can now find appreciations of purgatory in the writings of Wesleyans and even Unitarian Universalists.[38] Should Kierkegaard join their ranks? That will depend on how we understand his thought, not least on the matter of justification. In what follows, I want to briefly consult Kierkegaard's view on matters of justification, and then go on to ask further structural questions about his dialectic, in an effort to determine whether his thought can appropriate a version of purgatory.

Kierkegaard's Lutheranism: A Prima Facie "No" to Purgatory

The Catholic doctrine of purgatory appears to trade on the coherence of a process of purification that is incomplete at the end of a human life. As Daphne Hampson writes, "Purgatory is that place in which the process can continue, given that we are as yet insufficiently changed to be united with God."[39] As such, the idea of purgatory seems more at home with the transformative character of grace that we often associate with Catholic ideas on justification. Thus, the Council of Trent writes, "In this justice received through the grace of Christ 'faith cooperating with good works,' they increase and are further justified. . . . And this increase of justice Holy Church begs for, when she prays: 'Give unto us, O Lord, an increase of faith, hope, and charity.'"[40] By contrast, we have considered the Lutheran World Federation's claim in the *Joint Declaration on the Doctrine of Justification* that "righteousness as acceptance by God and sharing in the righteousness of Christ is always complete."[41] It will be necessary now to ask where Kierkegaard's understanding of redemption converges with and diverges from a Lutheran conception. In this section, we will briefly glimpse some convergences with the traditional Lutheran perspective.[42]

Hampson insists that there has been widespread misunderstanding of the Lutheran understanding of justification in Catholic circles. As I hope not to be party to it, my interpretation of the Lutheran framework will owe much to her perceptive work. In interpreting the Lutheran framework over against the medieval Catholic view that Luther inherited and then discarded, Hampson notes that in the case of the Catholic view, "the human is understood as a kind of derived substance, which has independence . . . existing in and for itself. Of such a substance (or essence) qualities or attributes can be predicated; hence the person, within Catholic theology, is said to be in a 'state' of grace or of sin, or equally one can speak of 'infused' virtues."[43] She goes on to write, "By contrast, Luther understands the person as one who is 'carried' by another. That power acts through him."[44] Hampson then argues that, for Luther, the Christian lives *extrinsically,* and through another, and so her righteousness is, unsurprisingly, gained in the same way.[45] Thus, the idea here is that the Christian gains her righteousness not through herself, since indeed Luther's thought problematizes a traditional substantialist conception of the self,[46] but rather, the righteousness is gained by the Christian's living in God's justice, and also in God's very self.

In Luther's system, accordingly, it is not that we are gradually infused with more and more love and thus take into ourselves more and more inherent righteousness. Rather, for Luther, "The Christian has the typically Lutheran double sense of self. Life is no longer held to be an Augustinian *via* to God, in which we are (internally) transformed through working with God's grace."[47] In this way, justification for Luther is not a "cooperation" with God's grace that allows human beings to be internally transformed, in a definitive way, from being *in themselves* sinners, to being *in themselves* righteous. Instead, from one point of view, the sinner remains totally a sinner, and from another, the person is totally just.[48] Luther gives an example of this double relationship by describing a layman performing all the functions of a priest (e.g., celebrating Mass). Luther even notes that this layman might perform the functions "more reverently and more properly than the real ones."

> But because he has not been consecrated and ordained and sanctified, he performs nothing at all, but is only playing church and deceiving himself and his followers. It is the same way with the righteous, good, and holy works which are performed either without or before justification. For just as this layman does not become a priest by performing all these functions, although it can happen that he could be made a priest without doing them, namely, by ordination, so also the man who is righteous by the Law is actually not made righteous by the works of the Law at all, but without them, by something else, namely, through faith in Christ, by which he is justified and, as it were, ordained, so that he is made righteous for the performance of the works of righteousness, just as this layman is ordained a priest for the performance of the functions of a priest.[49]

Luther's point here seems to be that works do not prepare the way for justification before God. Instead, justification comes through "something else" entirely, which is ultimately Christ's righteousness (which is spotless), imputed to the believer precisely insofar as he does not trust in his own merits.[50] At that point the works of the believer are, from the human point of view, still on a par with the works of the unjustified, but from the divine point of view, the works are the works of love and the fruit of the spirit (which, note, have no role whatever in the prior justification of the believer). In this way, the believer is at one and the same time justified and a sinner, *simul iustus et peccator.*

In fact, in one of the clearest ways in which Kierkegaard's thought models Lutheranism on this point, the Lutheran "law" is a negative dialectic in human action, which is to say that it makes us aware of our failure, but is impotent, in and of itself, to do anything to remedy the situation.[51] There is no positive, progressive movement toward justification, only a negative awareness of its absence. Thus, for Luther, as Hampson has it, "The human being does not make progress; life is not a *via*. After all what could 'progress' mean if one is speaking in terms of trusting not in one's own righteousness, but in God?"[52] Similarly, in Kierkegaard's work, only when the individual's final attempt to obtain her eternal happiness in relationship to God by her own efforts is brought to naught can the god in time perform the soteriological work of bringing about a new creation.

In Johannes Climacus's work *Concluding Unscientific Postscript,* for example, guilt-consciousness discovers the eternal impossibility of an individual relating herself to her eternal happiness (*CUP,* 526), because "eternity sentences forever the very first time" (*CUP,* 533). It is important, however, to note that guilt does not arise from simply committing "sins," but rather, from being in a state of trying, as part of the ethical life (this is Climacus's Religiousness A, which is also called the "ethico-religious") to relate to an eternal God and one's eternal happiness by one's own temporal efforts, a situation Climacus thinks is simply hopeless. This is why guilt is, as Climacus notes, "total" (*CUP,* 529).

For this reason, Climacus thinks it is a mistake to talk about particular guilt, or a guilt that was incurred with respect to a particular sin. To talk this way is actually to reinforce the situation of being guilty in the total sense, just as for Luther, to trust in one's own works was to inhibit one's own justification. Climacus writes, "If it is true of any category, it is true of *guilt:* it traps. Its dialectic is so cunning that the person who totally exonerates himself simply denounces himself, and the person who partially exonerates himself denounces himself totally" (*CUP,* 529, italics original). The idea here seems to be that, in the first place, one's claim to be totally exonerated is simply a statement of pride, which shows that one's individual works are, in reality, sinful. In the second place, one's claim to partial justification is itself an admission of no justification at all, since justification does not admit of degree. Further, the attempt by forms of Christianity to make guilt commensurable in the external with particular actions, so that one could obtain forgiveness for one act by doing something to, as it were, cancel the guilt of the other, is, in Climacus's Lutheran model, a theological mistake. It is this sort of tendency that prompts Climacus to write, "There is much in Catholicism that can serve as examples of this" (*CUP*, 522). We noted before that penance in the Catholic tradition is not to be understood as "payment" for sin. Still, it must be admitted, as Hampson notes, that there is a greater tendency in Catholicism to talk of particular sins, whereas in Lutheranism and certainly in Kierkegaard, there is a tendency to set off faith and sin as two "rubrics" (*SUD*, 105).[53]

Climacus's Lutheranism is further reinforced by his insistence that hidden inwardness is true religiousness. He writes, "True religiousness, just as God's omnipresence is distinguishable by invisibility, is distinguishable by invisibility, that is, is not to be seen. The god to whom one can point is an idol, and the religiousness to which one can point is an imperfect kind of religiousness" (*CUP*, 475). This idea reinforces the fact that a particular external act could be performed excellently well by a libertine and by a religious person (just as a person could perform an outwardly righteous act, while trusting in her own efforts, and thus belong to the rubric of sin).[54] This appears to give further support in Kierkegaard's works for the famed Reformation slogan, "*simul iustus et peccator*" ("at the same time justified and a sinner").[55] The Catholic doctrine of purgatory, however, would seem to rule out this "total" sense of the Reformation slogan, according to which one is both totally a sinner and totally justified at the same time. This is because purgatorial punishments, in the Catholic tradition, seem to presuppose a cleansing process whose effects definitively, but gradually, transform the interior person.[56] Does all of this mean that Kierkegaard's thought is fundamentally opposed to the idea of purgatory?

Kierkegaard's Hybrid Model

There are reasons to think that a Kierkegaardian picture of justification has strong elements in common with a Lutheran doctrine along such lines. Kierkegaard's picture, as glimpsed in the *Postscript,* appears to support the Lutheran vision of *simul iustus et peccator*. This is likely to be Kierkegaard's meaning when he notes, "The confusion with us is that we are at the same time the Pharisee and the publican" (*JN*, 1:265 / DD: 191). It is worth noting, however, that this entry was penned in 1839, early in Kierkegaard's career, and there are clear shifts in Kierkegaard's writings, not least in terms of his increased exposure to, and more critical reception of, Luther's own work. Particularly after 1848, Kierkegaard often demurs from Luther on various points. For instance, in 1849, he writes, "The conclusion of Luther's sermon for Quinquagesima Sunday on 1 Corinthians 13, where he makes out that faith is superior to love, is sophistry. On the whole Luther always interprets love only as love toward one's neighbor, just as if it were not also a duty to love God. Essentially Luther had substituted faith for love toward God and then called love— love toward one's neighbor" (*JP*, 3:2480 / *SKP*, X-1 A 85). This constitutes a theological disagreement with Luther, of the sort that may have repercussions for our question, and it will figure in the discussion below.

Another instance where the later Kierkegaard is what we might call "creative" with his Lutheranism can be seen when he fancifully imagines Luther himself resurrected and interrogating Kierkegaard about his faith (*FSE*, 16–24). There the resurrected Luther encounters Kierkegaard and upbraids him for his lack of faith, shown clearly by the lack of *recognizable* Christian action (*FSE*, 19). Here, we should recall how the espousal of the religiousness of hidden inwardness was one way that Climacus converged with the *simul iustus et peccator* slogan. Thus, a departure, however subtle, from this type of hidden inwardness may have repercussions for Kierkegaard's receding embrace of its correlate conception of justification. While Kierkegaard is not as open in his disagreement with Luther here as he is in the above journal entry, Kierkegaard eventually argues that if Luther himself were to appear in nineteenth-century Denmark, he would have the Apostle James's letter "drawn forward" a little, in clear contrast to the historical Luther's famous denunciation of that epistle (*FSE*, 16).

This illustrates how Kierkegaard moves away from (the historical) Luther on points related to the Christian life. The clearest way in which this is so is in relation to the gift motif over against the pattern (or prototype) motif. For Kierkegaard, Luther correctly emphasizes that Christ the Redeemer is a gift to humanity, because in Luther's time, Christ as pattern was accentuated, everything became works, and the gift was forgotten. By contrast, Kierkegaard explicitly notes, "I am quite conscious of the fact that I have moved in the direction of Christ as pattern" (*JP*, 3:2503 / *SKP*, X-2 A 30). This is significant, because the dialectic of the gift is different from the dialectic of the pattern. A gift is given or not given, received, or refused. A pattern, by contrast, typically represents points of convergence and divergence, something that is more conformed to a pattern exhibiting more of the former, and less of the latter. That is to say, we can imagine a *process* more clearly when a pattern is invoked. Below I will consider what significance these two divergences from Luther (on love for God and on the gift and pattern issue) have for Kierkegaard's thought.

Let us first examine the question of whether one can have love for God in Kierkegaard's thought and what such a thing might mean. Hampson notes that the typical Lutheran framework has it that, "The relation to God is one of 'faith,' to the neighbor of 'love.'"[57] She writes further that "it does not come naturally to the Lutheran tradition to envisage an inter-relationship between the human and God. To think that one could stand before God, in dialogue with God, would be for Luther to misunderstand the nature of God."[58] Thus, the fact that Kierkegaard can speak this way, explicitly endorsing a reciprocal relationship with God, is part of his Lutheran innovation, according to Hampson, and indeed, an innovation that makes him capable of deeper conversation with the Catholic tradition, where the relationship with God is understood as love.[59]

Love for God in Kierkegaard's work, is, as I think Hampson rightly suggests, a kind of higher eros.[60] We have discussed the love of God in chapter 3, but for our purposes here, the thing to notice is that one's relationship to God is the only relationship that should have the characteristic that, for Kierkegaard, particularly signals erotic love, namely, a higher degree of love for God than for others. Indeed, for all of Kierkegaard's pseudonymous and signed insistence that a human being is nothing before God,[61] this love of God is part of a "reciprocal relationship" (*CD*, 127). Hampson cautions that we should not read this type of reciprocal relationship as a kind of Thomistic communication of being, as does Heinrich Roos.[62] However, despite her really excellent work in the main, Hampson's worries here are overdrawn.

Hampson here is working to preserve her view that Kierkegaard has no truck with a scholastic metaphysics. She writes, "If one considers God's almightiness, says Kierkegaard, the creature *coram deo* is nothing. It is not that the human and God possess some quality, Being, in common. It is only on account of God's love that the human being can stand before God."[63] Yet, she is responding to Roos's citation of a passage from Kierkegaard where God's omnipotence and goodness in creating an independent individual are identified.[64] This suggests that separating God's "almightiness" and God's love may not be available as a way to avoid nonstandard metaphysical commitments for a Lutheran.[65] My point is simply that Kierkegaard appears to want a sense of *both* the Lutheran insight about a creature as nothing *coram deo* (the claim can be understood in different ways, but in the main it is hardly unique to the Lutheran tradition),[66] and a sense that the creature has an existence, radically indebted to, but, in another sense, independent from, God. Thus, Kierkegaard's approach to metaphysics is likely to be unsurprising to readers who have followed this book thus far: metaphysical disputation is not the central spiritual point, but this does not mean that its results are spurious for quite so simple a reason.

For this reason, Kierkegaard's theological anthropology is best understood as post-metaphysical, but not as anti-metaphysical. With regard to a Catholic or a Lutheran anthropology, then, Kierkegaard appears to be attempting to steer a middle course. The self that is a "relation's relating to itself," which, in doing so, relates to God, is not a piece of metaphysical furniture, like a body-soul composite, *but it does presuppose such a metaphysical entity* as a necessary condition (*SUD*, 13). Kierkegaard's notion of the self is in this sense both descriptive and normative, since being a self means success in the project of achieving wholeness. It is, of course, the case that Kierkegaard thinks this impossible without divine assistance, yet some of the ways Kierkegaard structures his dialectic are amenable to an interpretation along the lines of a redemptive process, which an independent human being is *really* undergoing. Hampson is thus correct when she notes that Kierkegaard, in contrast to Luther, comes "to think of life as some kind of *via*."[67]

There are several different ways to cast this *via* for Kierkegaard, all suggesting movements that are not so obviously compatible with a righteousness (or perhaps sanctification) that is "always complete."[68] One way is by referencing Christian discipleship, as is done in Anti-Climacus's *Practice in Christianity*. There, Anti-Climacus insists upon imitation, rather than admiration, of Christ. While he notes that it is blasphemy to want to *be Christ* (*PC*, 106), he nevertheless insists that human beings can express the truth that Christ is. He writes, "Being the truth is identical with knowing the truth, and Christ would never have known the truth if he had not been it, and nobody knows more of the truth than what he is of the truth" (*PC*, 205–206). Here again we see that the discipleship motif of pattern allows some compatibility with a process, which was harder to glimpse in Luther's preference for the motif of gift.

Another way to cast the redemptive process appears in one of Kierkegaard's discourses, titled "One Who Prays Aright Struggles in Prayer and Is Victorious—in That God Is Victorious." There, Kierkegaard writes, "God can imprint himself in him only when he himself has become nothing. When the ocean is exerting all its power, that is precisely the time when it cannot reflect the image of heaven, and even the slightest motion blurs the image; but when it becomes still and deep, then the image of heaven sinks into its nothingness" (*EUD*, 399). There are clear similarities here with John of the Cross, whose metaphors for purgation include wiping a window clean of smudges so that it can transparently reflect the light of the sun.[69] The fascinating thing about these largely compatible images is that they seem to be available, no doubt with some tinkering, to both Catholic and Lutheran partisans. God's own light makes the window, or the ocean, bright, but we can participate in the process by either not raging against the light (as with the ocean), or wiping the smudges clean (as with the window). In either case, there is a purifying process in which the believer participates. This kind of image can help us to make sense of Kierkegaard's claim that "there is an increasing openness in relation to God" (*JP*, 1:272 / *SKP*, X-2 A 320).[70]

A final case of a process motif in Kierkegaard's work is the case of the struggle between the "first self" and the "deeper self" in the discourse "To Need God Is a Human Being's Highest Perfection." In that discourse, Kierkegaard describes the struggle of the first self with the deeper self. It is clear that there is freedom; that the deeper self can lose the battle, and yet the deeper self is not an external party, but the very self. Kierkegaard writes, "The first self sits and looks at all the beckoning fruits, and it is indeed so clear that if one just makes a move everything will succeed,[71] as everyone will admit—but the deeper self sits there as earnest and thoughtful as the physician at the bedside of the sick, yet also with transfigured gentleness, because it knows that this sickness is not unto death, but unto life" (See *EUD*, 314–15). Although Kierkegaard published this discourse nearly five years prior to *The Sickness unto Death* (published in 1848), such imagery is likely to have played an important role in the writing of that text, especially since the passage here interprets the redemptive process as a "sickness unto life," and the title of that later work inverted the biblical passage (Jn 11:4) that is being referenced here. The struggle between the first self and the deeper self is clearly portrayed as a struggle that moves through stages. Gradually, reconciliation is brought about between the deeper self and the first self.

These images can help us to interpret Kierkegaard's comparatively early (1836) insistence that

> conversion goes slowly. As Franz Baader rightly observes, one has to walk back by the same road he came out on earlier. It is easy to become impatient: if it cannot happen at once, one may just as well let it go, begin tomorrow, and enjoy today; this is the temptation. . . . This is why we are told to work out our salvation in fear and trembling, for it is not finished or completed; backsliding is a possibility.—No doubt it was in part this unrest which drove people to seek zealously to become martyrs, in order to make the test as brief and momentarily intense as possible, a test which is always easier to endure than a prolonged one. (*JP*, 1:420 / *SKP*, I A 174)

While Kierkegaard is casting the issue here in terms of a more typically Lutheran sense of needing to begin again constantly,[72] he also seems to think of the process of conversion itself as being one that is undertaken slowly and perhaps with some reluctance. Perhaps this gradually receding reluctance is where the movement to faith can be construed as a process. It is also felicitous to note a considerable agreement here between Kierkegaard and Karl Rahner, who writes that conversion

> means standing firm and grasping the unique situation which is only found at this particular moment "today," not soothing oneself with the idea that it will come again, that the chance of salvation is always available. It is the sober realization that every conversion is only a beginning and that the rest of daily fidelity, the conversion which can only be carried out in a whole lifetime, has still to come.[73]

Here, both Kierkegaard and Rahner reject any sense of being able to simply have done with the ongoing struggle that is conversion. To understand this notion of conversion it is worth noting that, for Catholicism, the justification that ultimately occurs in conversion is "both an event and a process."[74] It occurs in baptism, but continues in important ways throughout life. Here Rahner insists that conversion is a process that takes place over an entire lifetime, and that, presumably, this process is what is brought to a close for many in purgatory.

Kierkegaard appreciates his Lutheran roots, but he also wants to affirm a kind of redemptive process. He does this, in part, because he wants to focus the reader's attention on the difficulty of *becoming* a Christian. It is a very interesting question whether Kierkegaard can consistently have all that he wants here.[75] He appears to want to hold, as the Lutheranism in him (and the dialectic of the *Postscript*) would have it, that the sinner must always begin anew, and yet he also discusses discipleship in terms of being and knowing more of the truth, and believes that the redemptive process can be glimpsed in terms of the struggle between the first self and the deeper self, a struggle that is a sickness "unto life." There is thus some reason for thinking that the element of process in Kierkegaard's dialectic can be cast in terms of a living purgatory (recall that Francis de Sales found purgation of the same sort to be found in purgatory to exist in daily life). Indeed, Judge William calls the spiritual struggle of the extraordinary person a "purgatory," and later claims that it is, to some extent, a struggle we all face (*EO,* 2:331–32). I now want to consider the question of purgatory more directly in terms of Kierkegaard's writings.

Purgatory in Kierkegaard? A Brief Assessment

It is time briefly to address our question of whether Kierkegaard can appropriate a version of purgatory into his thought. Purgatory in the Catholic tradition, one should recall, is not a "second chance," but the purification necessary, *after having once received the initial grace of justification,* because of lighter sins subsequently committed or temporal punishments later accrued for sins.[76] In this sense, it can have to do with an increase in justification. As for other reasons for purgatory in the Catholic tradition, such as venial sins, there appears not to be much in

Kierkegaard's corpus that corresponds to this idea, as he seems to hold that sins are on a par with one another.[77] So also with the idea of praying for the dead, which suggests the kind of petitionary prayer one does not often find in Kierkegaard's work.[78] Instead of these two avenues, I want to argue briefly that there are two other areas for profitable discussion between Kierkegaardians and Catholics with respect to purgatory. The first has to do, somewhat surprisingly perhaps, with temporal punishments for sins. The second has to do more with the distinction between explicit and implicit faith, a topic that has not been discussed in any of the dogmatic definitions on purgatory.

In my view, Kierkegaard will simply have no patience with a bookkeeping arrangement that inflicts an external punishment of a certain severity for every external misdeed. However, it must be noted that this is not the way the contemporary Catholic Church has interpreted its own doctrine of "temporal punishments" for sin, as we saw earlier. Instead, Catholicism has seen these as unhealthy or inordinate attachments to creaturely things over against God. Kierkegaard has a very early (1834) journal entry that reflects a similar concern: "This expression [forgiveness of sins] is always used where justification is discussed. Consequently it does not seem to signify the remission of sins as much as it signifies the loosening of sins. That is—by the act of justification man is placed in the right relationship; in this way the relationship to his sins is, so to speak, cut off. But man can still very well continue to feel their after-effects" (*JP*, 1:411 / *SKP*, I A 6). Kierkegaard may perhaps mean a certain progress in sanctification here (as opposed to an increase in justification), but a certain progress in the spiritual life might still be necessary to fight against the aftereffects.[79]

Kierkegaard elsewhere notes that temporal suffering occurs in life, and, although he appears not to link the occurrence of the suffering to sin in every case,[80] he does indicate that it can have purifying effects. He writes:

> The one time of suffering is a passing through that leaves no mark at all upon the soul, or, even more glorious, it is a passing through that completely cleanses the soul, and as a result the purity becomes the mark the passing through leaves behind. Just as gold is purified in the fire, so the soul is purified in sufferings. But what does the fire take away from the gold? Well, it is a curious way of talking to call it losing; in the fire the

gold loses all that is base—that is, the gold gains through the fire. So also with all temporal suffering, the hardest, the longest; powerless in itself, it is incapable of taking away anything, and if the suffering one lets eternity rule, it takes away the impure, that is, it gives purity. (*CD*, 102)

Perhaps Kierkegaard would prefer to restrict the struggle against the aftereffects to the earthly life (although we are never given a sustained theological *argument* for this claim in Kierkegaard's work).[81] Another option, the road taken by Wesley, might be to insist that the remaining sanctification could take place in the instant of death. However, taking this option, as Walls notes, would itself be to converge significantly with strains of Catholic eschatological thought.[82]

Another possibility for Kierkegaardians to consider is the distinction in contemporary Catholic theology between explicit and implicit faith. This distinction is the cornerstone of the Church's inclusivism with regard to salvation. Further, *Lumen Gentium* insists that those who have not *yet* arrived at an explicit knowledge of God may still achieve salvation, and that what is good and true among them can be considered a preparation for the gospel.[83] With respect to Kierkegaard, one might think that the implicit struggle to arrive at an explicit knowledge of God might be characterized as, in part, a struggle, against a very real temptation within oneself to disallow the "deeper self" to lead the "first self" out of its predicament. Earlier we saw Benedict XVI discussing how the justifying faith of the sinner is a "basic option" that "is buried under a great deal of wood, hay and straw." Similarly, in Kierkegaard, we might interpret the deeper self and its patient persistence with the first self as the manifestation of a kind of implicit, or nascent, faith that answers, in important ways to the implicit, or "buried," faith that such a Catholic writer as Benedict XVI holds to really justify.

What would happen if death put a hold on this struggle, already begun in earnest? The Catholic tradition seems to hold that it would need to be continued after the grave, with a certainty that the mercy of God would put a blessed end to it. Kierkegaard also believes in an eternal happiness devoid of struggle (*WL*, 194). Is it psychologically plausible to insist that Kierkegaard's purifying process can be simply brought to a close by God? This is an especially urgent question given the intimate connection that Kierkegaard thinks exists between a human being and God, who always respects the freedom that is the individual's very self (*SUD*, 29).

While I cannot argue for this claim here, David Brown has persuasively argued (though without reference to Kierkegaard) that the answer is that this "abrupt transition" is not plausible.[84] The question of purgatory, considered in light of Kierkegaard's innovative brand of Lutheranism, is never given a serious hearing in Kierkegaard's corpus. I suspect that the reasons for why Kierkegaard never considered it have more to do with Kierkegaard's Lutheran heritage than with theology proper. Perhaps it is time for Kierkegaardians to raise the question anew.

Indeed, the fact that Kierkegaard sees conversion as a slow process, together with Kierkegaard's and Catholicism's endorsements of the Augustinian doctrine of original sin,[85] also makes it difficult to imagine a just God condemning the ordinary run of human beings, where even those who are explicitly Christian find it difficult to allow a living faith to emerge without any of the "wood, hay, and straw" that weigh us down. Kierkegaard's thought curiously allows two different trajectories that are not obviously reconcilable. One, deeply imbued with Kierkegaard's Lutheranism, finds the presence of despair already the manifestation of a fundamental (and in some sense, damnable) rebellion.[86] Another trajectory appears to interpret this same movement to wholeness as a process and a struggle that would seem to admit of a really redemptive progression. It seems to me that the presence of both of these trajectories indicates that Kierkegaard wishes to prize his Lutheran heritage, but also to recognize that, even in the "negative dialectic" of the ethical, "one needs grace again in relation to grace" (*JP*, 2:1472 / *SKP*, X-2 A 198).

‡

Kierkegaard's thought combines two different elements that are in tension with one another. Kierkegaard's traditional Lutheranism gives support to the traditional Lutheran view of justification and thus militates against an understanding amenable to the doctrine of purgatory. On the other hand, as others have noted, Kierkegaard transforms his Lutheran heritage in marked ways. Because of this, there is a tendency in Kierkegaard's work to interpret the sinner's justification (or perhaps sanctification) as an ongoing process. One might raise interesting questions about whether this vision is ultimately coherent, but I suspect that at least one motivation for it is. By affirming that the Christian life is one of process and growth, Kierkegaard meets us where we are, insisting, in particular to the individual Christian, that her life was always already guided by grace, and that small steps, even along the law's negative dialectic, are ultimately the quelling of the storm that allows God's light to shine in us. This insistence brings with it serious reasons to consider the possibility of a Kierkegaardian doctrine of purgatory.

EIGHT

Kierkegaard and the Communion of Saints

The one knight of faith cannot help the other at all.

JOHANNES DE SILENTIO

The emphasis with which Kierkegaard describes the "individual" in his or her relationship to God may sound splendid, yet it nevertheless adds up to an obvious loss for the communion of saints.

HANS URS VON BALTHASAR

Can Balthasar's accusation above be sustained with justice?[1] Is it the case that Kierkegaard is an individualist of the sort that Silentio's pseudonymous passage would seem to suggest he is, or does Kierkegaard himself have more to say on this question than does his pseudonym? The nascent or "buried" faith Benedict XVI discusses bears some interesting comparisons with Kierkegaard's motifs of process in redemption. Yet, after recalling, this time under the papal seal, his earlier concept of purgatory, Benedict asks this question of his concept of purgatory: "if 'Purgatory' is simply purification through fire in the encounter with the Lord, Judge, and Savior, how can a third person intervene, even if he or she is particularly close to the other?"[2]

Benedict's answer to this question draws on his convictions that "no one lives alone. No one sins alone. No one is saved alone."[3] He goes on to say, "As Christians we should never limit ourselves to asking: how can I save myself? We should also ask: what can I do in order that others may be saved and that for them too the star of hope may rise? Then I will have done my utmost for my own personal salvation as well."[4] When we apply this to the question of purgatory it raises the question of commerce between the blessed in heaven, those undergoing purification in purgatory, and the pilgrim Church on earth.[5] Kierkegaard never seems to have dealt in any great detail with this question, but there is reason to suspect he would not have received it very favorably, both because he seems not to have dealt much with the present state of the dead and because his Lutheran heritage is not always amenable to the transfer of spiritual benefits.[6]

On this latter point it is worth noting that, although Luther can be portrayed as more of an individualist than he was, it is clear that an important aspect of his reform was to call Christians to more personal accountability for their own standing before God. On this point, when Luther was discussing the practice of offering a Mass for someone else, he writes, "Therefore, let this irrefutable truth stand fast: Where there is a divine promise, there every one must stand on his own feet; his own personal faith is demanded. . . . It is absolutely impossible to commune on behalf of anyone else."[7] Of course, it does not follow for Luther that there is anything wrong or ineffective about intercessory prayer, since Luther distinguishes communing on behalf of a person (which he rejects) and praying, in the course of a Mass, for a person (which he accepts).[8] Although we have no systematic treatment of intercessory prayer from the pen of Kierkegaard, I know of no reason why he could not accept it, and this practice might secure certain benefits for the living.[9]

Thus, putting aside for the time being the question of whether benefits can be sought for the dead, let us recall that St. Francis de Sales insisted that penance and contrition could also be called a certain kind of "purgatory," as "everything can be that serves to purge away our offences."[10] For the Catholic tradition, only venial sins and temporal punishments for sin are cleansed in purgatory, as opposed to permanently unrepented and fully consensual mortal sins, which are given their recompense in hell. Yet, there are two ways in which this purification can be expanded. First, as we have noted, the purification of "purgatory" may occur in this life as well. Second, the exchange in purifying "spiritual goods" that the Catholic Church understands by the communion of saints allows the benefits of certain works and prayers of the faithful to be applied to others. Thus, the *Catechism of the Catholic Church* states, "Recourse to the communion of saints lets the contrite sinner be more promptly and efficaciously purified of the punishments for sin."[11] Let us leave to one side, then, the question of whether, in the life of faith, we can help others *after death;* to what degree can we say that we can help others *in this life,* for Kierkegaard?

To judge by the received view of Kierkegaard as an individualist par excellence, the answer would seem to be that we cannot help others along the path of faith. After all, as we have seen, Silentio insists that the one knight of faith cannot help the other at all. Further, Kierkegaard himself often insisted on the primacy of the individual alone before her God. Indeed, in what appears to be a very minimal concession, Kierkegaard himself explains that the most one can do for another is, somewhat paradoxically, to help an individual stand *by herself* (WL, 275). We will consult this important and suggestive passage later. Meanwhile, before discussing what potential Kierkegaard's thought has in this regard, it will be useful to have an account of what kind of "exchange" the Catholic tradition prizes in its view of the communion of saints. I argue that while Balthasar's accusation has some purchase from the Catholic point of view, it can be partially mitigated by a fuller understanding of Kierkegaard.

The Communion of Saints: A Catholic Account

John Paul II, in his discussion of social sin, noted that there exists a "law of descent," "whereby a soul that lowers itself through sin drags down with itself the Church and, in some way, the whole world."[12] However sobering such a truth would be, however, there is a related idea that also won the late pope's approval, namely, a "law of ascent," according to which, "every soul that rises above itself, raises up the world."[13] It is this law that John Paul II connects with the communion of saints. While nearly all Christians are at burden to accept some version of the "communion of saints," since the term, as part of the Nicene Creed, is firmly entrenched in the Christian tradition, there are still some marks that distinguish the Catholic understanding of the communion of saints.

In the Catholic tradition, there are traditionally three "states" of the Church. There are the blessed in heaven (sometimes called the Triumphant Church), the faithful departed still undergoing purification in purgatory (sometimes called the Suffering Church), and the fellowship of those of us in the "wayfaring" state on earth (sometimes called the Militant Church). The most obvious difference between the three groups is that the third group includes individuals who quite possibly may not reach eternal beatitude with God, whereas those in purgatory will reach heaven, and those in heaven are no longer being purified. Nevertheless, these three groups form "one Church," as Vatican II insisted.[14] In fact, according to the same text, all three states of the Church "sing the same hymn of glory to our God." The unity of this Church is quite staggering; according to *Lumen Gentium,* it includes all nations at the present time and all those united with the Church in any of its three states.[15] We read, "All those from every tribe and tongue and people and nation who have been redeemed by the blood of Christ and gathered together into one Church, with one song of praise magnify the one and triune God."[16]

While we have noted that Kierkegaard usually is silent about the present state of the dead, and thus whether and how there might be communion with them, he gives us an interesting passage to consider when reflecting on whether we join the heavenly throng of angels in one hymn of praise. In a late journal entry (1855), he writes:

> But what, specifically, does God want? He wants souls able to praise, adore, worship, and thank him—the business of angels. Therefore God is surrounded by angels. . . . No, the angels please him, and what pleases him even more than the praise of angels is a human being who in the last lap of this life, when God seemingly changes into sheer cruelty and with the most cruelly devised cruelty does everything to deprive him of all zest for life, nevertheless continues to believe that God is love, that God does it out of love. Such a human being becomes an angel. (*JP,* 6:6969 / *SKP,* XI-2 A 439)

Clearly, Kierkegaard does not mean that a human being simply swaps species and *becomes* an angel. Rather, it seems that what he means is that a human being who does God's will in being brought to the "extremity of life-weariness" at the end of life and recognizing this as God's loving will partakes in the business of angels. This person's praise is dear to God, and it fittingly joins in worship with the choirs of angels. Now we will have occasion to note that Kierkegaard can be unjustly lampooned as a more strident individualist than he actually was, but it is also worth noting the contrast here between Vatican II's claim that the entirety of the Church (earthly and heavenly), especially in the communal celebration of the Eucharist, is united at all times and places, and Kierkegaard's singling out a particular sort of individual for giving the kind of worship that joins him to the heavenly throng. On the one hand, this is a clear difference in emphasis between *Lumen Gentium,* Vatican II's *Dogmatic Constitution on the Church,* and Kierkegaard's work, which constantly calls us to a deeper private devotion to God. On the other hand, as we will see, the Catholic tradition simply prizes a wider unity of Church than Kierkegaard appears willing to countenance.

Accordingly, *Lumen Gentium* goes on to note, "Therefore the union of the wayfarers with the brethren who have gone to sleep in the peace of Christ is not in the least weakened or interrupted, but on the contrary, according to the perpetual faith of the Church, is strengthened by communication of spiritual goods."[17] On this point, Christoph Schönborn writes, "The exchange of spiritual goods is both ascending and descending: from the saints in heaven to us through their intercession, and from us to them through our veneration."[18] Preeminent among those interceding for the faithful is, of course, the Virgin Mary, which is why *Lumen Gentium* follows its chapter 7 on "The Eschatological Nature of the Pilgrim Church and Its Union with the Church in Heaven," with a final chapter 8 on the role of Mary.

What is true of the saints with regard to their intercession is true of Mary in a more exalted fashion.[19] For the most part, the same applies the other way around: what is true of Mary is true of the (rest of the) saints in a less-exalted fashion.[20] Still, Mary is singled out for a title such as "Mediatrix," which often raises the hackles of some Protestant readers.[21] No doubt part of the reason such readers would have for worrying about such a title would be a biblical text such as 1 Timothy 2:5–6, where we read, "For there is one God. There is also one mediator between God and the human race, Christ Jesus, himself human, who gave himself as ransom for all." Both *Lumen Gentium* and John Paul II, in his encyclical *Redemptoris Mater,* cite this passage and explain the Catholic view in response to it. *Lumen Gentium* notes, "The maternal duty of Mary toward men in no wise obscures or diminishes this unique mediation of Christ, but rather shows His power. For all the salvific influence of the Blessed Virgin on men originates, not from some inner necessity, but from the divine pleasure."[22] John Paul II comments on this that Mary's mediation is "mediation in Christ."[23]

A quite early (1836) journal entry from Kierkegaard relates to such mediation:

> Christianity is essentially the consciousness of the mediated relation-ship through which man must always approach the divine—thus, for example, to pray in Jesus' name, that is, to pray in a way that involves the consciousness that each one of us is a link in the development of a race, for only in this way can a person place himself in a relationship to God, whether he acts or prays. For this reason almost all nations have had someone or other in whose name they prayed. But it was limited to them, because the consciousness of the whole world did not merge in them, but only a national consciousness, a local consciousness—thus praying through the saints, the Catholics praying through the mother of God, are cases in point. (*JP*, 1:419 / *SKP*, I A 172)[24]

Here we notice that Kierkegaard sees mediation as a crucial way in which all of us must relate to God. Still, the mediation seems to be through Christ, whose mediation concerns "the whole world," and is therefore, we might say, global. This global mediation involves the consciousness that each of us is a "link in the development of a race," and there seems to be some truth to this. For in Christ are the "firstfruits" of the living from the dead, and it is *in* Christ that Christians claim to have their resurrection (1 Cor 15:20–23). Christ goes before, but Christians seek to follow after, and to be united with him in his very resurrection.

However, Kierkegaard goes on to point out the limited scope of cer-tain "local" mediations. The idea here seems to be that these other me-diations do not have a fittingly universal reach. One presumes that one stands before God as redeemed by Christ (which, to some extent, applies to the whole human race), but it may be less than seemly to imagine someone standing before God qua citizen of, say, Copenhagen.[25] One gets the sense that one's national consciousness ought to hang on one a bit more loosely than one's consciousness as a Christian. This, too, seems broadly correct.[26] It would, however, be premature to make any norma-tive conclusions about whether certain mediations would be illegitimate on this basis. Furthermore, it would be a leap to suggest that the only legitimate component of one's "Christian consciousness" is a conscious-ness of one's being redeemed by Christ. In fact, for Catholics, Mary's mediation in Christ, subordinate though it undeniably is, is considered to be active with respect to every grace obtained through Christ. On this point, Pope Leo XIII writes:

> The eternal Son of God, when He wished to assume the nature of man for the redemption and glory of man, and for this reason was about to enter upon a kind of mystic marriage with the entire human race, did not do this before He received the wholly free consent of His designated mother, who, in a way, played the part of the human race itself. . . . Therefore, no less truly and properly may it be affirmed that nothing at all of the very great treasure of every grace . . . nothing is imparted to us except through Mary, God so willing; so, just as no one can approach the highest Father except through the Son, so no one can approach Christ except through His Mother.[27]

Mary's consent to bear the Son of God fixes her place in God's plan of redemption, and she plays this role for the whole human race. Indeed, *Lumen Gentium* cites similar claims from the Church Fathers, such as St. Irenaeus, from whom we read, "Being obedient, [she] became the cause of salvation for herself and for the whole human race."[28]

I think, therefore, that there are at least two things a Catholic might wish to note about the above discussion. First, there is no obvious reason given for why Christ's "global" mediation could not tolerate (or, indeed, prefer) the cooperation of other forms of mediation that participate in Christ's own mediation to such a degree that these other forms might also be "global" and even belong to one's "Christian consciousness" in the relevant way. The Catholic Church asserts that it is this way with Mary's mediation "in Christ." Christ's and Mary's mediations are es-sentially different from one another, because the influence of the lat-ter "flows forth from the superabundance of the merits of Christ, rests on His mediation, depends entirely on it and draws all its power from it,"[29] but this need not isolate the latter from the former, since both are linked.

The second thing that I think a Catholic might point out in response to Kierkegaard's journal entry above is that the mediation and interces-sion of other saints is also "in Christ." Still, it is not the case that every saint cooperates in every grace in the way that Mary does. So, while some saintly mediation may be "local" in some ways, its availability is still, in some sense, global for the Christian. I may include members of my family as wayfaring people who draw me closer to Christ, and this is not likely to be true of a person living on the other side of the world whom I have not met. Still, the exchange of spiritual goods that is possible with the broader communion of saints (especially the blessed) is in no way restricted to those saints who called my locale home. I am as free to petition St. Cyprian of Carthage for assistance as I am to call on St. Thérèse of Lisieux. Schönborn writes, "The truth that all salvation proceeds from Christ does not exclude the fact that he founded a community whose members share in his power as mediator."[30] Indeed, *Lumen Gentium* insists that, just as Christians can pray for one another and thus benefit one another in this life, so our "companionship" with the saints, whose love and veneration we can undertake, and whose petitions to God we can secure, also "joins us to Christ."[31]

One might ask why one would "clutter" the mediation of Christ with such seemingly ancillary mediations within it. The answer that *Lumen Gentium* unmistakably provides is simply that God wills it that way, since all of Mary's mediation, and presumably all saintly mediation (as it applies in each case) along with it, originates purely from the "divine pleasure."[32] We are assisted on our way by those who tread the path of faith with us, or who have already arrived at its beatific goal, and this is because God prefers that we should be so assisted.

At this point, we should ask how to respond to Benedict XVI's worry about the entry of the third person into the purification process. On this point, Benedict writes, "Certainly, Jesus Christ is the true light, the sun that has risen above all the shadows of history. But to reach him we also need lights close by—people who shine with his light and so guide us along our way."[33] The catechetical instruction I might receive from a priest or layperson and the kind encouragement I receive from a friend are probably some of the clearest ways in which we can imagine someone shining with the light of Christ, encouraging us to humble ourselves under God's purifying grace in this life. While this kind of mediation may be difficult to imagine in purgatory, it is also unlikely to be as controversial as the mediation one can receive through indulgences.

The power of the Church to grant indulgences was dogmatically established by the Council of Trent in 1563.[34] Luther's critique of indulgences eventually went so far as to argue that the pope was unable to grant indulgences, and this was too far from the Catholic point of view.[35] Still, there were gross excesses in the practice of indulgences, and since Luther's time, the Church has instituted certain reforms of the practice. One of the clearest recent discussions of this can be found in Pope Paul VI's 1967 apostolic constitution *Indulgentiarum Doctrina*.[36] There, Paul VI writes, "In an indulgence in fact, the Church, making use of its power as minister of the Redemption of Christ, not only prays but by an authoritative intervention dispenses to the faithful suitably disposed the treasury of satisfaction which Christ and the saints won for the remission of temporal punishment." Thus, in order to acquire an indulgence for oneself or to offer its effects for others, one must be properly disposed.[37] This typically includes, among other things, that the person be in the state of grace and that the person receive communion and make confession of sins either shortly before or shortly after performing the prescribed work. These remarks can give the idea that indulgences are a simple economic transaction between God and a particular human being, as if the whole thing were a bookkeeping arrangement of the sort that Kierkegaard and others would deplore. However, Paul VI writes that "indulgences are in fact free gifts, nevertheless they are granted for the living as well as for the dead only on determined conditions."[38]

The communion of saints can be of great help to the Catholic faithful, through the prayers of saints in glory, the prayers and works of the living faithful for the dead in purgatory, or the prayers and works of the living faithful for other members of the pilgrim Church on earth.[39] However, the efficacy of any and all of these derives entirely from the merits of Christ and the pleasure of God. On the face of it, this would seem to suggest that God's pleasure in purifying individuals in purgatory and on earth can take precedence over the individual's freedom. Yet, one of the reasons that we suspected Kierkegaard might be amenable to a doctrine of purgatory was that God could not externally impute the abrupt transition from sinner to saint without violating the individual's freedom. Is this not precisely what Benedict XVI and the Catholic tradition mean to do, in seemingly allowing the work of a third person to commute some or all of the temporal punishments due to sin for another person?

One solution to this question that will not work for the contemporary Catholic tradition is to claim that the temporal punishments for sin were externally imposed from without by God in the first place, and so they can simply be removed, without further ado, by a similar act of fiat. As we noted in chapter 7, the temporal punishments for sin are not understood as being quite so contingently connected to the relevant sin. The punishment is supposed to follow *from the nature of sin itself.*[40] But if it is the very nature of sin itself that supports the punishment, this would seem to accentuate the problem. How can a third party (in addition to the individual and God) remove the punishment if its connection to the sin itself is intrinsic? One can't very well alter the past, and pretending that the sin never took place will hardly serve to benefit the soul of a sinful individual.

In order to answer this question, we should refer back to our discussion in the last chapter. There we discussed sin's consonance with another malady, namely, addiction. We noted there that each sin is itself an unhealthy attachment, and, in a certain way, addiction, to creatures. In this sense, sin is its own punishment, just as virtue is often heralded as its own reward. We further noted that many who suffer from addiction cannot eliminate all of its symptoms simply by an act of resolve. Instead, there are certain actions and experiences that serve to rehabilitate a person and to put away her inordinate attachments to creatures. To take up the model of addiction and apply it to the case of temporal punishments for sin, we might consider the temporal punishments as we would symptoms of withdrawal in the case of the addict.

This analogy can help us a bit in responding to the objection. For symptoms of withdrawal from addiction can be mitigated by various means. Some symptoms may be nearly impossible to offset entirely, but this fact speaks to the inability of the medical sciences (perhaps in their current state) to allay every possible physical malady rather than to the nature of addiction and its symptoms of withdrawal. Some symptoms of withdrawal can be partially assuaged by the kind of medication that one can take freely. In this case, the rehabilitation has oneself as its source. But it should also be admitted that one who suffers from symptoms of withdrawal from addiction can also be aided considerably by the presence and assistance of friends and kindly acquaintances. This can be through a kind word, a gentle touch, or care in nursing one back to health. Further, there is no reason why a third party could not administer medical care in such a way as to compromise neither the freedom of the person (who does or would desire such care) nor the integrity of the healing process. Indeed, it is not even obvious that this needs to take place with the patient's knowledge, so long as there is good reason to suspect that the patient implicitly consents to it.[41] In fact, in some cases of addiction (notably for nicotine), medicine can be developed whose purpose is primarily to lessen the craving for the source of the addiction. One must indeed be suitably disposed for this regimen to be effective, but there is no reason why the simple lessening of the craving could not be administered by a third person. Indeed, earthly friendship too can be a healing balm, and it *must* be administered by a "third party." Can such care be administered for a person without her knowledge? There clearly are cases of this, where a person is still ravaged by the illness that follows a serious addiction, and is nursed to health by a strange person in a strange place. The similarity of this account to one of the chief reasons for purgatory, namely, temporal punishments, and for the indulgences that can mitigate the experience of these temporal punishments seems to me to be at least a prima facie reason for allowing the possibility that a third person could play a role, even if purgatory is understood, as in Benedict XVI, as an individual encounter with the Lord.[42]

Kierkegaard's view of indulgences seems generally to be quite negative, though nearly all of his references to the concept discuss abuses that have not formed part of the Church's considered judgment on indulgences. For instance, he writes, of the view he associates with indulgences, "If you want to be saved, it will cost 4 marks and 8 shillings and a tip to the priest; if you want to be completely saved, then 5 marks; but that you will be saved is absolutely guaranteed and you will get a receipt" (*JP*, 3:2539 / *SKP*, X-4 A 371). When indulgences are themselves claimed to be efficacious routes to salvation, rather than the lightening or abrogating of the temporal punishments due to sin (where the eternal punishment had already been cleansed), we have indeed gotten beyond the proper Catholic understanding of them. It should be noted that it is, of course, an entirely fair complaint that, especially during the Reformation period, high-ranking officials of the Church were complicit in (and in many cases instigated) this departure from the correct Catholic understanding of indulgences.

A bit more revealing passage from Kierkegaard comes at *JP*, 2:1476 / *SKP*, X-3 A 72, where Kierkegaard is talking about indulgent relaxation of the Christian requirement. Although he is probably not talking about ecclesial indulgences in the strict sense, it hardly seems likely that the connection has escaped his notice. There, he writes, "Therefore, the requirement is what must be proclaimed. The teacher has to declare the requirement and in this way incite unrest. He dare not scale down the requirement. Indulgence [*Indulgentsen*] must not be proclaimed. Indeed, it cannot be proclaimed, since it is completely different for different people in their innermost private relationship with God." Kierkegaard's claim here appears to be that "indulgence" in the God-relationship cannot be proclaimed from outside because one individual's God-relationship is incommensurable with another individual's God-relationship. Some pre–Vatican II missals come to mind here, since many claimed that a certain number of hours or days in purgatory could be abrogated by the saying of a particular prayer.[43] It seems likely that this sort of thing would come in for the criticism Kierkegaard gives above, to the effect that it is impossible for an indulgence to cover a certain amount of time for all individuals because there is no currency that every God-relationship honors (and even if there were, the "exchange rates" need not be equal across individual lives).

In response, I think a Catholic should ask for a positive construal of the God-relationship, rather than rest content with the claim that one individual's God-relationship is incommensurate with another individual's God-relationship. As Benedict XVI reminds us, "no man is an island,"[44] and we are not so radically separated from one another that one individual's relationship to God is an entirely new universe. It is unclear why the encounter with Christ of which Benedict speaks is not personal *enough* (even if perhaps not utterly private), and we have seen that the Catholic understanding of the communion of saints can still be defended on this understanding. In the next section, then, we will consider just how far Kierkegaard's account is from allowing us to assist one another in the life of faith.

Kierkegaard and Intercession in the Life of Faith

Since Kierkegaard has a rather silent attitude toward what the faithful departed are currently experiencing, it seems probable that he would not think much of the exchange in spiritual goods that the Catholic tradition sees between the three states of the Church. However, that exchange is an instance of a broader sort of exchange in spiritual goods that the Catholic tradition in any case thinks can take place between those of us who remain on earth. It is therefore the case that the Catholic tradition would assert that Silentio's claim that "the one knight of faith cannot help the other at all" (*FT,* 72) is false. Of course, this view was articulated by a pseudonym, and Kierkegaard's own view may be, and in fact is, more nuanced.

Yet, as Gregory R. Beabout and Brad Frazier have argued, it is not without reason that Kierkegaard is often thought to be an individualist.[45] Indeed, Kierkegaard sometimes argues that Catholicism is an indulgent discharge from the God-relationship, representing a failure of self-sufficiency, concentration, or even nerve. In one entry he claims that some "more recent humorists" became Catholic out of desire for a community and "a sense of direction [*en Holdning*] which they themselves lacked" (*JN,* 1:219 / DD: 24). He also writes:

> There are altogether very few people capable of bearing the *Protestant* view of life. And the latter, if it is really to give strength to the *common man,* must either constitute itself in a smaller community (separatism, conventicles, etc.) or approach Catholicism, in order in both cases to develop the shared carrying of life's burdens in a social life, which only the most gifted individuals are able to dispense with. (*JN,* 1:245 / DD: 108, emphasis original)

The idea here seems to be that a social life is a kind of "concession to human weakness," something that Kierkegaard actually claims at *JP,* 2:1377 / *SKP,* IX A 315.

Beabout and Frazier, however, rightly point out that this is best seen as an extreme toward which Kierkegaard tended, rather than as his considered view. They note that "[Kierkegaard] was often so at odds with Danish Christendom that he went to extremes to attack the eclipse of personal responsibility, as he saw it."[46] This attack can be glimpsed most clearly in Kierkegaard's work *Two Ages.* There, Kierkegaard argues that we have "idolized" the "positive principle of sociality" (*TA,* 86) and that this has resulted in a "leveling" of the individual before God. He writes that "we are willing to keep Christian terminology but privately we know that nothing decisive is supposed to be meant by it. And we will not be repentant, for after all we are not demolishing anything" (*TA,* 81). Here, Merold

Westphal helpfully notes, "The fatal flaw of the Hegelian philosophy and of [Kierkegaard's] 'present age' is a tendency toward self-deification of the We."[47] Westphal goes on to write, "Kierkegaard seeks to unsocialize the individual in order to undeify society."[48] When outward society is deified, the crucial role for the inward individual is lost. Beabout and Frazier are quite right to note that inwardness must be expressed in the external world, but Kierkegaard believes that the message his age needs to hear is that "character is inwardness" (*TA*, 78). Without the inwardness of an individual before God, we are unable to come together for a purpose, as in any genuinely passionate revolution, because the individual is too far absorbed in "the public" (see esp. *TA*, 92–96).

Thus, despite the fact that there are passages in Kierkegaard's authorship that suggest that he regards the "solitary self" as the height of personhood, there is evidence to believe that this is not Kierkegaard's considered view. As Kierkegaard puts it, in the "highest form" of religion, "the individual relates first to God and then to the community; but this former relation is the highest, so long as he does not slight the latter" (*JN*, 2:261 / JJ: 430). Thus, Kierkegaard decries the kind of societal leveling that prevents us from engaging in *genuine* community, but we still might wish for a bit more positive account of how we may help one another in community.

Beabout and Frazier help themselves to Westphal's notion of Religiousness C to discuss how Kierkegaard's later writings show that Christian faith issues in external action. They write, "While Religiousness B focuses on faith, Religiousness C emphasizes the works that ought to derive from faith."[49] I believe that the term "Religiousness C" is a bit infelicitous, and so I will not adopt it,[50] but this does not mean that there is no insight to be gained from the attention that the term asks us to give the post-Climacus writings, notably *Works of Love*. Westphal takes the term to refer to some of Kierkegaard's later texts where inwardness is not blocked by "the public" and can be expressed in loving action. Insofar as it directs our attention to the later texts as representative of Kierkegaard's considered views, I think Westphal's account can be quite helpful. In what way, then, can Kierkegaard's later work show that there is a positive role for community in the life of faith?

If we mean to ask this question with regard to any overt ecclesiology in Kierkegaard, we will meet with considerable challenges. Bruce

Kirmmse is certainly right that there are interpretive obstacles that any attempt at detailing a positive Kierkegaardian ecclesiology faces. Indeed, Kirmmse goes so far as to claim that Kierkegaard's "final view of the Church" holds that "1) true Christianity is too unsocial for any concept of congregation; and 2) the concept of congregation has been the 'ruination of Christianity.'"[51] We have already seen that there is some support for this reading in Kierkegaard's texts. Indeed, Kierkegaard writes, "The congregation is a composition of eternity within time. This is evident in the medium. The congregation is in the medium of being, which implies growth and composure. The single individual is in the medium of becoming—and this earthly existence is a time of testing—therefore there is no congregation here" (*JP*, 2:2011 / *SKP*, IX A 450). Despite the fact that Kierkegaard appears to regard the "congregation" as an impossibility in this earthly life, there are at least two important things to note about this. First, Kierkegaard's reception of the category of the "congregation" is very contingently, and very culturally, tied to the frequent use of this category by one of his Danish opponents, N. F. S. Grundtvig.[52] Thus, when Kierkegaard decries the "congregation," he needn't be seen as rejecting every meaning that term could possibly have. Second, Kierkegaard clearly does believe in the "Church militant," which, in contrast to "the congregation," is "*in the process of becoming*" (*PC*, 211, emphasis mine). The militant aspect of the Church will cease in heaven, where Christians can no longer be accused of impatience for the Church Triumphant (*PC*, 211–32, and *WL*, 194), but in this life the true Church must be militant. Thus, there are some ways in which we can still imagine Kierkegaard as a faithful, if critical, servant of the Church, as Michael Plekon insists.[53] However, even Plekon rightly acknowledges that "any judgment about the late Kierkegaard must be a wager based on how one reads the texts he leaves."[54] To go beyond these contributions in the direction of ecclesiology proper would be little more than guesswork.

Ecclesiology as a whole, however, is not our primary concern in this concluding chapter. I am happy to concede that there are ways in which the ecclesiology of the Catholic tradition will part ways with whatever we can discern in Kierkegaard along these lines. Yet, in this chapter ecclesiology derives its importance from its connection with the communion of saints, and, further, from the connection that idea bears with what the Catholic Church has called an "exchange in spiritual goods." Let us, then, return to our central question: To what degree can one individual help another along the path of faith, for Kierkegaard?

Along these lines, I think there is one place in Kierkegaard's writings where an interesting suggestion is made, and another place that may help in developing the interesting suggestion. The suggestion I refer to occurs in the same text where Silentio claims that one knight of faith cannot help the other at all, namely, *Fear and Trembling*. There, Silentio articulates what might have happened "if Abraham had doubted" in the course of the *Akedah*. Silentio contends that if Abraham had doubted he would have done something that Silentio admits would have been "great and glorious" (*FT*, 20), but that would not have been an act of faith, as Silentio understands that term. If Abraham had doubted, Silentio tells us, he would have gone to Moriah *alone,* and "would have thrust the knife into his own breast" (*FT*, 21). Commenting on what would have happened if this possibility had been actualized, Silentio writes, "He would have been admired in the world, and his name would never be forgotten; but it is one thing to be admired and another thing to become a *guiding star that saves the anguished*" (*FT*, 21, emphasis mine).

It is not much of a leap here to infer that it is the actual Abraham (or, at any rate, Abraham as Silentio actually understands him) that is the guiding star that saves the anguished, and this is presumably because he was faithful where the other fictional Abraham impostor substituted something in faith's place. If this inference is valid, however, then it is hard to resist the conclusion that all knights (or "ladies") of faith are also "guiding stars that save the anguished." If Silentio accepts this claim, then it follows forthwith that Mary is also a "guiding star the saves the anguished," since Mary is the only other biblical individual whose faith Silentio explicitly cites and dwells on at some length. It is also worth noting that Pope Benedict XVI has been quite fond of calling Mary the "star of hope," of late,[55] and this connection is worth analyzing briefly.

Silentio writes, "[Mary] needs worldly admiration as little as Abraham needs tears, for she was no heroine and he was no hero, but both of them became greater than these, not by being exempted in any way from the distress and the agony and the paradox, but became greater by means of these" (*FT*, 65). The faith in Abraham seems to consist in his ability to receive Isaac back with joy after having given up every human hope of having him returned, and having rested all his earthly hope therein. The agony seems to be in the anxiety of maintaining his hope after all human possibilities were exhausted. Where then is Mary's agony? Silentio says that what is great in Mary is not that she was "the favored one among women," but instead seems to locate her greatness in the bearing of Jesus. This has the support of Kierkegaard's journals, where Kierkegaard gives way to acclamation of her acceptance of this role in the Annunciation (Lk 1:26–38). In that entry, Kierkegaard notes that her willingness "to become nothing, a mere instrument," is remarkable. He also notes that as part of this willingness she "will live [her] life scorned by other maidens, treated as a frivolous, conceited wench or a poor, half-crazy wretch or a loose woman, and so on" (see *JP*, 3:2672 / *SKP*, X-4 A 454, and *JP*, 3:2674 / *SKP*, XI-1 A 40). As much as I, along with Silentio, find it "revolting" to note these facts (*FT*, 65), we must remember that Gabriel hardly went about discouraging the Israelites from thinking poorly of Mary, and this fact reminds us that she would be exposed to disgrace, and conflict with the prevailing ethical order. Some Church Fathers claimed that Isaac's imagined acquiescence in the *Akedah* was itself an expression of virtue.[56] In Mary's scenario, Joseph would be the clearest such cohort, since he believed, as he was instructed to do, that Mary's pregnancy was by virtue of the Holy Spirit. Yet Mary must undergo this trial in silence just as Abraham needed to do. Along these lines, the Catholic theologian Monika Hellwig helpfully writes, "In response to Joseph's anguish Mary, the Church, is silent, because there is nothing that she can say."[57]

Along with Abraham, Mary is said to have become great "by means of" the paradox (*FT*, 65). In the terms of *Fear and Trembling*, this should mean that she became great by virtue of the absurd. Where can we find the absurd in Mary's case? I suggest that we turn to the *Magnificat* (Lk 1:46–55), where Mary sings "[The Lord] has helped Israel his servant, remembering his mercy, according to his promise to our fathers, to Abraham and to his descendants forever" (1:54–55). Thus, God has chosen to redeem his people precisely in the context of what appears as a disgrace among them, namely, Mary's virginal conception. On the one hand, to complete the double movement, Mary must, in some sense, renounce the hope of God's redemption in the creation of a disgrace among his people. On the other hand, to complete the double movement, Mary must hold fast to the possibility of redemption through divine (and not human) means, namely, the birth of the Messiah to a virgin mother. Mary's obedience takes place in virtue of the absurd—that God will redeem his people precisely through the creation of a scandal among them. Indeed, it was in virtue of this very "disgrace" that Mary was to say that all generations would call her blessed (Lk 1:48).

Kierkegaard himself affirms that Mary's consent at the Annunciation was quite voluntary (*JP*, 3:2672 / *SKP*, X-4 A 454), and this is important in understanding what resources for discussing the communion of saints he might have. In the same entry, Kierkegaard notes the way in which "gentle piety—not without gracefulness" has described the Annunciation, dwelling on the thought that "when the angel had spoken to Mary, it was as if the whole creation cried to Mary: O do say 'Yes'! Hurry and say 'Yes'!, etc." Similarly, Benedict XVI notes that, without Mary and her free consent, "the entire process of God's stepping into history would fail of its object."[58] Still, in the same entry under discussion, Kierkegaard quite rightly notes that Mary cannot become the chosen instrument of God without divine assistance.

Now Kierkegaard does not appear to render a verdict on the doctrine of Mary's immaculate conception (as much as a positive verdict seems unlikely), though it is worth noting that Luther's reception of the doctrine is a matter of some controversy, since it cannot be denied that he held Mary in high honor.[59] The interesting thing for our purposes, however, about the doctrine of Mary's immaculate conception, is that it espouses the view that Mary is redeemed by, and in anticipation of, Christ's merits. The *Catechism of the Catholic Church* thus states, "In fact, in order for Mary to be able to give the free assent of her faith to the announcement of her vocation, it was necessary that she be wholly borne by God's grace."[60] Pope Pius IX's bull *Ineffabilis Deus,* which dogmatically established the doctrine, notes that "the most Blessed Virgin Mary, at the first instant of her conception, by a singular grace and privilege of Almighty God, in virtue of the merits of Christ Jesus, the Savior of the human race, was preserved immaculate from all stain of original sin."[61] For our purposes, the important thing to note about this doctrine is not so much that Mary was immaculate (for I think that Kierkegaard would likely reject this claim), but that Mary was redeemed by the merits of Christ, and yet these were temporally posterior to the consent she gave to make such merits possible.

Kierkegaard asserts that Mary needs grace to be able to give her consent, and whether such grace was needed in the measure that the Catholic tradition asserts is not a matter on which we need dwell for our purposes. An interesting question, though, is whether Kierkegaard would agree that Christ's merits account for the *availability* of the requisite grace. If such graces were simply provided by God's fiat,[62] unconnected with Christ's merits, then Mary would still be cooperating in making future redemption, in virtue of Christ's merits, available to others in the communion of saints. I do not see how Kierkegaard could deny such a claim. If such grace as is requisite for *Mary's consent* were to spring from Christ's anticipated merits, then Mary would actually be consenting, in a somewhat paradoxical fashion, to her own redemption. In the latter case, Mary is, with the paradoxical help of God's grace, helping *herself* to be able to stand before God redeemed by Christ. In the former case, which at any rate seems undeniable for a Christian who believes in Mary's voluntary consent, Mary is helping *others* to stand before God as redeemed by Christ. Mary is participating in the economy of salvation in an important way, but her paradoxical faith presumably cannot take place utterly outside its historical context. Here we are back to Abraham, whose faith resulted in the establishment of the Jewish people, whose Messiah Jesus came to be. These are indeed guiding stars to save the anguished.

Our examination of the suggestion that Abraham and Mary could be "guiding stars to save the anguished" should direct us to another place where Kierkegaard discusses the relevance of others' participation in the life of faith. In the discourse "Love Does Not Seek Its Own," Kierkegaard discusses "the work of sacrificially giving of oneself" (*WL*, 265). On the one hand, Kierkegaard has harsh words for an "exchange," and here we should be mindful that the Catholic tradition frequently cites an "exchange of spiritual goods." On this point, Kierkegaard writes, noting the exchange of rings between husband and wife as an example, "an exchange by no means abolishes the distinction '*mine* and *yours*,' because that for which I exchange myself then becomes mine again" (*WL*, 267, italics original). Kierkegaard seems to be arguing here that since I receive a ring in the same instant that I give one, and it is reasonable to *expect* this kind of reciprocity in the course of a marriage vow, such an exchange retains a *mine* and a *yours*. Instead, Kierkegaard notes that love abolishes the possessive categories of *mine* and *yours*. This does not, of course, mean that love abolishes the necessary categories of you and I, without which love cannot actually be what it is, a work of sacrificial *giving* (*WL*, 266). Rather, there should be the genuine giving of love, but this giving should not take place in such a way that reciprocity is expected, the other feels beholden for the love, the other feels a need to compensate for the generosity extended, or anything of that sort.

This is why Kierkegaard emphasizes that one should not give in such a way that "I am saying, 'He stands simply and solely through my help'—[since] then, of course, he is not standing by himself, then he has indeed not become his own master; then, after all, it is to my help that he owes all this—and he is aware of it. To help a human being in this way is really to deceive him" (*WL*, 274). Rather, Kierkegaard praises an effort by one human being to say of another, "This person is standing by himself—through my help" (*WL*, 275). This may at first appear to be a rather minimal concession to human sociality. In reality, it is not minimal at all. As Ferreira explains, however, there are some obstacles that the proper reading needs to overcome. For instance, Kierkegaard writes, "The greatest benefaction, therefore, cannot be done in such a way that the recipient comes to know that it is to me that he owes it, because if he comes to know that, then it simply is not the greatest beneficence" (*WL*, 275). We must read this passage carefully and in proper context, however.

Notice that what the other person cannot come to know is that "it is to me that he owes" any kind of exchange. What we should think of in this context is not so much that I ought to go about concealing my physical identity when I offer loving help to a neighbor, but that I should always give in such a way as to note that I am myself only giving what God has given to me. On this point, Ferreira writes:

> Kierkegaard is not recommending that we give a "gift" that should not seem like a gift. Rather, this deliberation elaborates another dimension of the notion of our "infinite debt" to the other—that everything we have is given, so what we give is already a gift, and what we give is what we owe to the other. . . . Unless I give to another in such a way that the other sees that what I have given has been a gift from God to me, a gift enabling me to give to another, and that it is ultimately to God that the recipient should feel indebted, then I have misled the recipient—and that is a form of harm.[63]

There is considerable textual support for Ferreira's important distinction. Seemingly to this very effect, Kierkegaard writes:

> Therefore, giving thanks to God, he declares: Now this individual is standing by himself—through my help. But there is no self-satisfaction in the last phrase, because the loving one has understood that essentially every human being indeed stands by himself—through God's help—and that the loving one's self-annihilation is really only in order not to hinder the other person's God-relationship, so that all the loving one's help infinitely vanishes in the God-relationship. (*WL*, 278)

What this reading amounts to is an understanding that the help of one human being for another is perfectly admissible in Kierkegaard's thought, so long as the one offering assistance and the one receiving it are in some way made to know and remember that all such gifts are possible only in the context of God's unmerited gift to us all. Indeed, Mary's consent at the Annunciation (which would have been impossible without God's grace) makes possible the redemption that humanity obtains through Christ, and this is, of course, a very great help.

Yet, despite the fact that this consent is a very great help to the humanity whose salvation is its goal, we must not forget something that Kierkegaard and the Catholic tradition completely agree about, namely, that "Mary's chief glory is in her nothingness."[64] This is particularly clear in what Balthasar says about Mary, when he goes so far as to claim that Mary does not know that she is sinless. He writes, "It is only the sinner who twists himself back onto his ego: the person who is sinless . . . does not know this backward glance but looks steadfastly at what is good, and 'no one is good but God alone' (Mk 10:18). It is precisely this lack of knowledge about her own sinlessness that makes Mary the 'seat of wisdom.'"[65] The consonance here with Kierkegaard's discussion of the arrow of love (*WL*, 182, also noted in chapter 3) is striking. It is only in sin that we look backward toward our own achievement. In love we look toward God, the source of our love.

This seems to be one of the many cases where what is true of Mary is true, albeit in a less-exalted fashion, of the rest of the saints. The rest of the saints, too, find their glory in their nothingness. Indeed, Balthasar notes that, in addition to Mary, all the "poor and humble" share the gift of the "light of wisdom" but "never experience [it] *as their own*."[66] All gifts from one to another are gifts given through the gratuitous love of

God. This, of course, is why Mary's intercession, the intercession of any and all of the saints, the whole system of indulgences, and any other garden-variety ways in which we help one another along the path of faith are all rooted, as we saw, in the "divine pleasure."[67] Just as there is an *objective* salvation history for Christians, in which Mary's contribution was, and is, unparalleled, there is also a *subjective* narrative for each of us.[68] Kierkegaard's thought has real strength in this regard, since perhaps no one has plumbed, with such depth, the subjective dimensions of the God-relationship as has Kierkegaard. Our reflections above on Silentio's treatment of Abraham and Mary and Kierkegaard's own discussion of Mary allow us to see a way in which individuals can play a beneficial role in the objective salvation history whose story Christianity is. Those who help, through their examples and prayerful concern, to provide for me a context in which my faith can flourish seem to be likewise "guiding stars to save the anguished." Accordingly, we can and do help one another in the life of faith, but the reason for why this help is efficacious is not that we are self-subsistent sources of such assistance, but that we give from out of what we have been given, and are still being given.

Now, of course, the *range* of activities that can be beneficially applied to another individual embarked on the life of faith for Kierkegaard is, to be sure, smaller than the range of such activities for the Catholic tradition. For the Catholic tradition, even individuals experiencing post-mortem cleansing in purgatory can be aided by the prayers and works of the faithful on earth. We have noted that there is reason to suspect that Kierkegaard would not accept this view. Further, there is a genuine question as to whether Kierkegaard's ecclesiology is robust enough (or indeed, whether he would have *wanted* it to be robust enough) to ground anything like properly ecclesial indulgences that could be applied either to the living or to the dead by external individuals. Still, I think that there is evidence that individuals can give others some assistance along the path of faith, for Kierkegaard.

What I think this means is that Balthasar's contention at the beginning of this chapter can easily be overstated. There are ways in which the communion of "saints" can enter into the picture. Given that there is a less-robust account of the commerce between the living and the dead in Kierkegaard's work, Kierkegaard may believe that St. Cyprian's contribution (to take a fittingly distant example) to my life of faith may be restricted to his overall historical contribution to objective salvation history. For Catholics, however, the saints can actually be appealed to right now, so that they can enter into one's subjective salvation history in addition. I think that Kierkegaard can accommodate both an objective and a subjective salvation history into which other individuals can enter, in the main. However, I think that his antecedent commitments to what may be a less-robust ecclesiology than the Catholic Church prizes, along with a rather silent (though largely negative) verdict on the question of commerce between the living and the dead, may indeed, from a Catholic point of view, "add up" to a loss for the Catholic understanding of the communion of saints.

‡

Despite the fact that Balthasar's contention can be overstated, I think Catholics would have to admit that there is something indisputably right about what he has said to begin this chapter. Kierkegaard's self-understanding is, in the main, that of a Lutheran Protestant. Catholics cannot help but anticipate, and find, certain lacunae, and even outright errors (from the Catholic point of view), in the writings of someone who understood himself in this way. Nonetheless, I do not think that the error in Kierkegaard's account regarding the communion of saints is to be sought primarily in his conception of the individual, but rather in his theological commitments regarding the Church (however difficult they may be to discern) and his views about the way in which the living are separated from commerce with the dead in a stronger way than the Catholic Church could espouse.

CONCLUSION

In this book I have tried to bring about dialogue between Kierkegaard and the Catholic tradition. Clearly, Kierkegaard is no crypto-Catholic. His work bears all the marks of an authentically Protestant and predominantly Lutheran origin. At the same time, he is deeply dissatisfied with the way the Lutheran establishment of his day fused Church and State, and engendered, as he thought, secularism under the guise of Christianity. To launch his vociferous attack required some radical steps, and his work on this front, while ostensibly Lutheran, also challenges the boundaries of Lutheran orthodoxy. In some cases, this brings him nearer to the Catholic tradition than Luther himself. In fact, as we have noted in chapter 4, Kierkegaard appears to see Luther as at least partially responsible for conflating religion and politics. What this may mean is that, for all the ways in which Kierkegaard and his pseudonyms can (I think accurately) be understood as postmodern, there is also a sense in which Kierkegaard longs for a premodern (indeed, pre-Constantinian) Christianity, at the expense of *some* of his traditional Lutheran moorings.

Further, there are points in Kierkegaard's work where what Kierkegaard means to say is captured well, or better, by an idea in the Catholic tradition. Although I anticipate the disagreement of scholars on various points here, what I have tried to do is to dialogue with Kierkegaard from within my own theological tradition. While I have my disagreements with Kierkegaard, there are also a number of important points where Kierkegaard and the Catholic tradition are engaged in a helpful dialogue and even rapprochement. There is certainly more of the latter on the question of natural reason in chapter 1 than the old canard that Kierkegaard is an irrationalist would have us believe. Although there is an ostensible disagreement on this and other issues, such as imperfect contrition in chapter 6, there is a deeper continuity in the more nuanced views that both Kierkegaard and the Catholic tradition put forward.

There are two major ways in which Kierkegaard really differs from the Catholic tradition, despite the fact that there is a great deal of dialogue possible within these areas. The first is in Kierkegaard's antipathy toward, or at least lack of, something akin to a Thomistic concept of nature. When Kierkegaard discusses nature, he seems to be accepting Luther's concept of nature, and, as Richard Marius notes, "[Luther] saw scarcely anything as a 'natural' phenomenon."[1] For Luther, the "natural" inclinations of (post-Fall) human beings are not good, but selfish and evil. I think this element of Kierkegaard's theological heritage helps to explain Kierkegaard's critical reception of Aristotelian love, natural theology's ability to know God without direct supernatural aid, and the natural human being's ability to obey natural law without direct supernatural aid. The manner of supernatural aid's arrival through the authoritative revelation of divine doctrine appears to be an area where Kierkegaard and the Catholic tradition have a great deal of underlying unity, despite the fact that Kierkegaard appears to be tempted toward Donatism in the administration of sacraments and preaching of the Word.

The other main area where Kierkegaard and the Catholic tradition are separated is in Kierkegaard's largely Lutheran conception of justification, which redounds to his conception of repentance, the Church, and his reception (or non-reception) of the concept of purgatory. I do not see wide disagreements between Kierkegaard and the Catholic tradition on the concepts of sin and hell, though harmony on this point (in chapter 5) helps us to glimpse the underlying unity that exists between the two, despite other related disagreements in the succeeding chapters. It is this underlying unity that enables this book to concern dialogue, and not just polemic.

These two main areas of nature and justification, I think, represent essential components for a uniquely Kierkegaardian theological and philosophical picture. They cannot simply be jettisoned without serious injustice to Kierkegaard's thought. For this reason, there will be dialogue and rapprochement, but conflict will remain. Who indeed could say whether Kierkegaard would have veered in a more Catholic direction if his prolific authorship had not been cut short by his untimely death? I confess that I have my doubts. His knowledge of the Catholic tradition per se was not deep, and in any case, he had deep misgivings about what he did know from the Catholic tradition. I would prefer to remember Kierkegaard as an individual who struggled to live a radically Christian life in a difficult time and place to live it. In his best moments he would simply have us return to God with all our hearts, for God is the source of grace and mercy. That sentiment is, of course, deeply Catholic and deeply Lutheran. I consider myself, in part, a Kierkegaardian, but I consider myself a committed Catholic with regard to my faith and theological commitments. I will part, and have parted, ways with Kierkegaard, but I hope to have done so in the inwardness to which he so correctly exhorted us, and which was, I believe, the essence of his true message. Kierkegaard should be ranked as one of Christianity's great teachers. Christians of every stripe have much to learn from him, and this is as true of Catholics as it is of anyone else.

NOTES

Introduction

1. The closest thing to an exception is Heinrich Roos's *Søren Kierkegaard and Catholicism*. However, Roos's book is quite short (62 pp.) and stays at the level of Catholic and anti-Catholic "tendencies" in Kierkegaard.

2. See Ferreira, *Love's Grateful Striving*, 11.

3. *Fides et Ratio*, 76.

4. *DH*, 3026 / *SCD*, 1806.

5. *Fides et Ratio*, 48.

6. Ibid., 76.

7. The source for this passage is *Lumen Gentium*, 11. See also John Paul II, *Ecclesia de Eucharistia*, 1. Consider also the fact that Luther claimed that the Mass was the "sum and substance" of the gospel (*LW* 36:56).

8. These form part 4 of *Christian Discourses* in the Princeton edition of *Kierkegaard's Writings*.

9. Niels Jørgen Cappelørn, however, is working on a project that discusses the dogmatic underpinnings of these discourses.

10. See Jack Mulder, Jr., "Cyprian of Carthage: Kierkegaard, Cyprian, and the 'Urgent Needs of the Times.'"

11. See *JP*, 6:6442 / *SKP* X-1 A 536, about *Practice in Christianity*.

12. I owe thanks to Søren Landkildehus for raising a worry about these terms in response to my delivery of a version of chapter 7. I have heard other scholars raise similar concerns in both the United States and in Denmark. Its most interesting form has to do with Kierkegaard's insistence that doubts about, say, the Ascension, are to be remedied not by reason but by a deeper imitation of Christ (see *FSE*, 66–70). Kierkegaard goes on to claim that reason can be positively harmful in the effort to bring about this imitation. See chapter 1 below for more on Kierkegaard and reason.

13. *The Lonely Labyrinth: Kierkegaard's Pseudonymous Works*, 6.

14. See Poole, *Kierkegaard: The Indirect Communication*, 7. For a fuller discussion of this tendency from an opposing perspective the reader is referred to

C. Stephen Evans, "Realism and Antirealism in Kierkegaard's *Concluding Unscientific Postscript*," and Evans, *Kierkegaard on Faith and the Self.*

15. See, for instance, *CUP,* 379–80; *PC,* 141; and *JP,* 6:6528 / *SKP,* X-2 A 184.

16. On this point, see *JP,* 1:482 / *SKP,* IX A 105.

17. See Brand Blanshard, "Kierkegaard on Faith," which opposes what it erroneously takes to be Kierkegaard's view for similar reasons.

18. *An Essay on the Development of Christian Doctrine,* 7.1.4, 290.

19. On Kierkegaard's view of the apostle, see chapter 4.

20. The pseudonym is H.H., on whom, see chapter 4.

21. Ch. 4, sec. 3, *An Essay in Aid of a Grammar of Assent,* 89.

22. Richard John Neuhaus, "Kierkegaard for Grownups," 28.

23. Attentive readers of Kierkegaard are, no doubt, already aware that Kierkegaard would have had no patience with a sort of adogmatic dabbling in his works. In fact, some of Kierkegaard's works are explicitly dogmatic, as shown by the longer title of *The Concept of Anxiety: A Simple Psychologically Orienting Deliberation on the Dogmatic Issue of Hereditary Sin.*

1. Kierkegaard and Natural Reason

The epigraph is from *An Essay in Aid of a Grammar of Assent* 4.3, 89.

1. Terence Penelhum's book *God and Skepticism* treats Kierkegaard as a fideist. More recently, Linda Zagzebski (*Philosophy of Religion: An Historical Introduction*) has claimed that Kierkegaard is a "radical fideist," a viewpoint that she associates with the claim that "faith is not only higher than reason, it is opposed to it" (59).

2. It is important to note in this connection, as M. Jamie Ferreira does, that "Kierkegaard never uses any Danish equivalent of 'leap of faith'" ("Faith and the Kierkegaardian Leap," 207).

3. See John Paul II, *Fides et Ratio,* 53.

4. C. Stephen Evans's books *Passionate Reason* and *Kierkegaard on Faith and the Self* are two of the best works that seek to rebut the charge that Kierkegaard is an irrational fideist, as opposed to a "responsible fideist," under which label Evans argues for including both Kierkegaard and Alvin Plantinga (203–204 in *Kierkegaard on Faith and the Self*).

5. In this chapter I will understand by "natural theology" that portion of the enterprise that attempts to prove God's existence without special revelation. I will sometimes use the phrase "natural reason" in a somewhat broader way, usually to indicate a natural awareness of God's existence, without necessarily having arrived at this awareness through discursive arguments.

6. *Fides et Ratio,* 48.

7. *DH,* 3026 / *SCD,* 1806.

8. See Linda Zagzebski, "Religious Knowledge and the Virtues of the Mind," esp. 207–208. Kierkegaard appears to be sympathetic to some versions of voluntarism with regard to belief, though not all. See *JP,* 2:1094 / *SKP,* I A 36. For more on this issue, see ch. 17 of Evans, *Kierkegaard on Faith and the Self.*

9. *LW* 31:376.

10. *LW* 54:183, #2938b. Some other choice words against "carnal reason" can be found in Luther's *The Bondage of the Will* (*LW,* vol. 33).

11. See especially Luther's *Disputation against Scholastic Theology, LW* 31:9–16.

12. See *JFY*, 140. Also, with regard to reason's tendency to actually nurture doubt in the life of faith, see *FSE*, 68.

13. William L. Rowe, *Philosophy of Religion: An Introduction*, 20. For Rowe, these are actually the two stages of the *cosmological* argument.

14. Ibid., 20.

15. Compare *CUP*, 203–204. We read there, "I observe nature in order to find God, and I do indeed see omnipotence and wisdom, but I also see much that troubles and disturbs. The *summa summarum* of this is an objective uncertainty."

16. While in one place he mentions Socrates as having given a version of the "physico-teleological demonstration for the existence of God" (*PF*, 44), this is hardly the only sort of proof under consideration.

17. The Catholic tradition tends to emphasize this brand of natural theology, i.e., a posteriori proofs for the existence of God, as opposed to a priori arguments. Although the latter form is especially exemplified in St. Anselm's famous ontological argument, this form is not as typical as the a posteriori proofs. No doubt part of the reason for this is St. Thomas Aquinas's long tenure as the semi-official theologian of the Church, coupled with the fact that he famously argued against Anselm's ontological argument. See Aquinas, *ST*, Ia.2.1, esp. reply to objection 2. Climacus gives a criticism of Spinoza's ontological argument in the note on *PF*, 41–42. Readers interested in this topic may wish to consult Robert C. Roberts, *Faith, Reason, and History*, 74–78, whose account of Climacus's discussion of the ontological argument seems to me to be on the mark in the main.

18. *ST*, Ia. 2.3.

19. See chs. 13, 15, 16, 18, and 37 of *Summa contra Gentiles, Book One: God*.

20. If Climacus's complaint is right, the teleological argument from governance will also presuppose a *moral* agent.

21. Though note well Luther's deep suspicion of Aristotle on such issues, which Kierkegaard seems to have inherited (see *LW* 44:200–201).

22. In previous publications, I interpreted this passage differently and in a way that was at odds with the interpretation offered by C. Stephen Evans in his "Realism and Antirealism in Kierkegaard's *Concluding Unscientific Postscript*," 157. I now believe that my earlier interpretation on this point was mistaken, despite the fact that I am not sure I can fully endorse Evans's suggestion to interpret this along the lines of a moral standard.

23. See *CUP*, 162–63 and 199–200. Also, on the topic of natural knowledge of God in Kierkegaard, see Robert C. Roberts's very helpful article "The Socratic Knowledge of God."

24. See *JP*, 2:1129 / *SKP*, X-1 A 367 for more on this point in Kierkegaard.

25. This, or something like it, was the worry of an anonymous reviewer for the journal *Faith and Philosophy,* in which an earlier version of this chapter is published under the same title. The reviewer wondered why we should care about Climacus's critique of natural theology if it is simply mistaken.

26. See Westphal, *Becoming a Self: A Reading of Kierkegaard's Concluding Unscientific Postscript*, 52.

27. *"In the Beginning . . .": A Catholic Understanding of Creation and the Fall*, 28.

28. See *CCC*, 155, which cites Aquinas's definition at *ST*, II-II.2.9 and *DH*, 3010 / *SCD*, 1791.

29. It is possible that Kierkegaard himself reacted to the overconfidence of the Hegelian system with an underconfident skepticism. See Anthony J. Rudd, "Kierkegaard and the Sceptics," esp. 87, where Rudd notes that a kind of natural knowledge of God through an "unsatisfied hunger" could have arisen from personal neurosis. In my view, the Catholic tradition should begin from the supposition that no such neuroses are present in ordinary cases, and let that be the standard for "objectivity" now conceived more positively.

30. *DH,* 3004/*SCD,* 1785. One might wonder (as the previously noted anonymous reviewer did) whether this canon requires demonstrative "proofs" or simply the knowledge garnered in one way or another from created things. I will not arrogate to myself the role of distinguishing where the heresy is to be found. However, the traditional position has been to affirm demonstrative arguments, especially the argument from causation. On this point, see Pope Pius X's anti-modernist oath (*DH,* 3538 / *SCD,* 2145) and Ludwig Ott, *Fundamentals of Catholic Dogma,* 13–17.

31. *CCC,* 36.

32. Ibid., 31.

33. Ibid., 34.

34. I have adapted this formulation slightly from Rowe's *The Cosmological Argument,* 258, and Rowe's formulation on *Philosophy of Religion,* 21.

35. Rowe, *Philosophy of Religion,* 32.

36. Ibid., 23, italics original.

37. See *Humani Generis* in *DH,* 3892 / *SCD,* 2320, where we read, "It is well known how much the Church values human reason, in what is concerned with definitely demonstrating the existence of one personal God."

38. *DH,* 3892 / *SCD,* 2320, italics mine.

39. Rowe, *Philosophy of Religion,* 31–32.

40. To deal in any depth with such an issue is simply outside the scope of this chapter. For my part, I find it preliminarily helpful to consider the fact that Plantinga rejects the need for Cartesian certainty (as it seems does Aquinas), but also notes the need for what he describes as psychological certainty in order for a belief to be known (see Plantinga, *Warrant and Proper Function,* 76–77).

41. *ST,* Ia.12.12.

42. See Hibbs's editor's introduction to the selection of Aquinas's writings titled *On Human Nature,* xi.

43. *ST,* Ia.12.13.

44. John I. Jenkins, *Knowledge and Faith in Thomas Aquinas,* 121.

45. Jenkins is clearly in dialogue with Plantinga here, a point he makes explicitly. By allowing for a certain kind of externalism here, I do not mean to contradict John Paul II's claim that "within visible creation, man is the only creature who not only is capable of knowing but who *knows that he knows,* and is therefore interested in the real truth of what he perceives" (*Fides et Ratio,* 25, italics mine). This might seem to include an internalist requirement for awareness of having met the conditions for knowledge. I think, however, that what the pope is actually insisting upon is that human knowledge is inherently self-reflexive (much in the way that inner sense perceives that the animal perceives, for St. Augustine in *On Free Choice of the Will* 2.4, 37). Thus, we are aware that our knowing faculty has been deployed, can ascertain, using the senses and other faculties, whether any impediments exist in

the way of its proper deployment, and are aware that our human existence is the right sort of context in which this knowing can take place.

46. The truth of a principle as basic as PSR is constantly presupposed, not argued for, in both Aristotle's procedure and Jenkins's interpretation of Aquinas.

47. Joe LaPorte is currently working on similar ideas, though with no connection to Kierkegaard. I have benefited a great deal from his helpful suggestions and criticisms.

48. When a crime is being investigated, one looks for such things as fingerprints, misplaced artifacts, and other identifying marks. One then moves to find a motive for the suspected individuals, constantly supposing that the weapons and identifying marks did not simply "pop" into existence as brute facts. I owe the crime scene example to William Rowe, who often uses this example in the context of discussing PSR.

49. For example, consider John Zeis, "Natural Theology: Reformed?" 50.

50. Stephen R. Grimm, "Cardinal Newman, Reformed Epistemologist?" Grimm notes a difference between Plantinga and Newman in that the former includes specifically Christian beliefs among those that could be properly basic, whereas the latter does not (515). It should also not escape our notice in this chapter that M. Jamie Ferreira has fruitfully compared Newman and Kierkegaard in her article "Leaps and Circles: Kierkegaard and Newman on Faith and Reason."

51. Ch. 5, sec. 1, *Essay in Aid of a Grammar of Assent,* 103.

52. Compare Luther's inability to understand why the vision of a sunrise does not persuade humanity of God's existence. See *LW* 54:72–73, #447.

53. See Plantinga, *Warranted Christian Belief,* 168–86.

54. Ibid., 173.

55. Ibid., 171n5.

56. Ibid., 175, emphasis original.

57. *ST,* Ia.12.11, reply to objection 3.

58. See, for instance, John Hick, "Religious Pluralism and Salvation," esp. 376.

59. Karl Rahner, *Foundations of Christian Faith,* 21.

60. Ibid., 20–21. See also *ST,* Ia.12.11, reply to objection 3, where Aquinas notes, "All things are said to be seen in God and all things are judged in Him, because by the participation of His light we know and judge all things."

61. *Foundations of Christian Faith,* 22.

62. Ibid., 52. Here is where Rahner seems closest to Plantinga.

63. Ibid., 53.

64. See, for example, ibid., 28–29.

65. *CCC,* 36.

66. See Evans, *Kierkegaard on Faith and the Self,* esp. chs. 10 and 11, esp. 185–88. My view seems to be somewhere in between his "ambitious" and "modest" epistemologies, since I don't think we need a reply for skepticism (which disqualifies my view from being "ambitious"), but I think there are also elements of "modest" epistemology that may be too modest for the Catholic tradition.

67. See, for instance, Thomas D. Sullivan, "Resolute Belief and the Problem of Objectivity." See also *CCC,* 153–65.

68. *Summa contra Gentiles, Book Three: Providence,* ch. 38, 125.

69. Ibid.

70. John Paul II, *Crossing the Threshold of Hope*, 135.

71. Of course, faith can more than compensate for the knowledge that everyday persons lack in comparison with the demonstrative knowledge of speculative theologians (see *Summa contra Gentiles*, 1.4 and 5). It is also important to note that John Paul II claims that the "atheistic interpretation of reality is one-sided and tendentious" (*Crossing the Threshold of Hope*, 198).

72. Evans, "Can God Be Hidden and Evident at the Same Time? Some Kierkegaardian Reflections," 246–47.

73. See *CUP*, 201.

74. Evans, "Can God Be Hidden and Evident at the Same Time?" 247.

75. *Lumen Gentium*, 16.

76. This does seem to be a spot where I disagree with Evans. See Evans, *Kierkegaard's Ethic of Love*, 160–61. Evans claims that natural knowledge of the love commandment springs from the presence of love (which is God) at the ground of the self. But I maintain that it is precisely this ground to which we have at best incomplete access prior to revelation. On this point I agree with John Davenport, in his essay "Faith as Eschatological Trust in *Fear and Trembling*," when he writes, "In the signed writings of his later years, Kierkegaard accepts both that our moral duties cannot fully be known without revelation, and that we cannot fulfill them without grace" (233).

77. See John Paul II, *Crossing the Threshold of Hope*, 83.

78. *Reconciliatio et Paenitentia*, 16.

79. See Benedict XVI, "*In the Beginning . . . ,*" 24.

80. See Pius XII, *Humani Generis*, esp. *DH*, 3875 / *SCD*, 2305, italics mine.

81. See Vatican II's *Gaudium et Spes*, 15.

82. *Crossing the Threshold of Hope*, 79–80.

83. *Gaudium et Spes*, 19.

84. Evans, "Can God Be Hidden and Evident at the Same Time?" 246.

2. Is Abraham a Hero?

The epigraph is from *Martyrdom of Saints Perpetua and Felicitas* in Musurillo, *The Acts of the Christian Martyrs*, 113.

1. *LW* 44:23.

2. See *CCC*, 1954–60, on the natural moral law.

3. I am grateful to John Lippitt for raising the question of whether I might be assuming too much in thinking that Perpetua's case does not manifest "insufficient gratitude for the gift of earthly life." While it is true that I do not argue for this claim, I think that to do so would be assuming the inordinately heavy burden of arguing for the permissibility of martyrdom, as Perpetua's case is archetypical of many cases of the martyrs.

4. I say this despite the fact that Kierkegaard acknowledges that Abraham's faith was not specifically Christian (*JP*, 1:12 / *SKP*, X-6 B 81), and that instead it is "the formal definition of faith." I think that Kierkegaard, in this journal entry, simply means, at least, that the necessary conditions for Abraham's faith are necessary conditions for Christian faith.

5. For one such discussion, see Ronald M. Green, "Enough Is Enough! *Fear and Trembling* Is *Not* about Ethics." For commentary on this trend in scholarship,

see John Lippitt, *The Routledge Philosophy Guidebook to Kierkegaard and Fear and Trembling*, esp. ch. 6.

6. For more on similar trends in patristic writers, see Jerome I. Gellman, *"Fear and Trembling:* Kierkegaard's Christian Work."

7. It is revealing in this connection to consider the *Catechism of the Catholic Church,* which points out that Christian Scripture has both literal and spiritual senses (the latter sense includes the "allegorical," the "moral," and the "anagogical" senses). The intent is to point out that it is often the case that one Scripture passage contains some aspect of all of these senses. I think a similar claim could be sustained about *Fear and Trembling* (see *CCC,* 115–19).

8. This is from Kosch's portion of a dialogue with John Lippitt. Kosch's portion is titled, "What Abraham Couldn't Say," in [*Proceedings of the Aristotelian Society*] *Supplementary Volume,* 82:59–78. Lippitt's response, "What Neither Abraham Nor Johannes de Silentio Could Say," follows on 79–99 of the same volume. The passage I have cited in the main text from Kosch's piece can be found on 61. I am grateful to John Lippitt for making available to me advance copies of these texts, and for reading an early draft of the present chapter.

9. The "hidden message" seems to be that "faith cannot be learned from another human being," and that "in order to survive in the terrain of faith the reader must eliminate [Abraham], along with every other example" (Kosch, "What Abraham Couldn't Say," 77). See also Lippitt's response, with which I find much agreement.

10. I will simply record my general agreement with Lippitt's response to Kosch, at least up until around 95 of Lippitt's response, when he draws on Stephen Mulhall's reading in the latter's *Inheritance and Originality,* esp. 354–88. Lippitt helpfully used a strategy of appealing to Kierkegaard's orthodoxy in interpreting Scripture to great effect in the first part of the article, but his endorsement of Mulhall's strategy undermines his ability to use Hebrews 11's discussion of Abraham. Briefly put, the issue is this: Mulhall claims that, on Silentio's reading, "the slightest grain of impurity" from sin makes it impossible for an individual to judge whether a putative demand to suspend ethically ordinary demands is in fact a divine command (see Lippitt's response to Kosch, 96, and Mulhall, 384). That may be implied by a very literal reading of one of Silentio's statements, and his often-mentioned naïveté concerning Abraham's lack of sin (see *FT,* 98). If we dismiss Abraham's sinlessness though, then even Abraham (on this view) is not in a position to judge that God's command to sacrifice Isaac is genuine. In that case, Abraham should have done exactly what Kant told him to do, namely, explain that humans are not epistemologically well-positioned enough to take such putative divine commands seriously (on Kant's view, see below). But one must choose between Kant's recommendation and Hebrews 11:19's approval of what it judges to be Abraham's actual reasoning process ("he reasoned that God was able to raise Isaac even from the dead"). Why not adopt the view of C. Stephen Evans, that God could reveal such a thing to an individual by causally determining her to believe it? On this point, see *Kierkegaard's Ethic of Love,* 310.

11. See, for example, *CUP,* 500, and *JP,* 1:11, 12 / *SKP,* X-6 B 80, 81.

12. Mooney, *Knights of Faith and Resignation,* 91.

13. See John Davenport, "Faith as Eschatological Trust in *Fear and Trembling.*" Davenport (to whom I owe thanks for making available an advance copy of his

work and for much helpful dialogue on the material in this chapter) makes it clear that Abraham does not believe, at any point, that he is called to murder Isaac, the moral meaning of murder including the permanent end of earthly life. See especially 201 and 268, where Davenport claims that Silentio's account entails the claim that "Abraham recognizes . . . that he can sacrifice Isaac *without* murdering him." I actually agree with Davenport about this, despite the fact that he cites my earlier article as disagreeing. See my "Re-radicalizing Kierkegaard: An Alternative to Religiousness C in Light of an Investigation into the Teleological Suspension of the Ethical." The fault is at least partially mine, though. I had not thought to make the distinction that murder (and thus attempted murder) entails the permanent end of (or the desire to bring about the permanent end of) a person's earthly life. I intend this chapter as a clearer statement of what I believe about *Fear and Trembling.*

14. "Morality as Anti-Nature," no. 1, *Twilight of the Idols,* in *The Portable Nietzsche,* 487.

15. Davenport was willing to grant this claim, which I will argue is Silentio's blind spot, as part of the "limits of Silentio's perspective." In correspondence, he wrote to me, "You might be right that Silentio only looks at faith in Abraham's case, or in general, as trusting in a eucatastrophe in 'this life,' though I believe the more general structure extending to the hereafter is implicit." I am unable to see that it is implicit, because of the claims that Silentio makes for faith at *FT,* 20, and other passages.

16. See Davenport, "Faith as Eschatological Trust in *Fear and Trembling,*" 222, where we read, "The structure of existential faith is more general than Christianity or Religiousness B." I am likewise reading Silentio's lesson on existential faith as one from which more than just Christians could profit, as Silentio's account spells out necessary conditions for existential faith, no matter how it is modeled.

17. The claim that such a fictional Abraham is a knight of infinite resignation is entailed by Davenport's own argument that the tragic hero is a subset of the category of infinite resignation (see "Faith as Eschatological Trust," 271n87), together with Silentio's understanding of the tragic hero on *FT,* 35.

18. See, for example, "Diapsalmata" and "Rotation of Crops," in *EO,* 1:17–43 and 281–300.

19. See Lippitt, *The Routledge Philosophy Guidebook to Kierkegaard and Fear and Trembling,* 47.

20. Ibid., 48.

21. In Abraham's case, this is the fulfillment of God's promise to bring progeny through Isaac. In the lad's case it is the love of the princess.

22. By "eternity" here I mean what Kierkegaard often means, the "eternal life" that is promised in Christian faith. I do not mean by this usage to imply that this existence does not involve temporal succession of one sort or another.

23. Mooney, *Knights of Faith and Resignation,* 52.

24. See *FT,* 54.

25. The Danish here is from *Sædelighed,* which corresponds to Hegel's *Sittlichkeit,* or ethical life in a societal context. See the Hongs' note 7 in *FT,* 346.

26. See Lippitt, *The Routledge Guidebook to Kierkegaard and Fear and Trembling,* 97–102, for discussion of the individual cases and how scholars interpret them in their original contexts.

27. The assumption is that, whatever one thinks of its merits, even Divine Command Theory *is* such an ethical theory.

28. See Kellenberger, *Kierkegaard and Nietzsche,* 33. I thus agree with Anthony Rudd when he writes, in a passage that Davenport also discusses, "Kierkegaard does not resolve the difficult in *Fear and Trembling* to which I have drawn attention—that if the God-relationship is simply regarded as the highest of the various goals towards which I am striving, then the relativization of other goals does not constitute a radical break with ethical thinking" (Rudd, *Kierkegaard and the Limits of the Ethical,* 150).

29. Kellenberger, *Kierkegaard and Nietzsche,* 33

30. This passage is from Kant's work *The Conflict of the Faculties,* which is found in English translation in Kant, *Religion and Rational Theology,* 283.

31. Lippitt, *The Routledge Philosophy Guidebook to Kierkegaard and Fear and Trembling,* 143.

32. The idea here is simply that the moral law against murder is unconditional and so no exception admits of a justification in terms of what might be achieved in a given situation. No condition or circumstance, no matter how dire, nullifies the unconditional requirement of the moral law. See the second section of Immanuel Kant, *Groundwork of The Metaphysics of Morals* in Kant, *Practical Philosophy.*

33. Ronald M. Green, *Kierkegaard and Kant: The Hidden Debt,* 89. Davenport cites this passage and later goes on to argue that there are agapic elements (of the sort that would later be found in *Works of Love*) in the ethical that is suspended. See Earl McLane, "Rereading *Fear and Trembling,*" for more on this claim. In this context, I agree with Merold Westphal's treatment that the "ethical" should be understood primarily as *Sittlichkeit* (see Westphal, "Kierkegaard and Hegel," esp. 107–10). Thus, I remain unpersuaded by the agapic argument above because if agapic ethics (considered as divine commands) are themselves absorbed into the "ethical" then there would be no higher τέλος than to follow them, but we have seen that there is a higher τέλος than the ethical.

34. Hegel writes, "In an ethical community, it is easy to say what man must do, what are the duties he has to fulfill in order to be virtuous: he has simply to follow the well-known and explicit rules of his own situation" (*Philosophy of Right,* 107, ¶150). Of course, this does not mean that Hegel is interested in a state composed of unthinking drones. On this point, see Stephen Houlgate, *Freedom, Truth and History: An Introduction to Hegel's Philosophy,* 120–21.

35. Hegel claims, "Once the state has been founded, there can be no longer any heroes" (*Philosophy of Right,* 245, addition to ¶93).

36. See *Philosophy of Right,* 219, ¶350.

37. See Hegel's introduction to *The Philosophy of History,* 30.

38. *Philosophy of Right,* 242, addition to ¶75.

39. See *Philosophy of Right,* 167, ¶270.

40. *Philosophy of History,* Introduction, 30.

41. See G. W. F. Hegel, "The Spirit of Christianity and its Fate," in *Early Theological Writings,* esp. 185–88.

42. The relevant passage here is, "For I certainly would like to know how Abraham's act can be related to the universal, whether any point of contact between what Abraham did and the universal can be found other than that Abraham

transgressed it" (*FT*, 59). This is why Davenport's claim that the category of tragic hero is a subset of the category of infinite resignation cannot solve the problem (see "Faith as Eschatological Trust in *Fear and Trembling*," 271n87). Certainly, Silentio's despairing imposture of Abraham is an instance of infinite resignation (which is entailed by Davenport's claim), but if it were also tragic heroism, then his deed would still have to belong to some "ethical." But then Abraham's act (which from the outward point of view would be identical with Silentio's imposture) would itself belong to the ethical, which is precisely what Silentio constantly denies.

43. See Evans, *Kierkegaard's Ethic of Love*, 74.

44. A related difficulty persists in the text. Silentio claims that he can understand, and even accomplish, the movement of resignation, but he cannot understand faith (*FT*, 34–35, 51–52). Yet it is precisely the movement of resignation that, according to Silentio, "no one can understand because it is a private venture" (*FT*, 115).

45. I acknowledge, of course, that the experience of particular martyrs will be different. Origen's definition of how the term came to be used will be of some use, though: "One who of his own free choice chooses to die for the sake of religion." See the entry on "Martyr; Martyrology," in Douglas, *The New International Dictionary of the Christian Church*, 638–39. That this might often result in the diminishing of hope for one's earthly life is hardly surprising.

46. See Musurillo's introduction to *Acts of the Christian Martyrs*, xxv.

47. *The Martyrdom of Saints Perpetua and Felicitas*, 4, 113.

48. Ibid., 5, 113.

49. I use the antiquated "lady" here simply to preserve some kind of parallel to Silentio's usage of "knight" in the cases of the knight of faith and the knight of infinite resignation.

50. Consider the fascination that Silentio attributes to an unknown man regarding the *Akedah* (*FT*, 9), and the fascination a similar unknown man has in relation to Christ's sacrificial death (*WA*, 55); the fact that both texts invoke the important but somewhat infrequent category of the double movement (*FT*, 36; *WA*, 60); similar episodes of the vexed pastor in relation to the congregant who actually proposes to do as his pastor says (*FT*, 28–29; *WA*, 67); and the fact that H.H. hardly by accident notes that the would-be martyr undertakes his task with "fear and trembling" (*WA*, 69);

51. See Merold Westphal, *Becoming a Self: A Reading of Kierkegaard's Concluding Unscientific Postscript*, 29.

52. See Tertullian's *Apology*, ch. 50, 227.

53. Some martyrs claim to have received dreams and visions on the order of special revelation about the times for their eventual martyrdoms. An example is St. Cyprian, who, according to his deacon Pontius, is said to have received such a vision. See Pontius's *Vita Cypriani*, chs. 12 and 13 (trans. Sister Mary Magdeleine Müller and Roy J. Deferrari), in Deferrari, *Early Christian Biographies*, 16–19.

54. See Aquinas, *ST*, I-II.94.2.

55. Stephen J. Pope, "Overview of the Ethics of Thomas Aquinas," 35.

56. See *ST*, I-II.94.4 and *CCC*, 1960.

57. *CCC*, 1954.

58. *ST*, I-II.94.5, Objection 2.

59. *ST,* I-II.94.5, reply to objection 2.

60. *ST,* I-II.93.3.

61. This is distinct from the position of Andrew of Neufchateau, which argues that Abraham's would-be action would be morally right if commanded by God, and yet still a murder. See Philip L. Quinn, "Divine Command Theory," 63.

62. *ST,* I-II.93.1. See also *ST,* I-II.93.6, where Aquinas explains how the eternal law governs and pertains to human agents who are sinful.

63. *ST,* I-II.91.2.

64. See Denis A. Goulet, "Kierkegaard, Aquinas, and the Dilemma of Abraham," at 177. Goulet, like many scholars of his day, pays no attention to the pseudonyms of Kierkegaard's authorship.

65. See Jon Stewart's *Kierkegaard's Relations to Hegel Reconsidered* for an argument that many of Kierkegaard's arguments were actually directed at the Danish Hegelians rather than Hegel himself per se.

66. *WL,* 53.

67. Goulet mentions this, somewhat after his accusations have already been made. See Goulet, "Kierkegaard, Aquinas, and the Dilemma of Abraham," 185.

68. Ibid., 184. See *ST,* II-II.104.4, reply to objection 2.

69. Goulet, "Kierkegaard, Aquinas, and the Dilemma of Abraham," 179.

70. The best treatment of Kierkegaard's often supposed irrationalism that I know of, though it is written with reference to Climacus's "paradox," is C. Stephen Evans, *Passionate Reason,* especially ch. 7.

71. There is a certain resemblance in the above to Norman Kretzmann's account of the *Akedah,* which, though unintentional, happily allows me to note my substantial agreement with Kretzmann's account. See Kretzmann, "Abraham, Isaac, and Euthyphro," at 418.

72. See Goulet, "Kierkegaard, Aquinas, and the Dilemma of Abraham," 178.

73. Davenport, "Faith as Eschatological Trust in *Fear and Trembling,*" 198.

74. Ibid., 203.

75. Ibid., 204.

76. This insistence is not difficult to locate in other places, but it is certainly a part of Silentio's account at *FT,* 20.

77. Davenport, "Faith as Eschatological Trust in *Fear and Trembling,*" 207.

78. Anthony J. Lisska, *Aquinas's Theory of Natural Law: An Analytic Reconstruction,* 114–15.

79. Ibid., 210.

80. Ibid., 33.

81. I am following the New American translation for the sake of consistency. The Greek is not gender-exclusive.

82. Accidental because the obedience entailed by resignation requires Abraham's hope in this life, but only because, *as it happens,* God made an earlier promise of progeny through Isaac.

3. The Order of Love

The epigraph is from *WL,* 19.

1. The two other passersby in the story, the priest and the Levite, in choosing not to ritually contaminate themselves by contact with a person "half-dead" (see Lv

21:1–3) "chose cult over compassion," to use Steven L. Bridge's words. For a brief but helpful account of this and the cultural context surrounding Jesus' use of this parable, see Steven L. Bridge, *Getting the Gospels,* 61–65.

2. I am primarily concerned in this chapter with the Thomistic tradition, but the latter has held a privileged position on the question of love's ordering for some time in the larger Catholic tradition. To some extent, this has even taken place with magisterial backing.

3. St. Augustine gives a quite similar example to the one discussed above. He writes, "Everyone must be loved equally; but, when you cannot be of assistance to all, you must above all have regard for those who are bound to you more closely by some accident, as it were, of location, circumstances, or occasions of any kind." See *Christian Instruction,* 1.28, in *Saint Augustine,* 48. Aquinas regarded similar texts to provide a source for his view (see *ST,* II-II.26.6, reply to objection 1), but it is likely that he meant to part ways, at least partially, with Augustine here. The two clearest magisterial sources that I know of on the ordering of love, and that are clearly inspired by Aquinas, include an affirmation (or rather denunciation of the opposite view) that God should be loved more than oneself (*DH,* 975 / *SCD,* 525), and the claim that we should love both Church and country but Church more. For this latter claim, see *SCD,* 1936a, and Leo XIII's encyclical *Sapientiae Christianae,* 5, which can be found on the Vatican's archive of papal documents (it is missing from newer editions of Denzinger).

4. When discussing Kierkegaard, I will use "Christian love" and "neighbor-love" interchangeably, since I believe they are interchangeable for Kierkegaard.

5. *LW* 31:367 and 365, respectively.

6. See *ST,* II-II.26. The entire question is devoted to distinctions and gradations in love.

7. If we follow Stephen J. Pope, "The Order of Love and Recent Catholic Ethics: A Constructive Proposal."

8. See Peter Lombard, *The Sentences: Book 1: The Mystery of the Trinity,* Distinction XVII. This is a point of interest, since the Catholic tradition, following Bonaventure and Aquinas, has tended to regard Lombard's view as at least "less probable," whereas Protestantism has received the idea more favorably. See Philipp W. Rosemann, "*Fraterna dilectio est Deus:* Peter Lombard's Thesis on Charity as the Holy Spirit," esp. 410.

9. See Aquinas, *On Charity,* art. 1, 21.

10. Ibid.

11. To bring this debate into full relief would require a different inquiry than the one in this chapter. I suspect one thing Kierkegaard might say, however, is that Aquinas is determined to make sure that love can be a habit (*On Charity,* art. 1, 22) toward which one can grow more and more inclined. Kierkegaard, on the other hand, wishes to separate love from habit, so that it is the simple performance of a commanded duty every time. On this point, see *WL,* 37, and Ferreira, *Love's Grateful Striving,* 37.

12. Kierkegaard writes, "To love without passion is an impossibility" (*WL,* 50), and yet it seems clear that this love is the love that is commanded. Kierkegaard does not conceive of love as a simple emotion into and out of which one can simply "fall," but whatever caring is associated with love, we need grace to bring it about.

Kierkegaard writes, "[W]hen eternity says, 'You shall love,' it is responsible for making sure that this can be done" (*WL*, 41).

13. Ferreira, *Love's Grateful Striving*, 37.

14. For an interesting comparison of Kierkegaard and Emmanuel Levinas on this point, see Ferreira, "Asymmetry and Self-Love: The Challenge to Reciprocity and Equality," esp. 56–57.

15. See *WL*, 52, and Ferreira, *Love's Grateful Striving*, 44.

16. See *WL*, 57, and Ronald M. Green and Theresa M. Ellis, "Erotic Love in the Religious Existence-Sphere," esp. 362.

17. See Francis's *The Love of God* 10.10, 428–29, and Augustine, *Confessions* 3.6.11, 43.

18. *ST*, II-II.26.3.

19. *Love's Grateful Striving*, 31.

20. *Nicomachean Ethics*, 8.2, 1155b19, in Jonathan Barnes, ed., *The Complete Works of Aristotle*, 2:1826. Some of the analysis of *Nicomachean Ethics* can also be found in Ferreira, *Love's Grateful Striving*, esp. 44–45.

21. *Nicomachean Ethics*, 8.3, 1156a10–14, 1827.

22. Ibid., 8.3, 1156b7–17, 1827.

23. Ibid., 9.3, 1165b13–17, 1842.

24. *LW* 44, 201.

25. See Ott, *Fundamentals of Catholic Dogma*, 219–36, for some helpful discussion.

26. *LW* 31, 15, Thesis 88.

27. Ibid., 12, Theses 41 and 50.

28. *Nicomachean Ethics*, 9.8, 1169a12, 1847.

29. Ibid., 9.8, 1168b6, 1847.

30. Ibid., 9.4, 1166a32, 1843.

31. Consider St. Bernard of Clairvaux's four stages in *On Loving God* (see *Bernard of Clairvaux: Selected Writings* for a full translation). The stages are, in ascending order, when a person loves herself for her own sake, when a person loves God for her own sake, when a person loves God for God's own sake, and when a person loves herself for God's sake (*On Loving God*, 8.23–11.30, 192–97). It seems to me that with regard to loving the other, Aristotle's friend reaches only somewhere in between the first and the second stages. Nevertheless, I think Kierkegaard, and ultimately Catholic thinkers who succeeded Bernard, such as Aquinas and Francis de Sales, believed that at least the third stage is what is required in order to actually succeed in loving God more than one loves oneself.

32. I suspect we can construct a somewhat inchoate view of love for God in Aristotle, and, owing to God's superiority in that system, perhaps we would be rationally required to love God more than we love ourselves in at least one sense (see for instance, *Metaphysics* Λ (12).7–10 in Barnes, *Complete Works of Aristotle*, 1694–1700). Still, for Kierkegaard and even Aquinas, I think there would still be two concerns. First, Aristotle's God is not a lover, and so even if our love were to participate in and reflect God's love, it would not be directed toward the neighbor. Second, it is not clear to me that, so construed, Aristotle's love for God would be the foundation of all of our other loves. I thank Carol Simon for some discussion on this point and for reading a draft of this chapter.

33. On this point, see Martin Andic, "Love's Redoubling and the Eternal Like for Like," esp. 18.

34. *The Love of God,* 10.11, 431. Fénelon was indebted to Francis de Sales's legacy in this work, but seems to have taken it too far. On this point, see Adams, "Pure Love," 174–92 and *DH,* 2351 / *SCD,* 1327. C. Stephen Evans seems to be making a similar point with regard to Kierkegaard in chapter 6 of his *Kierkegaard's Ethic of Love,* esp. 144–46.

35. It is important to note that this kind of love does not *remove* the dissimilarities of earthly life; it simply does not consider them as relevant features in the execution of neighbor-love (*WL,* 70).

36. See Ferreira, *Love's Grateful Striving,* 45.

37. Patrick Stokes, "Kierkegaardian Vision and the Concrete Other," 400.

38. See Buber, "The Question to the Single One" in Buber, *Between Man and Man,* and Adorno, "On Kierkegaard's Doctrine of Love." K. E. Løgstrup has also been influential in this regard. See Løgstrup, *The Ethical Demand.*

39. Adorno, "On Kierkegaard's Doctrine of Love," 420.

40. By way of example, consider Kierkegaard's claim that "[a]s far as thought is concerned, the neighbor does not even need to exist" (*WL,* 21). See Pia Søltoft, "The Presence of the Absent Neighbor in *Works of Love*" for a friendly interpretation of this passage.

41. Purvis, "Mothers, Neighbors and Strangers," 19.

42. Ibid.

43. Ibid., 26.

44. Ibid.

45. Ibid.

46. Ibid., 26–27, emphasis original.

47. Ibid., 27–28.

48. Ibid., 32.

49. Consider Kierkegaard's contrast between spontaneous love and Christian love (*WL,* 36–37), and his claim that love should be extended to all equally (*WL,* 49 and 63).

50. See Evans, *Kierkegaard's Ethic of Love,* 145.

51. Kierkegaard had some of the same reservations about maternal love that he had about erotic love and friendship (see *JP,* 3:2425 / *SKP,* X-1 A 635), but he recognizes that it can also be truly beautiful (*JN,* 2:19 / JJ: 199).

52. Ferreira, *Love's Grateful Striving,* 21.

53. Ibid., 259–60.

54. It is not clear whether Purvis intends to direct this charge specifically against Kierkegaard.

55. Purvis, "Mothers, Neighbors and Strangers," 28 and 32.

56. For the most part, I will use the word "love," or especially "Christian love" or "neighbor-love," to refer to Kierkegaard's views, and "charity" or "Christian charity" to refer to Aquinas's views. When I use "love" in a Thomistic context, I will try to make it clear that the context is Thomistic.

57. Pope, "The Order of Love and Recent Catholic Ethics," 260. Pope is referring to *ST,* II-II.23.1, where Aquinas explains how and why we are to love everyone.

58. *ST*, II-II.26.6. Stephen J. Pope indicates that this view sounds a great deal like Augustine's view, noted earlier. See Pope, *The Evolution of Altruism and the Ordering of Love*, 61.

59. *ST*, Ia.1.8, reply to objection 2.

60. *ST*, II-II.26.6.

61. On nature, see James M. Gustafson, "Nature: Its Status in Theological Ethics."

62. *CUP*, 573, 584; *FSE*, 76; *PF*, 19. While Kierkegaard's conception of this change of the subject and not in the subject is radical, it is a rebirth of what we "always already" were, and were originally intended to be. It is, as the Kierkegaard of the *Upbuilding Discourses* would put it, the manifestation of our "deeper self" (*EUD*, 314–19). For an important discussion of this point, see George Pattison, "Philosophy and Dogma," 161.

63. Pattison, "Philosophy and Dogma," 161.

64. *ST*, Ia.75.4.

65. Pope, *The Evolution of Altruism and the Ordering of Love*, 55.

66. Ibid., 58.

67. It is important to note, as we will in chapter 7, that here is a characteristic difference between Lutheranism and Catholicism, in that the latter is more ready to talk about particular sins and their gravity, while Lutheranism and indeed Kierkegaard prefer to talk about the "rubrics" of sin and faith (*SUD*, 105).

68. See *JFY*, 140, on the "natural man." By contrast, Aquinas will nearly always argue that while specifically Christian doctrines cannot be proven using natural reason, their truth is in some sense "suitable." For more on this, see Aquinas's treatment of such doctrines in book 4 of *Summa contra Gentiles*.

69. See also *JP*, 6:6433 / *SKP*, X-1 A 517.

70. See Pattison, "Philosophy and Dogma," 159–60. For Kierkegaard, we have constructed a sinful (though ultimately false) self, and this self must die. The desires of this sinful self are precisely what are at issue.

71. Evans, *Kierkegaard's Ethic of Love*, 207.

72. I owe my thanks to Steve Evans for help in thinking through these issues, despite the fact that I cannot agree with the view that he takes here.

73. See Evans, *Kierkegaard's Ethic of Love*, 208. The passage Evans quotes is from *WL*, 52.

74. See Evans, *Kierkegaard's Ethic of Love*, 204.

75. See Ferreira, *Love's Grateful Striving*, 104.

76. See *Nicomachean Ethics*, 9.4, 1166b13–29, 1844.

77. Ibid., 9.9, 1169b10, 1848.

78. Although Kierkegaard claims that paganism has no knowledge of the command to love the neighbor (*WL*, 44), I agree with Evans (*Kierkegaard's Ethic of Love*, 156–64) in thinking that this claim is not essential to Kierkegaard's overall project. The question of whether a person is *aware* of the duty to love one's neighbor and its theological foundation is not of primary importance; what is important is whether love has what Kierkegaard thinks is the proper structure *in fact*. Failing that, for Kierkegaard, we do not love.

79. Ignore for the moment our contemporary disagreements with Aristotle about whether this would be a relationship of equality.

80. See Augustine, *Christian Instruction*, 1.23, 43.

81. Ferreira, *Love's Grateful Striving*, 35.

82. *ST*, II-II.26.6, reply to objection 1.

83. Susan C. Selner-Wright, "The Order of Charity in Thomas Aquinas."

84. Pope writes, "The neighbor in real need in fact claims prima facie priority over all others, and hence in cases of urgent need we ought to care for strangers rather than friends" (Pope, "The Order of Love," 282). See also *ST*, II-II.31.3, reply to objection 1.

85. Selner-Wright, "The Order of Charity in Thomas Aquinas," 21. One might consider Paul's claim that "I could wish myself accursed and separated from Christ for the sake of my brothers, my kin according to the flesh" (Rom 9:3). On this point, see *ST*, II-II.27.8, and ch. 7 of Edward Collins Vacek, *Love, Human and Divine: The Heart of Christian Ethics*.

86. *ST*, II-II.26.4, reply to objection 1.

87. *ST*, II-II.26.4, emphasis mine.

88. Christopher Toner, "Was Aquinas an Egoist?" 604.

89. Pope, *The Evolution of Altruism and the Ordering of Love*, 62.

90. *ST*, II-II.26.6, reply to objection 1.

91. *ST*, II-II.26.7.

92. Ibid.

93. Ibid.

94. Ibid.

95. *ST*, II-II.26.8.

96. Ibid.

97. See *ST*, II-II.26.10.

98. For some helpful discussion, see John Lippitt, "Cracking the Mirror: On Kierkegaard's Concerns about Friendship."

99. Steel, "Thomas Aquinas on Preferential Love," 456.

100. *DH*, 2351, 2355 / *SCD*, 1327, 1331.

101. Vacek, *Love, Human and Divine*, 204.

102. See ibid. This is one of several alternatives for the act of contrition. See James Socias, *Daily Roman Missal*, 2180 and 2253. For more on the topic of contrition, see chapter 6.

103. Vacek, *Love, Human and Divine*, 205.

104. Adams, "Pure Love," 184.

105. Ibid., 182.

106. *Deus Caritas Est*, 1.

107. Ibid., 7.

108. Ibid.

109. Ibid., 14.

110. Ibid., 17.

111. See also *JP*, 1:773 / *SKP*, III A 4; and *JP*, 4:5038 / *SKP*, XI-2 A 239.

112. *The Love of God*, 10.10, 427.

113. Avery Cardinal Dulles, "Love, the Pope, and C.S. Lewis," 20.

114. I understand a common good here to mean something like a good that can be possessed by indefinitely many people without thereby subtracting from each

person's share in it. My thanks are owed to Carol Simon for pointing out the need to be explicit on this point.

115. *ST,* II-II.26.4, reply to objection 3. I do not mean that Kierkegaard's and Aquinas's views are the same on this apostolic dictum, but I cannot venture an interpretation of either in this space.

116. *ST,* II-II.26.3, reply to objection 3, italics mine.

117. See chapter 6 and *JP,* 3:2390 / *SKP,* III A 137. Though, nonetheless, as I argue in chapter 6, this is also a movement from an initial love of God that may still be selfish in important respects to a real love for God after redemption in Christ.

118. Daphne Hampson notes this in her *Christian Contradictions,* 260.

119. Josef Pieper, *Faith, Hope, Love,* 244–45.

120. See Michael S. Sherwin, *By Knowledge and By Love: Charity and Knowledge in the Moral Theology of St. Thomas Aquinas,* 54.

121. Pieper, *Faith, Hope, Love,* 235.

122. This is a loose paraphrase from Matthew 25:31–46.

4. The Catholic Moment?

The epigraph is from Merton, *New Seeds of Contemplation,* 111.

1. This doctrine is littered throughout Luther's writings, but one instance is at *LW* 44:129.

2. See Lowrie's translation of some of Kierkegaard's late writings, titled *Attack upon Christendom,* 300, for a particularly clear statement to this effect. Frederick Copleston also questions (somewhat more in passing) whether Kierkegaard might have become Catholic if he had only lived longer. See *A History of Philosophy,* 7:350. See Walter Lowrie, *Kierkegaard,* 2:523–31, and Heinrich Roos, *Søren Kierkegaard and Catholicism,* for more on Kierkegaard's relation to Catholicism.

3. For more on the pseudonym H.H. see Jacob Bøggild, "H.H.—Poet or Martyr?"

4. See David Law, "Resignation, Suffering and Guilt" on Religiousness A.

5. Note, however, that Climacus himself claims that he is not a Christian (*CUP,* 466).

6. The Danish text has *Mand* here, but for an interesting argument that some of the women in Kierkegaard's works practice apostolic authority, see Mark Lloyd Taylor, "Practice in Authority: The Apostolic Women of Søren Kierkegaard's Writings." In the Catholic tradition this issue is more complicated. In the narrowest sense of the word "apostle," only the original twelve are apostles. In a broader sense, bishops and popes can use apostolic authority. These first two groups would include only men. In a sense that is broader still, however, we can talk about apostolic orders of women religious and indeed the lay apostolate (see Vatican II's *Apostolicam Actuositatem*). In what follows the discussion is often focused on the first two senses above, and so when appropriate, will sometimes be gender exclusive. The appendix to Deborah Halter, *The Papal "No": A Comprehensive Guide to the Vatican's Rejection of Women's Ordination,* brings together magisterial sources on the question of women's ordination, despite the fact that I think the main text of her book is often slanted against these documents.

7. Note that Climacus, in discussing the ways in which the apostle is exceptional, notes that he or she, in the paradoxical-dialectical, is directly related to other people, and directly related to God (*CUP*, 605). The direct relation is paradoxically higher in the case of the apostle, which it would not be in the ordinary case.

8. There is a controversy over whether Climacus's Religiousness B is the last moment of the dialectic. Merold Westphal has argued that there is an additional moment that he has called Religiousness C. See his "Kierkegaard's Teleological Suspension of Religiousness B" for a good discussion of this view. This is not the place to weigh in on the controversy, since I have already registered my view elsewhere (see my "Re-radicalizing Kierkegaard"). At any rate, the point here is that, whatever the last moment of Kierkegaard's dialectic (whether it be Religiousness B or C), the apostle is not another rung on that ladder.

9. In the margin of this entry, Kierkegaard claims that the sort of authority that such people, notably bishops, have is "the concept of authority in immanence," in contrast to the paradoxical authority of the apostle.

10. Stephen N. Dunning points out that "there is no way to judge the apostle's claim simply by the content of his message" ("Who Sets the Task? Kierkegaard on Authority," 28). This seems correct; however, it would appear that, while one cannot evaluate a message by its content, one can nonetheless evaluate whether it is spoken with authority when one considers the life of the person who utters it. In fact, Kierkegaard seems to be engaged in just this sort of examination when it comes to Adolph Adler (see *The Book on Adler* and Dunning's essay for more on this point).

11. As late as 1847 Kierkegaard claimed that he had never "really" read anything by Luther (*JP*, 3:2463 / *SKP*, VIII-1 A 465), though the references to Luther (and to particular passages from his works) in Kierkegaard's journals pick up steadily after that time.

12. See James Collins, *The Mind of Kierkegaard*, 216, and *M*, 41–45.

13. See *JP*, 3:2481 / *SKP*, X-1 A 154; *JP*, 3:2751 / *SKP*, IX A 362; and *JP*, 3:3182 / *SKP*, XI-1 A 532. Also, see *JP*, 3:2548 / *SKP*, XI-1 A 108, which claims that Luther replaced the pope with "the public."

14. Kierkegaard once called Luther "the master of us all" (*JP*, 3:2465 / *SKP*, VIII-1 A 642).

15. See Luther's essay "Concerning the Ministry," *LW* 40:7–44.

16. Ibid., 11.

17. See Luther's essay "The Keys," *LW* 40:321–77.

18. Luther's essay "The Babylonian Captivity of the Church," esp. *LW* 36:46–57, is a worthy source here, though I think there would be some justice to the accusation that Luther was not as clear as he could have been on this matter.

19. See "Concerning Rebaptism," *LW* 40:225–62.

20. In 1848 Kierkegaard notes that Luther is "somewhat confused" (*JP*, 3:2467 / *SKP*, IX A 11) and a year later remarks, "the more I look at Luther the more I am convinced that he was muddle-headed" (*JP*, 3:2481 / *SKP*, X-1 A 172).

21. "The Private Mass and the Consecration of Priests," *LW* 38:139–219; quotation from 152.

22. On these points, see Ernest B. Koenker, "Søren Kierkegaard on Luther."

23. Kierkegaard's critiques do not change the fact that his theology is Lutheran in important ways. See Hermann Deuser, "Kierkegaard and Luther: Kierkegaard's 'One Thesis,'" 210.

24. Catholicism regards the bishops ("with priests as co-workers") as the successors of Christ's apostles, who themselves possess a kind of apostolic authority, certainly with respect to the teaching of doctrine in harmony with the larger episcopal college. See *CCC*, 861–62 and 888–92. It could be objected that my treatment of this issue uses Catholic sources, but approaches the issue in such a way that any Christian church that acknowledges authority based on apostolic succession could have also been used (e.g., the Orthodox Church). I simply grant the point as far as it goes. Nonetheless, there has been significant discussion in Kierkegaard scholarship over whether Kierkegaard's apostle aligns him with Catholicism's treatment of that matter, and it is this question that has given rise to the present chapter.

25. Gerald O'Collins and Mario Farrugia, *Catholicism: The Story of Catholic Christianity*, 101.

26. *CCC*, 860.

27. When talking about broader senses here, it is important to recall the lay apostolate.

28. O'Collins and Farrugia, *Catholicism*, 100.

29. Ibid.

30. *DH*, 2804 / *SCD*, 1641.

31. Dunning, "Who Sets the Task?" 21.

32. Hugh Pyper, "The Apostle, the Genius and the Monkey: Reflections on Kierkegaard's 'The Mirror of the Word,'" 131.

33. As Robert Perkins has pointed out to me, there may be conceptual differences between the Hebrew prophet's message and the Christian apostle's. Kierkegaard does invest the distinction between the Old and New Testaments with some importance with regard to prophecy (*JN*, 2:12 / *EE*: 33), but he clearly thinks that the episode in question here is a discharge of Nathan's divinely commissioned authority (*FSE*, 39). At this point in our discussion, however, the decisive thing about authority is its ability to communicate directly, rather than indirectly.

34. Pyper writes, "It would also be mistaken to see this retort of Nathan's as a direct statement in contrast to the indirectness of the parable. The device only works because David was initially led to distance himself from the man in the story by the skillful indirection of Nathan's reference. It is only because David was convinced that he was *not* the man that his faculty of judgement could be exercised" ("The Apostle, the Genius and the Monkey," 132–33). While Pyper is right that the whole episode, and not just one part, is quite effective in showing David the need for repentance, and is thus a successful discharge of Nathan's prophetic commission, Nathan does not, in Kierkegaard's account, appear successful at first. Indeed, Kierkegaard tells us that "authority" is used only when Nathan grows "weary of this impersonality and objectivity" (*FSE*, 39). This highlights the fact that Nathan, in Kierkegaard's account, originally intended his indirect story to do more than it was in fact doing. Perhaps Nathan thought that his "genius" in indirect communication would, on this occasion, be quite enough to show an otherwise holy king the error

of his ways (it does, after all, take some gumption to directly assert one's prophetic authority before the Lord's anointed). Nathan then had to directly (or at least more directly) assert his authority by having done with timidly hoping that David would understand the point of his hypothetical tale, and explain that the point was to convict David of that of which he must now be (more) directly accused.

35. Pyper, "The Apostle, the Genius and the Monkey," 131.

36. This is an affirmation of the serious and difficult burden placed on an apostle, not of Pelagianism, unless Pelagianism is interpreted so as to rule out *any* human component in faith or apostolic ministry, which component Kierkegaard appears to clearly accept. There is, no doubt, a more *practically effective* discharge of the apostolic commission when the apostle has a bit of dialectically orienting genius (which in any case would ultimately come from God) to bring to bear on the issue, though genius comes in degrees, and responsibility for preparing one's listeners probably does as well.

37. Before Gregory's time, both St. Gregory of Nazianzus and St. John Chrysostom penned works on the priesthood, both on the occasion of having been reluctantly elected to a sacerdotal office. Gregory of Nazianzus's work is said to have had a direct influence on Gregory the Great's treatise (see the "Introduction" to Gregory the Great's *Pastoral Care*).

38. Gregory the Great, *Pastoral Care,* 90.

39. Ibid., 94–95.

40. Ibid., 138, emphasis original.

41. Ibid.

42. St. John Chrysostom provides perhaps an even better example of the different ways to bring people back from sin in his *Six Books on the Priesthood,* 58.

43. Gregory enumerates a number of sins, those who are subject to which should not be considered for the priestly office. He even claims that "a man who is still ravaged by his own sins, cannot expiate the sins of others" (*Pastoral Care,* 44). Although this might seem to flirt with Donatism, Gregory often denounced what he labeled as Donatism early in his papacy, and so perhaps we should not be too hasty on this point. For more on this topic, see the entries "Donatist Bishops" and "Donatus, Donatism," in *Augustine through the Ages: An Encyclopedia.*

44. Gregory the Great, *Pastoral Care,* 30–31.

45. Ibid., 72.

46. Ibid., 73.

47. See, especially, *DH,* 912 / *SCD,* 486.

48. See J. N. D. Kelly, *Early Christian Doctrines,* 410. See also Ludwig Ott, *Fundamentals of Catholic Dogma,* 342, and *DH,* 1612 / *SCD,* 855.

49. Fitzgerald et al., *Augustine through the Ages,* 281.

50. See Letter 185, ch. 38, in *Augustine: Letters 165–203,* 178.

51. Augustine, *Letters 165–203,* 157.

52. The notion of the Church Militant is approvingly used by Catholic authors who antedate Kierkegaard's time. For instance, St. Francis de Sales (1567–1622) frequently used it in his polemic pamphlets against the Calvinists of Geneva. See pt. 1, ch. 8, of his *The Catholic Controversy,* 46–53.

53. I say this despite the fact that some Catholic writers, as one might expect (with St. Francis de Sales being notable among them), have tended to regard Do-

natism as applying more liberally to other factions of the Reformation, for instance to certain forms of Calvinism (see ibid., pt. 1, ch. 11, 65).

54. Augustine, *Letters 165–203*, 164. Recall that Luther follows Augustine on this point. See also *DH*, 123 / *SCD*, 53.

55. Augustine, *Letters 165–203*, 171.

56. Kierkegaard seems to approach the question at one point (*JP*, 2:1924 / *SKP*, XI-1 A 4), but does not answer it. Kierkegaard also seems to repudiate too much reliance on the sacraments, as being a retreat from the subjective to the objective (*JP*, 4:5047 / *SKP*, XI-1 A 556). The "Discourses at the Communion on Fridays" (*CD*, 247–300) include the most sustained of Kierkegaard's reflections on Holy Communion. However, these reflections are certainly not dogmatic theology in the strict sense, and indeed may well get Kierkegaard into significant dogmatic trouble. See Michael Plekon, "Kierkegaard and the Eucharist," for a friendly interpretation, though.

57. Compare St. Thomas Aquinas on the sacraments, who argues that gravely wicked priests do in fact sin in administering sacraments, but nonetheless are genuine instruments of Christ (provided they are still tolerated in the Church) by whose power all sacraments are truly accomplished, and that therefore such wicked and actively sinning priests can genuinely effect the sacraments. See *ST*, III.64.5, and 6. Here it might be important to remember that Kierkegaard himself effectively refused Holy Communion on his deathbed, indicating that he was willing to take it only from a layman. See Bruce H. Kirmmse, *Encounters with Kierkegaard: A Life as Seen by His Contemporaries*, 125–26.

58. Plekon notes that Kierkegaard appears anti-sacramental in one journal entry (*JP*, 4:5047 / *SKP*, XI-1 A 556), but goes on to argue that this is a misunderstanding ("Kierkegaard and the Eucharist," 221). Plekon tries to argue Kierkegaard free from the "theological trap of requiring the faith of the communicant to make the sacrament valid and the presence of Christ real" (229), which is particularly troublesome when viewed alongside the journal entry he cites (*JP*, 4:3936 / *SKP*, X-2 A 50). While I think Plekon succeeds in showing that Kierkegaard is not simply anti-sacramental, I am not yet convinced that he has rescued Kierkegaard from this and other theological traps having to do with the sacraments.

59. See Plekon, "Kierkegaard and the Eucharist," 228, and *CD*, 300.

60. See pt. 1, ch. 3, of *The Catholic Controversy*, 24.

61. John Paul II, *Pastores Gregis*, 2.11.

62. Ibid., 2.23.

63. Ibid., 3.31.

64. See *CCC*, 892, and Vatican II's *Lumen Gentium*, 25. In the most extreme case, there are the very rare *ex cathedra* pronouncements by the pope, the bishop of Rome (for instance, Pope Pius XII's 1950 apostolic constitution *Munificentissimus Deus*, which defined the dogma of the Assumption of the Virgin Mary). There is a large controversy about how to read *Lumen Gentium* when it comes to less-authoritative pronouncements and the *obsequium religiosum* enjoined upon the faithful with respect to such pronouncements. For a good variety of different opinions on this controversy, see William W. May, *Vatican Authority and American Catholic Dissent: The Curran Case and Its Consequences*.

65. On this point, H.H. writes, "Authority is a specific quality either of an apostolic calling or of *ordination*" (*WA*, 99, emphasis mine). This, however, need not

contradict the view that one can possess a fragile authority in virtue of ordination, but the ordination may not be sufficient to guarantee authority.

66. Steve Evans has suggested to me that the earlier writings on authority, such as *The Book on Adler,* bring forward a more orthodox perspective than the later writings. I would agree, for the most part, noting that "On the Difference between a Genius and An Apostle," on which we have dwelt earlier in this chapter, seems to be, in the words of the Hongs, an "epitomization" of *The Book on Adler* (see *BA,* viii). In that essay, I think there are shades of the rigorism and Donatism that will later appear more readily, but that important essay is much less troubling for orthodox Christians and Catholics than the later writings.

67. See Plekon, "Kierkegaard at the End: His 'Last' Sermon, Eschatology and the Attack on the Church," and chapter 8 below. Steve Evans has suggested to me that Kierkegaard's loneliness and declining health help to explain the more troubling extreme-sounding passages, and I find this a helpful way to consider the matter.

68. While Kierkegaard seems to guard himself by saying, "the thesis may well be posited," he seems to feel the sting of such questioning of Christ's apostles (for which he defends himself) later in a footnote from another article in *The Moment* (*M,* 341).

69. Recall that this is what Luther was also criticized for doing (*JP,* 3:2481 / *SKP,* X-1 A 154).

70. See Matthew 16:19.

71. This might seem to suggest that I believe no individual can be granted eternal salvation (and thus remission of sins) without the ordinary physical manifestation of the sacrament of baptism. For more on the Church's present (and complex) understanding of this point, see the International Theological Commission's 2007 document, *The Hope of Salvation for Infants Who Die without Being Baptized.* See also chapter 5, especially the section on Hans Urs von Balthasar's contribution to the question of theological universalism.

5. Must All Be Saved?

The first epigraph is from *JN,* 2:95 / *FF:* 149. The second epigraph is from Josef Pieper, *The Concept of Sin,* 42.

1. I wish to make it clear that I am not adopting any stance on the wider authorship of Balthasar. I am merely taking the broad approach toward possible universal salvation, of which he is merely the most famous representative in the contemporary Catholic tradition, to be a point of dialogue for the Catholic tradition and Kierkegaard.

2. See Balthasar, *Dare We Hope,* 88, 250, and *JP,* 6:6496 / *SKP,* X-2 A 44.

3. See, for example, *M,* 181.

4. Balthasar discusses these comments in his "A Short Discourse on Hell," included in the English translation of *Dare We Hope.*

5. For instance, see Pope John Paul II's statement to a general audience dated Wednesday, 28 July 1999. There the English text reads, "Eternal damnation remains a real possibility, but we are not granted, without special divine revelation, the knowledge of *whether or which* human beings are effectively involved in it" (emphasis mine). See also Pope John Paul II's *Crossing the Threshold of Hope,*

185–87, where John Paul II explicitly invokes Balthasar and himself claims that the Catholic Church has made no pronouncement regarding the fate of any particular individual, even Judas. There is a significant controversy about whether certain other aspects of Balthasar's theology should rest in the good graces of the Catholic magisterium. I am not registering a view on this matter. On this point, see Alyssa Lyra Pitstick, *Light in Darkness: Hans Urs von Balthasar and the Catholic Doctrine of Christ's Descent into Hell.* See also the exchange between Pitstick and Edward T. Oakes in "Balthasar, Hell, and Heresy: An Exchange," and "More on Balthasar, Hell, and Heresy."

6. Richard Marius seems to have it that Luther was more terrified at the prospect of death itself than damnation. See Marius, *Martin Luther: The Christian between God and Death,* esp. 60–63.

7. I believe that certain portions of Kierkegaard's thought, pseudonymous or signed, *come close* to requiring the rejection of Strong Universalism (SU). I will, however, confine myself to the more modest aim of arguing that Kierkegaard's texts provide the partial resources, which are especially strong when paired with those of the Catholic tradition, for a critical response to SU.

8. I will sometimes use the term "empty hell" purely for convenience. Neither Kierkegaard's position (on which see below) nor Balthasar's position requires that hell be any kind of literal place. See Balthasar, *Dare We Hope,* 127 and 166.

9. *ST,* Ia.25.3.

10. See *CCC,* 1035.

11. Socias, *Daily Roman Missal,* 2329.

12. See, for instance, the Council of Quiersy's statement, "Omnipotent God wishes *all men* without exception to be saved . . . although not all will be saved" (*DH,* 622 / *SCD,* 318). The force of the latter unconditional statement can be mitigated somewhat by the realization that this council was not ecumenical and by the fact that future ecumenical councils usually prefer the conditional claim that if anyone should die in a state of mortal sin (*DH,* 1306 / *SCD,* 693) or outside the bounds of the Catholic Church (*DH,* 1351 / *SCD,* 714) then that person would end up in hell. For a discussion of how it is possible (leaving aside the question of independent plausibility) to maintain CMT despite these challenges, see below.

13. See "The Doctrine of Everlasting Punishment," 21–23. I shall not comment on or question his definition of "theism" since its precise usage is not important for my purposes in this chapter.

14. Paul Jensen, in a careful discussion of Talbott, distinguishes between hard (I use "strong" here) and soft universalism, rightly citing Talbott as an example of the former. Hard universalism, according to Jensen, is the view that "no person *can be* finally lost," and soft universalism, according to Jensen, is the view that "no person *will be* finally lost" (see "Intolerable but Moral? Thinking about Hell," 236). With respect to John Paul II's earlier statement to a general audience, it would seem that he rejects SU (or Jensen's hard universalism), but might find it in principle possible that soft universalism could be true (with respect to, at any rate, human individuals).

15. "Three Versions of Universalism," 56.

16. I will be arguing for the conjunction of (1)–(4) together with ◊(5') and ◊(5") (see below), but I wish to note that, despite the way these propositions are worded,

I will not be staking anything in this chapter on the distinction between the claim that all human individuals (but not all angelic individuals) may possibly be reconciled with God and the claim that all individuals, human and angelic, may possibly be reconciled with God. I personally hold the former claim, as does the *Catechism* (see *CCC*, 391–95), but I will not be arguing for that more nuanced position in this chapter.

17. Note that this is a more nuanced position than I gave in my article ("Must All Be Saved? A Kierkegaardian Response to Theological Universalism") of which this chapter is a further development.

18. Both $\Diamond(5')$ and $\Diamond(5'')$ have a strictly logical character in and of themselves. However, if CMT is to have the kind of theological significance that Balthasar is interested in, it must, in addition, be *epistemically* possible (given what we know) that one possible world in which all find their ultimate beatitude is the actual world. Balthasar, along with John Paul II, argues that Scripture is not absolutely definitive even about the perdition of Judas. Perhaps Kierkegaard would disagree. If so, then he would cling to the purely logical forms of $\Diamond(5')$ and $\Diamond(5'')$, and dispute the *epistemic* possibility of logically contingent universal salvation in the actual world.

19. "The Doctrine of Everlasting Punishment," 37.

20. For some interesting criticism of Talbott's examples, see Charles Seymour, "On Choosing Hell."

21. "The Doctrine of Everlasting Punishment," 38.

22. Ibid., 39. For a longer treatment of this same type of argument, see Eric Reitan, "Eternal Damnation and Blessed Ignorance: Is the Damnation of Some Incompatible with the Salvation of Any?" As we have said in chapter 3, Aquinas would wish to bring some nuance to Talbott's claim that supremely worthwhile happiness requires that I learn to love my enemies as I love my own daughter.

23. I thank Steve Evans for helpfully insisting that I make my view on God's objective reality clearer here.

24. See also, for instance, *SUD*, 80; *JP*, 2:1349 / *SKP*, VII-1 A 201; and *JP*, 2:1449 / *SKP*, XI-2 133.

25. Clearly, there are ways in which God's existence is both external and not external. See Evans, "Realism and Antirealism in Kierkegaard's *Concluding Unscientific Postscript*."

26. See the entries that the Hongs group together as *JP*, 4:4893–919. As the Hongs' work groups entries by topic and not by date of entry or notebook, such designations for the above entries are quite different. A representative entry is *JP*, 4:4894 / *SKP*, X-3 A 393.

27. See Timothy P. Jackson, "Arminian Edification: Kierkegaard on Grace and Free Will."

28. See John Calvin, *Institutes of the Christian Religion*, bk. 3, ch. 22, sec. 1, 212–14; also *The Canons of Dort*, First Main Point, art. 9. See also Aquinas, *ST*, Ia.23.5. I do not mean to equate Calvinism and Thomism, however, which have distinct positions on these matters. I have temptations toward Thomism, but I think Arminianism or Molinism will make better sense of Kierkegaard's view. See Robert C. Koons's "Dual Agency" for a suggestive discussion of Thomism.

29. Or so Thomas P. Flint thinks in his "Two Accounts of Providence," 148.

30. The Catholic position is generally understood as one that affirms God's foreknowledge of future contingents, in accordance with Vatican I, on which see *DH,* 3003 / *SCD,* 1784.

31. Sin is defiance before God, so it is "intensified defiance" (*SUD,* 77).

32. See *Protagoras,* 359d, in *Plato: Complete Works.*

33. Pieper cites this, calling it "the right answer" to Socrates' question (*The Concept of Sin,* 32).

34. In order to substantiate what I mean by "ultimate cause," perhaps it will be helpful to recall Aristotle's distinction between someone's doing something in an ignorance for which she is responsible, and someone's doing something in an ignorance for which she is not responsible. On this distinction, see *Nicomachean Ethics* 3.5, 1758-60.

35. See *SUD,* 95. Also, Kierkegaard himself notes that Kant's theory of radical evil has only the fault that it "does not definitively establish that the inexplicable is a category." He goes on to note that "everything turns on this" (*JP,* 3:3089 / *SKP* VIII-1 A 11).

36. See Walls, *Hell: The Logic of Damnation,* esp. ch. 5.

37. Ibid., 128-29.

38. If one wants to find the priority of intellect over will, I doubt the best place to look is in Kierkegaard's work. Nonetheless, even if certain Thomistic theses (to say nothing of divergent Catholic views in the Franciscan tradition) rejecting the will's autonomy are true, there is still a good deal that Kierkegaard and such Christian thinkers can share in common when it comes to the concept of sin. Aquinas seems to hold that the trouble with sin is that one fails to attend to the rule that would govern one's behavior in the best way and then acts without regard to the rule. He writes, "And the very fact of not actually giving heed to such a rule considered in itself is not evil, neither a fault nor a penalty because the soul is not bound nor is it always possible to actually give heed to a rule of this kind; but it first takes on the nature of fault from this that without actual consideration of the rule it proceeds to such a choice, just as the carpenter does no wrong in not always having in hand a measure but in proceeding to cut without using the measure" (Aquinas, *On Evil,* question 1, art. 3, 22). This seems to hold that the trouble is not a false set of information either, but the failure to attend to the right information, and then the choice is made without actually consulting the right information.

39. I do not mean that the subject cannot present the choice to himself as an apparent partial good, but the apparent good must still be understood, in some sense, to be less-good than the better choice. In this sense, Milton's Satan, who *says* it is better to reign in hell than serve in heaven, must at some level *know* that it isn't, or he is subject to the Socratic analysis of sin (instead of book 1 of *Paradise Lost,* I would suggest dwelling a bit more on Satan's opening speech in book 4). Walls's insistence that this lesson is lost seems a very infelicitous way to put this. By contrast, consider Laura Waddell Ekstrom's model of indeterminist free agency, on which a choice that fails to select the "most rational" option still counts as "reasonable" given that it resulted from a process of reflective preference-forming. On this account, Satan's choice of hell would count as "reasonable" despite the fact that he acted quite defiantly against his better judgment. I see no reason why I could not call a defiant choice "reasonable" in this sense (despite the fact that I continue to see it as

inexplicable how one just does form this overriding preference for a less-rational option). See Ekstrom, *Free Will: A Philosophical Study,* esp. 127–29.

40. Pieper, *The Concept of Sin,* 42. See also *CCC,* 1861, which calls mortal sin "a radical possibility of human freedom."

41. See *JP,* 1:733 / *SKP,* XI-1 A 270, where Kierkegaard claims that the demoniac resists the solution, while knowing what it is, "at least with a kind of clairvoyance."

42. In *The Works of Bernard of Clairvaux,* vol. 7: *Treatises III.* The Latin title is *De gratia et libero arbitrio.* I recognize that Kierkegaard and his pseudonyms had some misgivings about the idea of *liberum arbitrium* (e.g., see *CA,* 112). For some discussion of this point, see Jackson, "Kierkegaard on Grace and Free Will," esp. 246–53. Some of this brief discussion on Bernard is reprinted with permission from my "Bernard of Clairvaux: Kierkegaard's Reception of the 'Last of the Fathers.'"

43. *On Grace and Free Choice,* 1.2, 54.

44. Nonetheless, Freedom of Choice is said to be more "orderly" in the just (*On Grace and Free Choice,* 4.9, 65–66).

45. *On Grace and Free Choice,* 9.30, 85–86.

46. *On Grace and Free Choice,* 7.23, 80. Here Bernard is following a long line of interpreters, among whom Augustine is the most notable. See Bernard McGinn's introduction to *On Grace and Free Choice* for more on this point.

47. McGinn writes, "The antecedent role of intellect is to illuminate the will through a true *judgment* [not missing after the Fall] . . . and to show the will what is expedient and licit through free *counsel.*" Because free counsel is gone after the Fall, humans cannot supply themselves with the proper motivation to pursue right actions. Although Bernard's standing in the Catholic tradition is high, I am not claiming that Bernard mirrors subsequent Catholic dogma on every point here, especially since he predates the Council of Trent. See the introduction to *On Grace and Free Choice,* 22, and Ott, *Fundamentals of Catholic Dogma,* 233–36.

48. See the introduction to *On Grace and Free Choice,* 23.

49. *On Grace and Free Choice,* 4.9, 65.

50. Bernard's insistence that the damned in hell continue to possess Freedom of Choice (*On Grace and Free Choice,* 9.30, 86) is a helpful supplement to Kierkegaard's understanding of hell and human freedom.

51. On this loss of dignity and its similitude to nonhuman animals, see also Michael Sherwin, *By Knowledge and By Love,* 106.

52. I am aware that what I take to be Kierkegaard's view, namely, "conditional predestination," will presuppose the coherence of middle knowledge. For a defense of middle knowledge, see Thomas P. Flint, *Divine Providence: The Molinist Account.*

53. *CCC,* 1058.

54. See Oakes's contribution in Pitstick and Oakes, "Balthasar, Hell, and Heresy," 29 (italics original). See also John R. Sachs, "Current Eschatology: Universal Salvation and the Problem of Hell," esp. 232, where we read, "[Balthasar's] is a pointed, but not extreme, position, quite consonant with Church teaching and the thought of most other major Catholic theologians."

55. Here, as throughout when I discuss Balthasar, I mean "possible" to indicate the epistemic possibility (given what we know prior to the eschaton) of (5″) in this world.

56. This seems to be Talbott's point in calling his position "Biblical Theism." See "The Doctrine of Everlasting Punishment," 23.

57. I do not mean, and I do not think Balthasar means, that there is no possibility for a wider understanding of these passages in a coherent view of the whole of Scripture that might be committed to a position on the issue of universalism. I just mean that "proof-texting" on this question won't decide the matter.

58. See *DH*, 1306 / *SCD*, 693.

59. *CCC*, 1856–61.

60. Pieper, *The Concept of Sin*, 72–73. The similarities to and differences from Kierkegaard's claim about the inability to tell whether a given deed is love or not at *WL*, 14, are interesting.

61. See *DH*, 1351 / *SCD*, 714.

62. On its sources in St. Cyprian, see my "Cyprian of Carthage: Kierkegaard, Cyprian, and the 'Urgent Needs of the Times.'"

63. See *CCC*, 846. Climacus simply reformulates it to "outside this condition there is no eternal happiness" (*CUP*, 586).

64. *Lumen Gentium*, 16. See also Vatican II's short declaration *Nostra Aetate*.

65. *Crossing the Threshold of Hope*, 83.

66. Ibid., 138, 140, italics original. John Paul II there cites Pope Paul VI's first encyclical, *Ecclesiam Suam*, as detailing the "circles of the dialogue of salvation."

67. This is clearest in ch. 3 of *Dare We Hope*, esp. 65.

68. Pieper, *Faith, Hope, Love*, 113. See also Balthasar, *Dare We Hope*, 27–28.

69. See ch. 7 of *A Short Discourse on Hell* (included in *Dare We Hope*), which bears the title "The Obligation to Hope for All."

70. Balthasar, *Dare We Hope*, 212.

71. See ibid., 166.

72. See ibid., 88 and 250.

73. Ibid., 190.

74. Ibid., 127.

75. Ibid., 53–58.

76. Ibid., 84.

77. Ibid., 237. For some of Kierkegaard's personal wrestlings with universalism, see *JP*, 4:4922 / *SKP*, XI-1 A 296.

78. See Andrei Buckareff and Allen Plug, "Escaping Hell: Divine Motivation and the Problem of Hell," for a version of this objection.

79. Buckareff and Plug call this "escapism." I will keep to the terminology introduced in my earlier article form of this chapter, but will give a more nuanced rebuttal.

80. See *Thus Spoke Zarathustra*, in *The Portable Nietzsche*, 127, in Zarathustra's Prologue.

81. *CCC*, 1856.

82. See Talbott, "The Doctrine of Everlasting Punishment," 26.

83. Buckareff and Plug, "Escaping Hell," 45.

84. *Dare We Hope*, 145.

85. Lewis was not, of course, a Catholic, but, importantly, Balthasar cites him often and with approval, making no mention of a view approaching "Holding Pattern Theism." See ibid., esp. 91–94.

86. See Buckareff and Plug, "Escaping Hell," 40. They consider their view to be an approximation of a suggestion in C. S. Lewis's *Great Divorce.* While Buckareff and Plug stop short of committing Lewis to this view, I want to note that I am not comfortable committing him to their "escapism," for two reasons. First, Lewis clearly and emphatically states that the sequence is a dream and not to be relied upon for doctrine (144). Second, there are indications in the book that time does not work in the dream the way it works in our human world. In one of the encounters that a ghost has with a "solid person," the solid person urges the ghost to join heaven, even implying that there will *not* be another chance, on the ground that, "this moment contains all moments" (109).

87. Ibid., 77.

88. Lewis, *That Hideous Strength,* 350.

89. *Nicomachean Ethics* 7.1, 1808–1809.

90. See Ott, *Fundamentals of Catholic Dogma,* 474.

91. See Ladislaus Boros, *The Mystery of Death,* for some especially provocative ways of thinking about this issue.

92. It is worth considering Timothy P. Jackson's discussion of the point that all persons have a genuine, if not identical, chance at "Glory." See Jackson, "Kierkegaard on Grace and Free Will," 240. This, in its turn, might also be interesting to consider alongside the Catholic tradition's claim that the reward of heaven admits of degree (see *DH,* 1305 / *SCD,* 693).

93. See *Dare We Hope,* 253.

94. See Aquinas, *ST,* II-II.26.13.

95. Talbott, "The Doctrine of Everlasting Punishment," 19.

96. I realize that I will have to reject Sachs's "asymmetry" thesis between the freedom of humans to choose yes or no in this life and the freedom of human beings to choose only their "yes" to God in a final and definitive way. Still, to mount an argument against this claim would require a wholly separate inquiry, and in any case would duplicate much of the foregoing. See Sachs, "Current Eschatology," 249.

6. On Being Afraid of Hell

The first epigraph is from *JP,* 3:2390 / *SKP,* III A 137. The second epigraph is from *Homilies on the Statues* 15.2, 249.

1. Socias, *Daily Roman Missal,* 2253.

2. As in John Paul II's apostolic exhortation, *Reconciliatio et Paenitentia,* 31n185.

3. *LW* 36:84.

4. See *LW* 54:259 and *SUD,* 105.

5. Kierkegaard owned the 4th edition of Karl Hase's *Hutterus redivivus oder Dogmatik der evangelisch-lutherischen Kirche,* in which the distinction between attrition (or imperfect contrition) and contrition is called a "Catholic distinction" (*Kath. Unterscheidung*). Hase goes on to claim that the Evangelical (Lutheran) Church does not accept the distinction (see 285). My thanks are owed to Niels Jørgen Cappelørn for pointing this out to me, and to Nick Perovich and the late John Quinn for further discussion of the point.

6. *DH,* 1678 / *SCD,* 898.

7. Karl Rahner, *Meditations on the Sacraments,* 58.

8. See, for example, *CCC*, 1454.

9. On personal unity, see George Connell, *To Be One Thing: Personal Unity in Kierkegaard's Thought*.

10. See *Republic* 361b–d, in *Plato: Complete Works*, 1001–1002.

11. Jeremy D. B. Walker, *To Will One Thing: Reflections on Kierkegaard's "Purity of Heart,"* 25.

12. For this discussion, see Immanuel Kant, *Groundwork of The Metaphysics of Morals,* in Kant, *Practical Philosophy*, 67–73. Ronald M. Green lists this work of Kant's as one that Kierkegaard "very likely read" (*Kierkegaard and Kant: The Hidden Debt*, 18–20). See also Ulrich Knappe, *Theory and Practice in Kant and Kierkegaard,* esp. 60, for a good discussion of the text's Kantian influences.

13. See *CCC*, 1033–37, and Ott, *Fundamentals of Catholic Dogma*, 481–82.

14. The sense in which purgatory is an eschatological training ground is the sense in which one prepares for a race one knows for certain one will be running. Where the analogy breaks down is that in this case, the race would itself be the reward of eternal beatitude.

15. *Reconciliatio et Paenitentia*, 31.

16. Ibid.

17. *DH*, 1676 / *SCD*, 897.

18. *DH*, 1678 / *SCD*, 898.

19. *DH*, 1705 / *SCD*, 915.

20. Ludwig Ott attributes this view to Luther, but fails to cite a text (see *Fundamentals of Catholic Dogma,* 429).

21. *LW* 31:50, Thesis 16.

22. Compare St. Catherine of Genoa: "Do not rely on yourself and say, 'I will confess myself and receive a plenary indulgence, and with that be cleansed of all my sins.' The confession and the contrition that is required for the plenary indulgence is such, and so demanding, that were you to realize it you would tremble in terror, more fearful of not having that grace than confident of being able to attain it" (see *Purgation and Purgatory*, 84).

23. "The Sacrament of Penance," 15.

24. *CCC*, 2001.

25. Richard M. Gula, *To Walk Together Again: The Sacrament of Reconciliation,* 217. See also Kenan B. Osborne, *Reconciliation and Justification: The Sacrament and Its Theology.*

26. This was a bone of contention for the Thomists and the Scotists. On this point, see Gula, *To Walk Together Again,* ch. 6, and Osborne, *Reconciliation and Justification,* ch. 6.

27. See Ott, *Fundamentals of Catholic Dogma,* 430, and *DH*, 2070 / *SCD*, 1146.

28. *Reconciliatio et Paenitentia*, 31.

29. *Reconciliatio et Paenitentia*, 31n185. It may be important to note, as John Paul II does, that, in a case of necessity when one is not able to go to confession, and is conscious of being in mortal sin, one "should first make an act of *perfect* contrition" (*Reconciliatio et Paenitentia*, 27, emphasis mine).

30. See Osborne, *Reconciliation and Justification,* 115.

31. See *CCC*, 1480–84.

32. Rahner, *Meditations on the Sacraments,* 57–58.

33. My thanks to Lyra Pitstick for helpful conversations on this point, even if I cannot guarantee that she would agree with everything I say here.

34. See Ott, *Fundamentals of Catholic Dogma*, 427.

35. See *DH*, 1526 / *SCD*, 798, and Ott, *Fundamentals of Catholic Dogma*, 430.

36. *ST*, II-II.26.3, reply to objection 3.

37. See *CCC*, 1453, 2001, and 2022.

38. See *CUP*, 584, for more on this point.

39. Recall that Kierkegaard never claims that it is double-minded to will the good out of a desire for the internal and homogeneous reward that is eternally joined to the good, and even studiously avoids making such claims, in direct contrast to his indictment of willing the good out of fear of eternal punishment (*UDVS*, 41).

40. See *CUP*, 573 and 584–85.

41. See *TDIO*, 23.

42. Climacus is not as clear as he could be about baptism (see *CUP*, 366 and 557), but the Catholic Church has, since the Council of Florence in 1439, reached the conclusion that baptism remits original sin along with all past sins and punishments for them, even calling the neophyte (newly baptized) a "new creature" (see *CCC*, 1265). Since the sacrament of penance reconciles one to the Church in nearly the same manner as baptism did, it is accordingly called a "second plank" after baptism (*DH*, 1702 / *SCD*, 912). This means, for our purposes, that the dialectic of Catholic confession is relevantly similar to the dialectic of Catholic baptism, which, in its turn, is relevantly similar to Kierkegaardian redemption.

43. It is also significant in this connection that Kierkegaard notes that "it is the good that out of love for the learner has invented the punishment" (*UDVS*, 51).

44. Kierkegaard's pseudonymous works do this in a way that is for the most part extra-sacramental, but that is a point I cannot address here.

45. On this point, see *UDVS*, 49.

46. Rahner, *Meditations on the Sacraments*, 58.

47. The existence of error or ignorance does not mean that our penitent is blameless. On this, see *SUD*, 87–96.

48. See *CCC*, 1033–37.

49. For the Catholic Church, the "fire" of hell may well be metaphorical. See Ott, *Fundamentals of Catholic Dogma*, 481, and a general audience of John Paul II (28 July 1999) on this.

50. My thanks are owed to M. Jamie Ferreira and Benjamin Olivares Bøgeskov for formulating this objection and helping me to gain some measure of clarity in responding to it.

51. On venial and mortal sin, see *CCC*, 1854–64, which discusses how venial and mortal sin respectively diminishes and destroys (in such a way as to require a new initiative of God's grace) charity or love in the hearts of human beings.

52. If one does accept venial sins, then there are sins one can actually commit that can cloud one's consciousness without destroying one's love of friendship for God.

53. See *CCC*, 1863.

54. See *Catechism of the Council of Trent*, 280.

55. See Hans Urs von Balthasar, "Mary in the Church's Doctrine and Devotion," in Balthasar and Joseph Cardinal Ratzinger, *Mary: The Church at the Source*,

112. Balthasar writes, "Who can so fully open his heart in confession that he lays bare the most secret recesses of his sin? No one can do it apart from the woman who, unburdened by any sin of her own, laid open before God the most hidden corners of her soul."

56. On this point, see de Letter, "Perfect Contrition and Perfect Charity."

57. *CCC*, 1855.

58. Ibid., 1856.

59. Though, see *JP*, 1:272 / *SKP*, X-2 A 320, and the next chapter, on an "increasing openness" to God.

60. See *CD*, 251–61 / *SKS* 10, 261–75.

61. My thanks are owed to Niels Jørgen Cappelørn for pointing out to me the relevance of this passage.

62. Kierkegaard uses this language of God awakening longing within the communicant at *CD*, 254. On Kierkegaard's views regarding the connection of Communion and confession, see *WA*, 133–34.

63. *JP*, 2:2032 / *SKP*, X-3 A 687.

7. The Sickness unto Life

The first epigraph is from *SUD*, 44. The second epigraph is from *Purgation and Purgatory and The Spiritual Dialogue*, 72.

1. *LW* 36:70.

2. Ibid., 67.

3. Ibid., 59.

4. See *LW* 31:347 and 351.

5. See *Joint Declaration on the Doctrine of Justification*, 39. As one can see from the *Declaration*, and the clarification that the Catholic Church hurried to issue about it, the fact that there was a joint declaration issued does not mean that all parties agreed on this point or others, though it was an important step. One should also note that the fact that Luther holds that justification is always complete does not mean that he thinks that the same is true for the process of becoming holy and sanctified, though he suggests that this process will be brought to its completion by God at "the last day, the day of the resurrection of the dead" (*LW* 31:358). Whether this would be an abrupt transition of the sort that would cut short purgatory is difficult to say, since, as I point out later, at the time of this treatise (*The Freedom of a Christian*, 1520), Luther still believed in purgatory.

6. See Daphne Hampson, *Christian Contradictions*, 284.

7. In his earlier writings, Luther accepted the doctrine of purgatory, as in his 1521 "Defense and Explanation of All the Articles," a response to the condemnatory bull *Exsurge Domine* (*LW* 32:95). There, we read, "The existence of purgatory I have never denied. I still hold that it exists, as I have written and admitted many times, though I have found no way of proving it incontrovertibly from Scripture or reason." Later in his career (1538) though, he remarks, "In short, God has set before us two ways in his Word, the way to salvation through faith and the way to damnation through unbelief. There is no mention of purgatory. Nor should purgatory be admitted because it obscures the benefits and grace of Christ." See *LW* 54:259.

8. See *SUD*, 21, and *WL*, 194, respectively.

9. The one explicit exception of which I am aware is *EO*, 2:331–32.

10. See Hampson, *Christian Contradictions*, 249, and *CUP*, 556.

11. Pt. 3, art. 2, ch. 1, in *The Catholic Controversy*, 353.

12. See *Lumen Gentium*, 48.

13. See *DH*, 838 / *SCD*, 456; *DH*, 1304–1306 / *SCD*, 693; and *DH*, 1820 / *SCD*, 983.

14. See Gregory the Great, *Dialogues* 4.41, 249.

15. *CCC*, 1472.

16. Le Goff, *The Birth of Purgatory*, 61.

17. See *City of God: Books 17–22*, 21.13, 373. See also James Jorgenson, "The Debate over the Patristic Texts on Purgatory at the Council of Ferrara-Florence, 1438," 321.

18. *CCC*, 1472.

19. See Patrick T. McCormick, *Sin as Addiction*.

20. Note that the *Catechism* asserts, "A conversion which proceeds from a fervent charity can attain the complete purification of the sinner in such a way that no punishment would remain" (*CCC*, 1472). Accordingly, it may be possible for some to eliminate, immediately and altogether, temporal punishments for sin, but for many it does not happen this way.

21. Peter C. Phan, "Contemporary Context and Issues in Eschatology," 519.

22. *CCC*, 2043.

23. See *Reconciliatio et Paenitentia*, 31.

24. C. S. Lewis, *Letters to Malcolm*, 108–109.

25. See Le Goff, *The Birth of Purgatory*.

26. *ST*, App. 1.2.2 (Appendix to the *Summa*).

27. *Purgation and Purgatory*, 78.

28. On this principle, see *CCC*, 1124.

29. See *The Martyrdom of Saints Perpetua and Felicitas*, 7 in Musurillo, *The Acts of the Christian Martyrs*, 115–17. See also Michael J. Taylor, *Purgatory*.

30. Aquinas uses this argument in the usually perfunctory "On the contrary" to establish the existence of purgatory (*ST*, App. 2.1.1). St. Francis de Sales claims, perhaps a bit hastily, that "[t]his argument is so correct that to answer it our adversaries deny the authority of the Book of Maccabees, and hold it to be apocryphal, but in reality this is for lack of any other answer" (pt. 3, art. 2, ch. 5, in *The Catholic Controversy*, 364).

31. See *DH*, 1820 / *SCD*, 983.

32. See The Congregation for the Doctrine of Faith, "The Reality of Life after Death," 502. The entry for the translation is found in the bibliography.

33. Joseph Ratzinger [Benedict XVI], *Eschatology: Death and Eternal Life*, 229. Thus, when Benedict XVI writes, in his 2007 encyclical *Spe Salvi*, "Some recent theologians are of the opinion that the fire which both burns and saves is Christ himself, the Judge and Savior," he means, at least in part, himself. See *Spe Salvi*, 47.

34. Ratzinger, *Eschatology*, 230.

35. Ibid., 231.

36. "Resurrection or Reincarnation? The Christian Doctrine of Purgatory," 83.

37. By contrast, see Aquinas, *ST*, App. 2.1.2. Later, though, Catherine of Genoa is very positive about purgatory, exclaiming that "[t]here is no joy save that in paradise to be compared to the joy of the souls in purgatory" (*Purgation and Purgatory*, 72). See also Peter Kreeft, *Everything You Ever Wanted to Know about Heaven . . . But Never Dreamed of Asking*, 53, and 62.

38. See Jerry L. Walls, "Purgatory for Everyone," some of which also appears in chapter 2 of his book, *Heaven: The Logic of Eternal Joy.* See also Carl R. Scovel, "The Blessings of Purgatory." Clark H. Pinnock also suggests that Protestants reexamine purgatory. See his response to Zachary Hayes in Crockett, *Four Views on Hell,* esp. 130.

39. Hampson, *Christian Contradictions,* 85.

40. *DH,* 1535 / *SCD,* 803.

41. See *Joint Declaration on the Doctrine of Justification,* 39.

42. While I do not mean to ignore the complex historical divides that occurred within the Lutheran tradition itself on this question, to go into them is beyond the scope of this chapter. I thank Jeff Tyler for noting this concern and for other help on points regarding Luther.

43. Hampson, *Christian Contradictions,* 11.

44. Ibid.

45. Ibid., 12.

46. See ibid., 18.

47. Ibid., 16.

48. The business of cooperation remains something of a Catholic sticking point. See Canon 4 in the Council of Trent's *Decree on Justification* (*DH,* 1554 / *SCD,* 814). See also the *Joint Declaration on the Doctrine of Justification,* 19–21. Indeed, this is one of the items in the *Joint Declaration* that the Catholic Church felt the need to further clarify, as in the *Response of the Catholic Church to the Joint Declaration,* 3.

49. See *LW* 25:235.

50. Later in the same passage discussed above, Luther notes that the sinner "may actually be more impeded by these works from coming to righteousness and to the works of grace."

51. Hampson, *Christian Contradictions,* 39. See also *LW* 31:348.

52. Hampson, *Christian Contradictions,* 51.

53. See ibid., 90.

54. Hampson argues that the Deer Park sequence in the *Postscript* is a case in point. See *CUP,* 472–78, and Hampson, *Christian Contradictions,* 258.

55. See Andrew J. Burgess, "Kierkegaard's Concept of Redoubling and Luther's *Simul Justus,*" esp. 49.

56. On the Catholic side of things, one should consider Karl Rahner's "Justified and Sinner at the Same Time."

57. Hampson, *Christian Contradictions,* 11.

58. Ibid., 30.

59. This occurs prior to, in the moment of, and indeed after, justification, though in different ways. See ch. 6 of the Council of Trent's Decree on Justification (*DH,* 1526 / *SCD,* 798).

60. Hampson, *Christian Contradictions,* 260. See also *WL,* 19.

61. On this point, see e.g., *CUP,* 461, and *JN,* 2:24 / *EE:* 67.

62. See Roos, *Søren Kierkegaard and Catholicism,* 16–17.

63. Hampson, *Christian Contradictions,* 263. I realize that Hampson has her eye on the analogy of being here, which might echo some of Karl Barth's famous concerns along these lines. However, I think that it would be anachronistic to attribute Barthian anxieties about the analogy of being to Kierkegaard if Kierke-

gaard's texts give us insufficient reason to suppose that he was similarly concerned. George Pattison notes what he calls a "subtle difference" between the analogy of being and Kierkegaard's view, but he also points out that Kierkegaard's concern is different from classical Lutheranism. See his "Philosophy and Dogma," 161.

64. *JP,* 2:1251 / *SKP,* VII-1 A 181; Roos, *Søren Kierkegaard and Catholicism,* 17. Hampson needs to argue this point because Roos claims, "This Kierkegaardian chain of thought is Thomistic through and through and is in complete opposition to the Lutheran point of view" (Roos, *Søren Kierkegaard and Catholicism,* 18). She notes, however, of the passage she discusses that it is "fascinating: quite unlike anything that we have seen within the Lutheran tradition" (*Christian Contradictions,* 261). Hampson thinks of Kierkegaard as a Lutheran with a twist, which seems right, but then why such strong apprehension about including insights parallel to Aquinas?

65. Hampson writes, "Roos quotes Thomas Aquinas: 'Since God possesses Being in its entire perfection, it follows that He is able to communicate it to others, giving His creatures the power to act self-existently.' But Kierkegaard never says anything of the sort!" (*Christian Contradictions,* 263). We are owed more of an argument here. What exactly does Kierkegaard never say? He does call God "unconditioned being" (*JP,* 4:4918 / *SKP,* XI-2 A 205). Is it the communication of Being that Kierkegaard never discusses? Then why does he write, "[distinctiveness] is God's gift by which he gives being to me, and he indeed gives to all, gives being to all" (*WL,* 271)? If one persists in thinking that Kierkegaard never claims that God gave creatures the power to act "self-existently," I would invite a comparison of (*JP,* 2:1251 / *SKP,* VII-1 A 181), and the very passage that Roos cited, namely, *On Spiritual Creatures,* art. 10, reply to objection 16. Neither Aquinas nor Kierkegaard means an impossible metaphysical independence of God's sustaining power. So what is the problem?

66. Consider St. John of the Cross in the *Ascent of Mount Carmel,* 1.4.3, in *John of the Cross: Selected Writings,* 66.

67. Hampson, *Christian Contradictions,* 266. Hermann Deuser also writes, "If Kierkegaard criticized the person Luther as well as Luther's concept of *sola gratia,* he did so because he wanted to see the *process* of becoming a Christian more emphasized than the status of *being* one" ("Kierkegaard and Luther," 208).

68. Walls (in "Purgatory for Everyone") seems interested in endorsing a version of purgatory that allows the postmortem process to be one of sanctification, and not of justification. I do not see a clean distinction between the two in Kierkegaard's work, and I think the process motifs I will identify seem to be talking as much about justification as anything else, but that may be one possible way to reconstruct a broadly Kierkegaardian view.

69. *Ascent of Mount Carmel,* 2.5.6–8, in *John of the Cross: Selected Writings,* 90–91.

70. In this journal entry, Kierkegaard still insists that the increase of inwardness "goes backward" so that "one discovers more and more deeply the infinite distance." This, no doubt, has to do with the negative dialectic of the law in Luther (or the ethical in Kierkegaard). Yet, both the Lutheran system and the Catholic system on this point can admit that one can, in a certain sense, fight against justification, and the question is ultimately where that puts the sinner who is fighting the battle on the point of death.

71. In this context, "succeed" appears to be referring to the success of the first self, which would be the "silencing" of the deeper self.

72. See Hampson, *Christian Contradictions*, 50.

73. See Karl Rahner's entry on "Conversion" in *Sacramentum Mundi*, 2:5.

74. See Peter Toon, *Justification and Sanctification*, 71.

75. See Hampson, *Christian Contradictions*, 283.

76. The Catholic Church maintains that baptism remits original sin, all actual sins, and all punishments for sins. Absolution (in confession), by contrast, "takes away sin, but it does not remedy all the disorders sin has caused" (see *CCC*, 1263 and 1459).

77. See *CD*, 63, for some support along these lines.

78. Consider *WL*, 355, where Kierkegaard says that it is "out of the question" that a dead person could change.

79. The other option for "aftereffects" might be concupiscence, but the aftereffects in this entry seem to belong to the person's own sins and not to have arisen from original sin.

80. Christ is to have undergone these sufferings (*CD*, 103).

81. Kierkegaard appears to think that the relevant suffering might last "as long as life" (*CD*, 101).

82. On Wesley, see Walls, *Heaven*, 53–54. On the convergence with Catholic thought, see Boros, *The Mystery of Death*, 135–41. "Convergence" is really the right word, though, since Catholic theologians of all stripes are now quite reticent to talk about a precise temporal duration for purgatory, but the International Theological Commission insisted that this is a "post-mortem" process. See its "Some Current Questions in Eschatology," 231–32.

83. *Lumen Gentium*, 16.

84. David Brown, "No Heaven without Purgatory."

85. I here suppose that Lee Barrett is right in arguing that Kierkegaard endorses the Augustinian doctrine to that effect. See Barrett, "Kierkegaard's 'Anxiety' and the Augustinian Doctrine of Original Sin."

86. See chapter 5 above and *SUD*, 14, where we learn that all despair can ultimately be traced back to the despair of defiance. See also *SUD*, 21, where we learn that the despairer is "nailed" to himself.

8. Kierkegaard and the Communion of Saints

The first epigraph is from *FT*, 71. The second epigraph is from "Catholicism and the Communion of Saints," 166.

1. I should note that the accusation takes place in the context of Balthasar's discussion of the communion of saints, not any sustained discussion of Kierkegaard. In the context in which the accusation appears, Balthasar does not give an actual argument for it.

2. Benedict XVI, *Spe Salvi*, 48.

3. Ibid.

4. Ibid.

5. These are the three groups that are typically thought to make up "the communion of saints" in Catholic thought. For more on this, see Schönborn, "The 'Communion of Saints' as Three States of the Church." See also *CCC*, 1475.

6. Kierkegaard, in considering one who is dead, claims that he or she is "no actual object" (*WL*, 347). I am not inclined to speculate on what Kierkegaard's precise view of the interim state is, because I believe that the texts are not conclusive. On the one hand, Kierkegaard claims that death is sleep (*TDIO*, 91), but he also emphasizes throughout the discourse "At a Graveside" that death is inexplicable, and, accordingly, approaches the question with circumspection. At any rate, Kierkegaard does regard death as in some way decisive (*TDIO*, 78), and so it is perhaps fair to say that Kierkegaard seems to regard the dead as separated from us on earth, at least for the time being.

7. *LW* 36:49.

8. Ibid., 50–51.

9. It is worth noting, however, that in one place, Kierkegaard appears to suggest that true prayer would not be of an intercessory sort, but simply an expression of docility before God (*JN*, 2:272 / JJ: 464).

10. Pt. 3, art. 2, ch. 1, in *The Catholic Controversy*, 353.

11. *CCC*, 1475. See also ibid., 1471, where we read that "the faithful can gain indulgences for themselves or apply them to the dead." I know of no reason why salutary acts of purgative significance (even without the ecclesial sanction of an indulgence) could not be applied to the plight of the living faithful. See also *DH*, 1448 / *SCD*, 740a. Readers (especially non-Catholic readers) are urged to keep in mind that such a transaction can be applied with any effect only to those in a state of grace, since indulgences and the like spiritual goods can remove only temporal punishments for sin and venial sins, not mortal sins. Thus, one can hardly live a depraved life, hoping all the while to be rescued by the coattails of the saints. I thank Lyra Pitstick for helpful conversation on this point.

12. *Reconciliatio et Paenitentia*, 16.

13. Ibid.

14. See Vatican II's *Lumen Gentium*, 49.

15. Although the texts I have quoted do not explicitly invoke the angels, it is clear that they form part of the one Church, as the categories of angels and saints overlap in the Catholic tradition, which can be seen by the fact that the archangels Michael, Gabriel, and Raphael are treated as saints (with a feast day of September 29). All the angels are explicitly invoked for aid in the penitential rite in the Order of Mass as well.

16. Ibid., 50.

17. Ibid., 49.

18. "The 'Communion of Saints,'" 173.

19. Though, of course, Mary is herself redeemed, as are all the rest of us, by the merits of Christ (see *Lumen Gentium*, 53). See ibid., 62, for a clear statement on Mary's subordinate role.

20. Obviously, for Catholics, there are exceptions to the claim that other saints bear resemblance to Mary in a less-exalted fashion: among the saints, only Mary was immaculately conceived, Mary was unique in being bodily assumed into heaven, and no other saint, with any ecclesiastical stamp, has been called "Queen of the Universe" (ibid., 59). None of these things admit of degree, and so none admits of a clear parallel in the case of other saints to whom they do not apply.

21. See ibid., 62.

22. Ibid., 60.

23. *Redemptoris Mater*, 38.

24. On praying in Jesus' name, see *JP*, 3:3441 / *SKP*, X-2 A 77.

25. On this point, consider *WA*, 100.

26. Recall chapter 3, where we noticed that one should love both Church and country, but Church should be loved more. See *SCD*, 1936a, and Leo XIII's encyclical *Sapientiae Christianae*, 5.

27. *DH*, 3274 / *SCD*, 1940a.

28. See *Lumen Gentium*, 56. Note that she may have in some way become the cause of her salvation, but this she would have been able to do only through the grace of God that prepared her for this.

29. *Lumen Gentium*, 60.

30. "The 'Communion of Saints,'" 174.

31. *Lumen Gentium*, 50.

32. Ibid., 60. Still, this need not simply be an act of arbitrary divine fiat, since, as we saw in chapter 2, the natural law is itself an expression of the Divine Wisdom. In that way, the command not to murder originates from the divine pleasure, since God selected to create human nature in the context where murder does not lend to human flourishing. Thus, the obligatory status of such a command issues from human nature, despite the fact that God was the author of human nature. Later, when I consider indulgences, I deny that God's arbitrary fiat can be the cause for the efficacy of indulgences. There, I claim that indulgences can be likened to various kinds of assistance to one recovering from an addiction. The analogy to natural law can be a bit misleading, though. Surely, it is an instance of God's *super*natural regard for human beings that he would have instituted an order of salvation according to which saintly humans can efficaciously intercede for others, and a Church in which indulgences can be applied to others. Nonetheless, there is a sense in which God could antecedently will these things to belong to the order of salvation without arbitrarily (through pure fiat) restricting their efficacy to particular individuals.

33. *Spe Salvi*, 49.

34. See *DH*, 1835 / *SCD*, 989. See also the bull *Exsurge Domine*, which condemns a number of propositions associated with Martin Luther on indulgences, in *DH*, 1451–92 / *SCD*, 741–81.

35. For a helpful discussion of Luther's treatment of indulgences, see ch. 6 of Martin Brecht, *Martin Luther: His Road to Reformation, 1483–1521*. Luther's view, of course, develops and changes, but in the *Ninety-Five Theses* he claims that the pope's remission of penalties for common sins in indulgences has a merely declarative, and not decisive, significance (*LW* 31, 26, Thesis #6).

36. See *Indulgentiarum Doctrina*, 8, for a frank admission that the excesses of Luther's age resulted in "the power of the keys" being "humiliated."

37. No doubt certain relevant conditions also apply to the recipients of such indulgences, since remission of temporal punishments for sins hardly seems relevant in the case of someone who remains in a state of mortal sin. To see why, consider that, on the point of death, the mortal sinner is destined for hell, where indulgences are of no effect.

38. Ibid., 10.

39. Indeed, as Schönborn points out, the veneration of the saints is also a gesture of love toward them.

40. *CCC,* 1472.

41. Note that this is precisely the situation of anyone to whom an indulgence could be fruitfully applied, since such application presupposes that one is in a state of grace.

42. Reconciling this account with a plenary indulgence (which takes away all the punishments due to sin, on which see *CCC,* 1471) is perhaps a bit more difficult. Still, there does not seem to be anything logically impossible about the suggestion that a drug could be discovered that could remove *all* the signs of a prior addiction to, say, nicotine. Recall that, for such an indulgence to be applied, the subject would be either in purgatory or, minimally, in a state of grace, so the subject would, as a foregone conclusion, desire the removal of any signs of addiction.

43. The clearest example I know of is from the *St. Joseph Daily Missal* of 1959. There, certain prayers to, for instance, St. Joseph, are indulgenced for time periods such as 7 years, 3 years, and 500 days (1315). This was changed in Paul VI's *Indulgentiarum Doctrina,* where norm 4 revised the practice so that indulgences would be granted only as "partial" or "plenary" and not as removing a specified number of days or years in purgatory. My thanks to Lyra Pitstick for help in this regard.

44. *Spe Salvi,* 48.

45. See Beabout and Frazier, "A Challenge to the 'Solitary Self' Interpretation of Kierkegaard."

46. Ibid., 93.

47. See ch. 3 of Westphal's *Kierkegaard's Critique of Reason and Society,* 33.

48. Ibid., 34. I have removed Westphal's original emphasis.

49. Beabout and Frazier, "A Challenge to the 'Solitary Self' Interpretation of Kierkegaard," 88.

50. Although I have my disagreements with Westphal's account, they are largely dialectical concerns, and needn't affect the fact that, say, *Works of Love,* and other texts of Kierkegaard's post-Climacus writings reflect Kierkegaard's own view. My own view of what really divides our readings is that Climacus is already too concerned about the "public" and open breaches of "legality" and that this makes his account too appreciative of the hiddenness of hidden inwardness (see *CUP,* 500). I have discussed why I think that this means that his account must be given a correction in "Re-radicalizing Kierkegaard: An Alternative to Religiousness C in Light of an Investigation into the Teleological Suspension of the Ethical." Westphal has responded, in "Kierkegaard's Religiousness C: A Defense," that I, in effect, contradict my own account by having the later authorship intensify inwardness, but reject Climacus's version of hidden inwardness (see 541). My only response to this complaint is that there is the truncated Climacan *hidden* inwardness, which Kierkegaard repudiates in the journals (see *JP,* 2:2125 / *SKP,* X-3 A 334, see also "Re-radicalizing Kierkegaard," 316–20), and the inwardness of the later authorship. I'll certainly admit that I could have been clearer on this point, but the essence of my contention has not changed. Climacan hidden inwardness is an illegitimate subterfuge that circumscribes the way in which faith can be expressed (no doubt part of the reason is that Climacus is not a Christian). The later authorship removes this barrier. In my view, a new dialectical moment (Religiousness C) is tantamount

to multiplying entities without necessity, since my account embraces outwardness through a signed correction to a pseudonymous mistake.

51. See Kirmmse, "The Thunderstorm: Kierkegaard's Ecclesiology," 98.

52. My thanks to Bob Perkins for pointing this fact out to me, in correspondence about an earlier version of chapter 4. For more on Kierkegaard and Grundtvig, see Morten Kvist, "N. F. S. Grundtvig's Conception of Historical Christianity: An Introduction to the Relationship between Kierkegaard and Grundtvig."

53. Plekon, "Kierkegaard at the End: His 'Last' Sermon, Eschatology and the Attack on the Church."

54. Ibid., 82.

55. See *Spe Salvi*, 49.

56. See especially St. Cyprian, as discussed in Jerome I. Gellman, "*Fear and Trembling*: Kierkegaard's Christian Work."

57. Monika K. Hellwig, *Understanding Catholicism*, 68. Compare *JP*, 3:2670 / *SKP*, VIII-1 A 338.

58. Joseph Cardinal Ratzinger [Benedict XVI], "God with Us and God among Us," in *God is Near Us*, 13.

59. See Beth Kreitzer, *Reforming Mary: Changing Images of the Virgin Mary in Lutheran Sermons of the Sixteenth Century*, esp. 123–25. The complication is, of course, due to the historical complexity of Luther's developing theology. It is, however, worthy of note that Luther petitions Mary for wisdom at the beginning of his commentary on the *Magnificat*. Indeed, in that same text, Luther appears to concede the title of "Queen of Heaven" to her, and to concede that she was "without sin" (see *LW* 21, esp. 298 and 327). Luther also solidly endorsed Mary's perpetual virginity (see *LW* 22, esp. 23).

60. *CCC*, 490.

61. *DH*, 2803 / *SCD*, 1641.

62. Kierkegaard cites the "power of the Holy Spirit" to overshadow Mary (*JP*, 3:2672 / *SKP*, X-4 A 454).

63. Ferreira, *Love's Grateful Striving*, 159–60.

64. See Thomas Merton, *New Seeds of Contemplation*, 170.

65. See Balthasar, *Mary for Today*, 70.

66. Ibid., italics mine.

67. Recall that this claim is rooted in *Lumen Gentium*, 60.

68. I do not intend there to be a hard-and-fast chasm between objective salvation history and subjective salvation history. I personally profit from reading St. Cyprian, whose works are part of objective salvation history, and this profitable reading may redound to my subjective salvation history in some fashion. Perhaps the real distinction between the categories is that, in objective salvation history, I can profit from the *historical legacy* of saintly individuals, whereas if I can petition them to enter into my subjective salvation history, I can profit from their *present action*.

Conclusion

1. Richard Marius, *Martin Luther: The Christian between God and Death*, 28.

BIBLIOGRAPHY

Adams, Robert M. "Pure Love." In *The Virtue of Faith and Other Essays in Philosophical Theology*, 174–92. Oxford: Oxford University Press, 1987.

Adorno, T. W. "On Kierkegaard's Doctrine of Love." *Studies in Philosophy and Social Science* 8 (1940): 413–29.

Andic, Martin. "Love's Redoubling and the Eternal Like for Like." In Perkins, *International Kierkegaard Commentary: Works of Love*, 9–38.

Aquinas, Thomas. *On Charity*. Trans. Lottie H. Kendzierski. Milwaukee: Marquette University Press, 1984.

———. *On Evil*. Trans. John A. Oesterle and Jean T. Oesterle. Notre Dame, Ind.: University of Notre Dame Press, 1995.

———. *On Human Nature*. Ed. Thomas Hibbs. Indianapolis: Hackett, 1999.

———. *On Spiritual Creatures*. Trans. Mary C. FitzPatrick and John J. Wellmuth. Milwaukee: Marquette University Press, 1969.

———. *Summa contra Gentiles, Book Four*. Trans. Charles J. O'Neil. Notre Dame, Ind.: University of Notre Dame Press, 1957.

———. *Summa contra Gentiles, Book One: God*. Trans. Anton C. Pegis. Notre Dame, Ind.: University of Notre Dame Press, 1975.

———. *Summa contra Gentiles, Book Three: Providence*. Trans. Vernon J. Bourke. Notre Dame, Ind.: University of Notre Dame Press, 2001.

Aristotle. *The Complete Works of Aristotle*. Ed. Jonathan Barnes. 2 vols. Princeton, N.J.: Princeton University Press, 1984.

Augustine. *Augustine: Letters 165–203*. Trans. Sister Wilfrid Parsons. New York: Fathers of the Church, 1955.

———. *Christian Instruction*. In *Saint Augustine*. 2nd ed. Fathers of the Church: A New Translation (Patristic Series), vol. 2. Washington, D.C.: Catholic University of America Press, 1950.

———. *City of God: Books XVII–XXII*. Trans. Gerald G. Walsh and Daniel J. Honan. New York: Fathers of the Church, 1954.

———. *Confessions*. Trans. Henry Chadwick. Oxford: Oxford University Press, 1991.

——. *On Free Choice of the Will.* Trans. Thomas Williams. Indianapolis: Hackett, 1993.

Balthasar, Hans Urs von. "Catholicism and the Communion of Saints." Trans. Albert K. Wimmer. *Communio* 15 (1988): 163–68.

——. *Dare We Hope that All Men be Saved?* Trans. Dr. David Kipp and Rev. Lothar Krauth. San Francisco: Ignatius Press, 1988.

——. *Mary for Today.* Trans. Robert Nowell. San Francisco: Ignatius Press, 1987.

Balthasar, Hans Urs von, and Joseph Cardinal Ratzinger. *Mary: The Church at the Source.* Trans. Adrian Walker. San Francisco: Ignatius, 2005.

Barrett, Lee. "Kierkegaard's 'Anxiety' and the Augustinian Doctrine of Original Sin." In Perkins, *International Kierkegaard Commentary: The Concept of Anxiety,* 35–61.

Beabout, Gregory R., and Brad Frazier. "A Challenge to the 'Solitary Self' Interpretation of Kierkegaard." *History of Philosophy Quarterly* 17 (2000): 75–98.

Benedict XVI (Pope) [includes references to Ratzinger, Joseph Cardinal]. *Eschatology: Death and Eternal Life.* Trans. Michael Waldstein and Aidan Nichols. Washington, D.C.: Catholic University of America Press, 1988.

——. *God Is Near Us.* Ed. Stephan Otto Horn and Vinzenz Pfnür. Trans. Henry Taylor. San Francisco: Ignatius Press, 2001.

——. *"In the Beginning . . .": A Catholic Understanding of Creation and the Fall.* Trans. Boniface Ramsey. Grand Rapids, Mich.: Eerdmans, 1990.

Bernard of Clairvaux. *Bernard of Clairvaux: Selected Writings.* Trans. G. R. Evans. New York: Paulist Press, 1987.

——. *The Works of Bernard of Clairvaux.* Vol. 7: *Treatises III.* Trans. Daniel O'Donovan. Kalamazoo, Mich.: Cistercian Publications, 1977.

Blanshard, Brand. "Kierkegaard on Faith." In *Essays on Kierkegaard,* ed. Jerry H. Gill, 113–25. Minneapolis: Burgess, 1969.

Boros, Ladislaus. *The Mystery of Death.* New York: Seabury Press, 1973.

Bøggild, Jacob. "H.H.—Poet or Martyr?" In Houe et al., *Anthropology and Authority,* 171–78.

Brecht, Martin. *Martin Luther: His Road to Reformation, 1483–1521.* Trans. James L. Schaaf. Philadelphia: Fortress, 1985.

Bridge, Steven L. *Getting the Gospels: Understanding the New Testament Accounts of Jesus' Life.* Peabody, Mass.: Hendrickson Publishers, 2004.

Brown, David. "No Heaven without Purgatory." *Religious Studies* 21 (1985): 447–56.

Buckareff, Andrei, and Allen Plug. "Escaping Hell: Divine Motivation and the Problem of Hell." *Religious Studies* 41 (2005): 39–54.

Buber, Martin. *Between Man and Man.* Trans. Ronald Gregor Smith. New York: Macmillan, 1965.

Burgess, Andrew J. "Kierkegaard's Concept of Redoubling and Luther's *Simul Justus.*" In Perkins, *International Kierkegaard Commentary: Works of Love,* 39–55.

Calvin, John. *Institutes of the Christian Religion.* Trans. Henry Beveridge. Grand Rapids, Mich.: Eerdmans, 1989.

The Canons of Dort. In *Ecumenical Creeds and Reformed Confessions,* 122–45. Grand Rapids, Mich.: CRC Publications, 1988.

Catechism of the Council of Trent for Parish Priests. Trans. John A. McHugh and Charles J. Callan. 1976; rept., Rockford, Ill.: Tan Books, 1982.

Catherine of Genoa. *Purgation and Purgatory.* Trans. Serge Hughes. New York: Paulist Press, 1979.

Chrysostom, John. *Homilies on the Statues.* Trans. John Henry Parker. London: Oxford, 1842.

———. *Six Books on the Priesthood.* Trans. Graham Neville. Crestwood, N.Y.: St. Vladimir's Seminary Press, 1977.

Collins, James. *The Mind of Kierkegaard.* Chicago: Regnery, 1953.

Congregation for the Doctrine of Faith. "The Reality of Life after Death." In *Vatican Council II: More Postconciliar Documents,* ed. Austin Flannery, 500–504. Grand Rapids, Mich.: Eerdmans, 1982.

Connell, George B. *To Be One Thing: Personal Unity in Kierkegaard's Thought.* Macon: Mercer University Press, 1985.

Connell, George B., and C. Stephan Evans, eds. *Foundations of Kierkegaard's Vision of Community.* Atlantic Highlands: Humanities Press, 1992.

Copleston, Frederick. *A History of Philosophy.* 9 vols. Vol. 7. New York: Image, 1965.

Crockett, William, ed. *Four Views on Hell.* Grand Rapids, Mich.: Zondervan, 1996.

Davenport, John. "Faith as Eschatological Trust in *Fear and Trembling.*" In Mooney, *Ethics, Love, and Faith in Kierkegaard,* 196–233.

Deferrari, Roy J. *Early Christian Biographies.* New York: Fathers of the Church, 1952.

De Letter, Prudentia. "Perfect Contrition and Perfect Charity." *Theological Studies* 7 (1946): 507–24.

Deuser, Hermann. "Kierkegaard and Luther: Kierkegaard's 'One Thesis.'" Trans. Gesche Linde. In *The Gift of Grace: The Future of Lutheran Theology,* ed. Niels Henrik Gregersen et al., 205–12. Minneapolis: Fortress Press, 2005.

Douglas, J. D., ed. *The New International Dictionary of the Christian Church.* Grand Rapids, Mich.: Zondervan, 1974.

Dulles, Avery Cardinal. "Love, the Pope, and C.S. Lewis." *First Things* 169 (2007): 20–24.

Dunning, Stephen N. "Who Sets the Task? Kierkegaard on Authority." In Connell and Evans, *Foundations of Kierkegaard's Vision of Community,* 18–32.

Ekstrom, Laura Waddell. *Free Will: A Philosophical Study.* Boulder, Colo.: Westview Press, 2000.

Evans, C. Stephen. "Can God Be Hidden and Evident at the Same Time? Some Kierkegaardian Reflections." *Faith and Philosophy* 23 (2006): 241–53.

———. *Kierkegaard on Faith and the Self.* Waco, Tex.: Baylor University Press, 2006.

———. *Kierkegaard's Ethic of Love: Divine Commands and Moral Obligations.* Oxford: Oxford University Press, 2006.

———. *Passionate Reason.* Bloomington: Indiana University Press, 1992.

———. "Realism and Antirealism in Kierkegaard's *Concluding Unscientific Postscript.*" In Marino and Hannay, *The Cambridge Companion to Kierkegaard,* 154–76.

Ferreira, M. Jamie. "Asymmetry and Self-Love: The Challenge to Reciprocity and Equality." In *Kierkegaard Studies Yearbook 1998,* ed. Niels Jørgen Cappelørn and Hermann Deuser, 41–59. Berlin: de Gruyter, 1998.

———. "Faith and the Kierkegaardian Leap." In Marino and Hannay, *The Cambridge Companion to Kierkegaard,* 207–34.

———. "Leaps and Circles: Kierkegaard and Newman on Faith and Reason." *Religious Studies* 30 (1994): 379–97.

———. *Love's Grateful Striving.* Oxford: Oxford University Press, 2001.

Fitzgerald, Allan D., et al., eds. *Augustine through the Ages: An Encyclopedia.* Grand Rapids, Mich.: Eerdmans, 1999.

Flint, Thomas. *Divine Providence: The Molinist Account.* Ithaca, N.Y.: Cornell University Press, 1998.

———. "Two Accounts of Providence." In *Divine and Human Action,* ed. Thomas V. Morris, 147–81. Ithaca, N.Y.: Cornell University Press, 1988.

Francis de Sales. *The Catholic Controversy.* Trans. Henry Benedict Mackey. Rockford, Ill.: Tan Books, 1989.

———. *The Love of God.* Trans. Vincent Kearns. Westminster, Md.: Newman Press, 1962.

Gellman, Jerome I. "*Fear and Trembling*: Kierkegaard's Christian Work." *Faith and Philosophy* 18 (2001): 61–74.

Goulet, Denis A. "Kierkegaard, Aquinas, and the Dilemma of Abraham." *Thought* 32 (1957): 165–88.

Green, Ronald M. "Enough Is Enough! *Fear and Trembling* Is *Not* about Ethics." *Journal of Religious Ethics* 21 (1993): 191–209.

———. *Kierkegaard and Kant: The Hidden Debt.* Albany: SUNY Press, 1992.

Green, Ronald M., and Theresa M. Ellis. "Erotic Love in the Religious Existence-Sphere." In Perkins, *International Kierkegaard Commentary: Works of Love,* 339–67.

Gregory the Great. *Dialogues.* Trans. Odo John Zimmerman. New York: Fathers of the Church, 1959.

———. *Pastoral Care.* Trans. Henry Davis. Westminster, Md.: Newman Press, 1955.

Grimm, Stephen R. "Cardinal Newman, Reformed Epistemologist?" *American Catholic Philosophical Quarterly* 75 (2001): 497–522.

Gula, Richard M. *To Walk Together Again: The Sacrament of Reconciliation.* New York: Paulist Press, 1983.

Gustafson, James M. "Nature: Its Status in Theological Ethics." *Logos: Philosophical Issues in Christian Perspective* 3 (1982): 5–23.

Halter, Deborah. *The Papal "No": A Comprehensive Guide to the Vatican's Rejection of Women's Ordination.* New York: Crossroad, 2004.

Hampson, Daphne. *Christian Contradictions.* Cambridge: Cambridge University Press, 2004.

Hase, Karl. *Hutterus redivivus oder Dogmatik der evangelisch-lutherischen Kirche.* 4th ed. Leipzig: 1839 [*ASKB* 581].

Hegel, G. W. F. *Early Theological Writings.* Trans. T. M. Knox. Gloucester: Peter Smith, 1970.

———. *The Philosophy of History.* Trans. J. Sibree. Amherst: Prometheus Books, 1991.

———. *Philosophy of Right.* Trans. T. M. Knox. Oxford: Oxford University Press, 1952.

Hellwig, Monika K. *Understanding Catholicism.* 2nd ed. New York: Paulist Press, 2002.

Hick, John. "Religious Pluralism and Salvation." *Faith and Philosophy* 5 (1988): 365–77.

Houe, Poul, Gordon D. Marino, and Sven Hakon Rossel, eds. *Anthropology and Authority: Essays on Søren Kierkegaard.* Amsterdam: Rodopi, 2000.

Houlgate, Stephen. *Freedom, Truth and History: An Introduction to Hegel's Philosophy.* London: Routledge, 1991.

International Theological Commission. "Some Current Questions in Eschatology." *Irish Theological Quarterly* 58 (1992): 209–43.

Jackson, Timothy P. "Arminian Edification: Kierkegaard on Grace and Free Will." In Marino and Hannay, *The Cambridge Companion to Kierkegaard,* 235–56.

Jenkins, John I. *Knowledge and Faith in Thomas Aquinas.* Cambridge: Cambridge University Press, 1997.

Jensen, Paul. "Intolerable but Moral? Thinking about Hell." *Faith and Philosophy* 10 (1993): 235–41.

John of the Cross. *John of the Cross: Selected Writings.* Ed. Kieran Kavanaugh. New York: Paulist Press, 1987.

John Paul II (Pope). *Crossing the Threshold of Hope.* Trans. Jenny McPhee and Martha McPhee. Ed. Vittorio Messori. New York: Alfred A. Knopf, 2003.

Jorgenson, James. "The Debate over the Patristic Texts on Purgatory at the Council of Ferrara-Florence, 1438." *St. Vladimir's Theological Quarterly* 30 (1986): 309–34.

Kant, Immanuel. *Practical Philosophy.* Trans. and ed. Mary J. Gregor. Cambridge: Cambridge University Press, 2005.

———. *Religion and Rational Theology.* Trans. and ed. Allen W. Wood and George Di Giovanni. Cambridge: Cambridge University Press, 1996.

Kellenberger, J. *Kierkegaard and Nietzsche: Faith and Eternal Acceptance.* New York: St. Martin's Press, 1997.

Kelly, J. N. D. *Early Christian Doctrines.* Rev. ed. San Francisco: Harper, 1978.

Kelly, Thomas A. F., and Philipp W. Rosemann. *Amor Amicitiae: On the Love That Is Friendship.* Leuven: Peeters, 2004.

Kierkegaard, Søren. *Attack upon Christendom.* Trans. Walter Lowrie. Princeton, N.J.: Princeton University Press, 1944.

———. *Purity of Heart Is to Will One Thing.* Trans. Douglas V. Steere. New York: Harper, 1956.

Kirmmse, Bruce H. "The Thunderstorm: Kierkegaard's Ecclesiology." *Faith and Philosophy* 17 (2000): 87–102.

———, ed. *Encounters with Kierkegaard: A Life as Seen by His Contemporaries.* Trans. Bruce H. Kirmmse and Virginia R. Laursen. Princeton, N.J.: Princeton University Press, 1996.

Knappe, Ulrich. *Theory and Practice in Kant and Kierkegaard.* Berlin: Walter de Gruyter, 2004.

Koenker, Ernest B. "Søren Kierkegaard on Luther." In *Interpreters of Luther: Essays in Honor of Wilhelm Pauck,* ed. Jaroslav Pelikan, 231–52. Philadelphia: Fortress Press, 1968.

Koons, Robert C. "Dual Agency: A Thomistic Account of Providence and Human Freedom." *Philosophia Christi* 4 (2002): 397–410.

Kosch, Michelle. "What Abraham Couldn't Say." In [*Proceedings of the Aristotelian Society*] *Supplementary Volume.* Vol. 82, 59–78. London: Williams and Norgate, 2008.

Kreeft, Peter. *Everything You Ever Wanted to Know about Heaven . . . But Never Dreamed of Asking.* San Francisco: Ignatius, 1990.

Kreitzer, Beth. *Reforming Mary: Changing Images of the Virgin Mary in Lutheran Sermons of the Sixteenth Century.* Oxford: Oxford University Press, 2004.

Kretzmann, Norman. "Abraham, Isaac, and Euthyphro." Reprinted in *Philosophy of Religion: The Big Questions,* ed. Eleonore Stump and Michael J. Murray, 417–27. Oxford: Blackwell, 1999.

Kvist, Morten. "N. F. S. Grundtvig's Conception of Historical Christianity: An Introduction to the Relationship between Kierkegaard and Grundtvig." Trans. K. Brian Söderquist. In *Kierkegaard Studies Yearbook 2005,* ed. Niels Jørgen Cappelørn and Hermann Deuser, 37–52. Berlin: de Gruyter, 2005.

Law, David. "Resignation, Suffering and Guilt." In Perkins, *International Kierkegaard Commentary: Concluding Unscientific Postscript,* 263–89.

Le Goff, Jacques. *The Birth of Purgatory.* Chicago: University of Chicago Press, 1981.

Lewis, C. S. *The Great Divorce.* New York: Harper, 2001.

———. *Letters to Malcolm.* New York: Harcourt, Brace, and World, 1964.

———. *That Hideous Strength.* New York: Scribner, 1974.

Lippitt, John. "Cracking the Mirror: On Kierkegaard's Concerns about Friendship." *International Journal for Philosophy of Religion* 61 (2007): 131–50.

———. *The Routledge Philosophy Guidebook to Kierkegaard and Fear and Trembling.* London: Routledge, 2003.

———. "What Neither Abraham Nor Johannes de Silentio Could Say." In [*Proceedings of the Aristotelian Society*] *Supplementary Volume.* Vol. 82, 79–99. London: Williams and Norgate, 2008.

Lisska, Anthony J. *Aquinas's Theory of Natural Law: An Analytic Reconstruction.* Oxford: Clarendon Press, 1996.

Lombard, Peter. *The Sentences: Book 1: The Mystery of the Trinity.* Trans. Giulio Silano. Toronto: Pontifical Institute of Mediaeval Studies, 2007.

Lowrie, Walter. *Kierkegaard.* 2 vols. New York: Harper, 1962.

Løgstrup, K. E. *The Ethical Demand.* Ed. Hans Fink and Alasdair McIntyre. Notre Dame, Ind.: University of Notre Dame Press, 1997.

Marino, Gordon, and Alastair Hannay, eds. *The Cambridge Companion to Kierkegaard.* Cambridge: Cambridge University Press, 1998.

Marius, Richard. *Martin Luther: The Christian between God and Death.* Cambridge, Mass.: Harvard University Press, 2004.

May, William W., ed. *Vatican Authority and American Catholic Dissent: The Curran Case and Its Consequences.* New York: Crossroad, 1987.

McCormick, Patrick T. *Sin as Addiction.* New York: Paulist Press, 1989.

McGinn, Bernard. Introduction to *On Grace and Free Choice.* In *The Works of Bernard of Clairvaux,* vol. 7: *Treatises III.*

McLane, Earl. "Rereading *Fear and Trembling.*" *Faith and Philosophy* 10 (1993): 198–219.

Merton, Thomas. *New Seeds of Contemplation.* New York: New Directions, 1972.

Mooney, Edward. *Knights of Faith and Resignation: Reading Kierkegaard's* Fear and Trembling. Albany: SUNY Press, 1991.

———, ed. *Ethics, Love, and Faith in Kierkegaard.* Bloomington: Indiana University Press, 2008.

Mulder, Jack, Jr. "Bernard of Clairvaux: Kierkegaard's Reception of the 'Last of the Fathers.'" In Stewart, *Kierkegaard and the Patristic and Medieval Tradition,* 22–45.

———. "Cyprian of Carthage: Kierkegaard, Cyprian, and the 'Urgent Needs of the Times.'" In Stewart, *Kierkegaard and the Patristic and Medieval Tradition,* 67–94.

———. "Must All Be Saved? A Kierkegaardian Response to Theological Universalism." *International Journal for Philosophy of Religion* 59 (2006): 1–24.

———. "Re-radicalizing Kierkegaard: An Alternative to Religiousness C in Light of an Investigation into the Teleological Suspension of the Ethical." *Continental Philosophy Review* 35 (2002): 303–24.

Mulhall, Stephen. *Inheritance and Originality.* Oxford: Oxford University Press, 2001.

Murray, Michael J. "Three Versions of Universalism." *Faith and Philosophy* 16 (1999): 55–68.

Musurillo, Herbert, ed. *The Acts of the Christian Martyrs.* Oxford: Oxford University Press, 1972.

Neuhaus, Richard John. "Kierkegaard for Grownups." *First Things* 146 (2004): 27–33.

Newman, John Henry Cardinal. *An Essay in Aid of a Grammar of Assent.* Notre Dame, Ind.: University of Notre Dame Press, 2006.

———. *An Essay on the Development of Christian Doctrine.* In Newman, *Conscience, Consensus, and the Development of Doctrine,* ed. James Gaffney. New York: Image, 1992.

Nietzsche, Friedrich. *The Portable Nietzsche.* Ed. and trans. Walter Kaufmann. New York: Penguin, 1982.

———. *Thus Spoke Zarathustra.* In *The Portable Nietzsche,* 103–439.

———. *Twilight of the Idols.* In *The Portable Nietzsche,* 463–563.

Oakes, Edward T., and Alyssa Lyra Pitstick. "Balthasar, Hell, and Heresy: An Exchange." *First Things* 168 (2006): 25–32.

———. "More on Balthasar, Hell, and Heresy." *First Things* 169 (2007): 16–19.

O'Collins, Gerald, and Mario Farrugia. *Catholicism: The Story of Catholic Christianity.* Oxford: Oxford University Press, 2003.

Osborne, Kenan B. *Reconciliation and Justification: The Sacrament and Its Theology.* Repr. Eugene, Ore.: Wipf and Stock Publishers, 2001.

Ott, Ludwig. *Fundamentals of Catholic Dogma.* Ed. James Canon Bastible. Trans. Patrick Lynch. 4th ed. 1955. Repr., Rockford, Ill.: Tan Books, 1960.

Pattison, George. "Philosophy and Dogma." In Mooney, *Ethics, Love, and Faith in Kierkegaard,* 155–62.

Penelhum, Terence. *God and Skepticism.* Dordrecht: Kluwer, 1983.

Perkins, Robert L., ed. *International Kierkegaard Commentary 4: Either/Or Pt. 2.* Macon, Ga.: Mercer University Press, 1997.

———. *International Kierkegaard Commentary 8: Concept of Anxiety.* Macon, Ga.: Mercer University Press, 1985.

———. *International Kierkegaard Commentary 12: Concluding Unscientific Postscript to* Philosophical Fragments. Macon, Ga.: Mercer University Press, 1997.

————. *International Kierkegaard Commentary 16: Works of Love.* Macon, Ga.: Mercer University Press, 1999.

Phan, Peter C. "Contemporary Context and Issues in Eschatology." *Theological Studies* 55 (1994): 507–30.

Pieper, Josef. *The Concept of Sin.* Trans. Edward T. Oakes. South Bend, Ind.: St. Augustine's Press, 2001.

————. *Faith, Hope, Love.* San Francisco: Ignatius Press, 1997.

Pitstick, Alyssa Lyra. *Light in Darkness: Hans Urs von Balthasar and the Catholic Doctrine of Christ's Descent into Hell.* Grand Rapids, Mich.: Eerdmans, 2007.

Plantinga, Alvin. *Warrant and Proper Function.* Oxford: Oxford University Press, 1993.

————. *Warranted Christian Belief.* Oxford: Oxford University Press, 2000.

Plato. *Complete Works.* Ed. John M. Cooper. Indianapolis: Hackett Publishing, 1997.

Plekon, Michael. "Kierkegaard and the Eucharist." *Studia Liturgica* 22 (1992): 214–36.

————. "Kierkegaard at the End: His 'Last' Sermon, Eschatology and the Attack on the Church." *Faith and Philosophy* 17 (2001): 68–86.

Poole, Roger. *Kierkegaard: The Indirect Communication.* Charlottesville: University Press of Virginia, 1993.

Pope, Stephen J. "Overview of the Ethics of Thomas Aquinas." In *The Ethics of Aquinas,* ed. Stephen J. Pope, 30–53. Washington, D.C.: Georgetown University Press, 2002.

————. *The Evolution of Altruism and the Ordering of Love.* Washington, D.C.: Georgetown University Press, 1994.

————. "The Order of Love and Recent Catholic Ethics: A Constructive Proposal." *Theological Studies* 52 (1991): 255–88.

Purvis, Sally B. "Mothers, Neighbors and Strangers: Another Look at Agape." *Journal of Feminist Studies in Religion* 7 (1991): 19–34.

Pyper, Hugh. "The Apostle, the Genius and the Monkey: Reflections on Kierkegaard's 'The Mirror of the Word.'" In *Kierkegaard on Art and Communication,* ed. George Pattison, 125–36. New York: St. Martin's Press, 1992.

Quinn, Philip. "Divine Command Theory." In *The Blackwell Guide to Ethical Theory,* ed. Hugh La Follette, 53–73. Oxford: Blackwell, 2000.

Rahner, Karl. "Conversion." In *Sacramentum Mundi: An Encyclopedia of Theology.* Vol. 2, 4–8. Ed. Karl Rahner et al. 6 vols. New York: Herder and Herder, 1968–70.

————. *Foundations of Christian Faith.* Trans. William V. Dych. New York: Crossroad, 2006.

————. "Justified and Sinner at the Same Time." *Theological Investigations.* Vol. 6, 218–30. New York: Crossroad, 1982.

————. *Meditations on the Sacraments.* New York: Seabury, 1977.

Ratzinger, Joseph Cardinal. See Benedict XVI (Pope)

Reitan, Eric. "Eternal Damnation and Blessed Ignorance: Is the Damnation of Some Incompatible with the Salvation of Any?" *Religious Studies* 38 (2002): 429–50.

Roberts, Robert C. *Faith, Reason, and History.* Macon, Ga.: Mercer University Press, 1986.

———. "The Socratic Knowledge of God." In Perkins, *International Kierkegaard Commentary: The Concept of Anxiety,* 133–52.

Roos, Heinrich. *Søren Kierkegaard and Catholicism.* Trans. Richard M. Brackett. Westminster, Md.: Newman Press, 1954.

Rosemann, Philipp W. "*Fraterna dilectio est Deus:* Peter Lombard's Thesis on Charity as the Holy Spirit." In Kelly and Rosemann, *Amor Amicitiae,* 409–36.

Rowe, William L. *The Cosmological Argument.* Princeton, N.J.: Princeton University Press, 1975.

———. *Philosophy of Religion: An Introduction.* 4th ed. Belmont, Calif.: Thomson, 2007.

Rudd, Anthony J. *Kierkegaard and the Limits of the Ethical.* Oxford: Clarendon Press, 1993.

———. "Kierkegaard and the Sceptics." *British Journal for the History of Philosophy* 6 (1998): 71–88.

Sachs, John R. "Current Eschatology: Universal Salvation and the Problem of Hell." *Theological Studies* 52 (1991): 227–54.

———. "Resurrection or Reincarnation? The Christian Doctrine of Purgatory." In *Reincarnation or Resurrection?* ed. Hermann Häring and Johann Baptist Metz, 81–87. London: SCM, 1993.

St. Joseph Daily Missal. New York: Catholic Book Publishing, 1959.

Schönborn, Christoph. "The 'Communion of Saints' as Three States of the Church: Pilgrimage, Purification, and Glory." *Communio* 15 (1988): 167–81.

Scovel, Carl R. "The Blessings of Purgatory." *Unitarian Universalist Christian* 57 (2002): 66–69.

Selner-Wright, Susan. "The Order of Charity in Thomas Aquinas." *Philosophy and Theology* 9 (1995): 13–27.

Seymour, Charles. "On Choosing Hell." *Religious Studies* 33 (1997): 249–66.

Sherwin, Michael S. *By Knowledge and By Love: Charity and Knowledge in the Moral Theology of St. Thomas Aquinas.* Washington, D.C.: Catholic University of America Press, 2005.

Socias, James, ed. *Daily Roman Missal.* Chicago: Midwest Theological Forum and United States Conference of Catholic Bishops, 2004.

Søltoft, Pia. "The Presence of the Absent Neighbor in *Works of Love.*" Trans. M. G. Piety. In *Kierkegaard Studies Yearbook 1998,* ed. Niels Jørgen Cappelørn and Hermann Deuser, 113–37. Berlin: de Gruyter, 1998.

Steel, Carlos. "Thomas Aquinas on Preferential Love." In Kelly and Rosemann, *Amor Amicitiae,* 437–58.

Stewart, Jon. *Kierkegaard's Relations to Hegel Reconsidered.* Cambridge: Cambridge University Press, 2003.

———, ed. *Kierkegaard and the Patristic and Medieval Tradition.* Aldershot: Ashgate, 2008.

Stokes, Patrick. "Kierkegaardian Vision and the Concrete Other." *Continental Philosophy Review* 39 (2006): 393–413.

Sullivan, Thomas D. "Resolute Belief and the Problem of Objectivity." In Zagzebski, *Rational Faith,* 110–39.

Talbott, Thomas. "The Doctrine of Everlasting Punishment." *Faith and Philosophy* 7 (1990): 19–42.

Taylor, Mark Lloyd. "Practice in Authority: The Apostolic Women of Søren Kierkegaard's Writings." In *Anthropology and Authority*, ed. Poul Houe, Gordon D. Marino, and Sven Hakon Rossel, 85–98.

Taylor, Michael J. *Purgatory*. Huntington, Ind.: Our Sunday Visitor, 1998.

Tertullian. *Apology*. Trans. T. R. Glover. Cambridge, Mass.: Harvard University Press, 1960.

Thompson, Josiah. *The Lonely Labyrinth: Kierkegaard's Pseudonymous Works*. Carbondale: Southern Illinois University Press, 1967.

Toner, Christopher. "Was Aquinas an Egoist?" *Thomist* 71 (2007): 177–208.

Toon, Peter. *Justification and Sanctification*. Westchester, Ill.: Crossway Books, 1983.

Vacek, Edward Collins. *Love, Human and Divine: The Heart of Christian Ethics*. Washington, D.C.: Georgetown University Press, 1994.

Walker, Jeremy D. B. *To Will One Thing: Reflections on Kierkegaard's "Purity of Heart."* London: McGill-Queens University Press, 1972.

Walls, Jerry. *Heaven: The Logic of Eternal Joy*. Oxford: Oxford University Press, 2002.

———. *Hell: The Logic of Damnation*. Notre Dame, Ind.: University of Notre Dame Press, 1992

———. "Purgatory for Everyone." *First Things* 122 (2002): 26–30.

Westphal, Merold. *Becoming a Self: A Reading of Kierkegaard's* Concluding Unscientific Postscript. West Lafayette, Ind.: Purdue University Press, 1996.

———. "Kierkegaard and Hegel." In Marino and Hannay, *The Cambridge Companion to Kierkegaard*, 101–24.

———. *Kierkegaard's Critique of Reason and Society*. Macon, Ga.: Mercer University Press, 1987.

———. "Kierkegaard's Religiousness C: A Defense." *International Philosophical Quarterly* 44 (2004): 535–48.

———. "Kierkegaard's Teleological Suspension of Religiousness B." In Connell and Evans, *Foundations of Kierkegaard's Vision of Community*, 110–29.

Zagzebski, Linda. *Philosophy of Religion: An Historical Introduction*. Oxford: Blackwell, 2007.

———. "Religious Knowledge and the Virtues of the Mind." In Zagzebski, *Philosophy of Religion*, 199–225.

———, ed. *Rational Faith*. Notre Dame, Ind.: University of Notre Dame Press, 1993.

Zeis, John. "Natural Theology: Reformed?" In Zagzebski, *Philosophy of Religion*, 48–78.

INDEX

Vacek, Edward Collins, 92, 242n85
Vatican I, 4, 14, 22, 24, 251n30
Vatican II, 1, 4, 211; *Apostolicam Actu-ositatem,* 243n6; *Gaudium et Spes,* 35, 232nn81,83; *Lumen Gentium,* 33, 144, 197, 203, 204, 206, 207, 227n7, 248n64, 258n12, 263nn19,28, 265n67; *Nostra Aetate,* 253n64

Walker, Jeremy D. B., 157, 158

Walls, Jerry, 137, 138, 197, 251n39, 259n38, 260n68, 261n82
Westphal, Merold, 21, 213, 235n33, 244n8, 264n50
Will, the, 22, 30, 32, 74, 89, 93, 95, 127, 133, 136, 137, 141, 147, 251nn38,39, 252nn42,47; willing the good, 156–62, 166, 167, 169–72, 256n39

Zagzebski, Linda, 14, 228nn1,8

JACK MULDER, JR., is Assistant Professor of Philosophy at Hope College. He is author of *Mystical and Buddhist Elements in Kierkegaard's Religious Thought* as well as other articles and book chapters on Kierkegaard's philosophy and theology.

Milton Keynes UK
Ingram Content Group UK Ltd.
UKHW020703250823
427470UK00012B/536